Books by Helen P. Rogers:

ne's Guide to Financial Planning
Security: An Idea Whose Time Has Passed

The Election

Othe

Every
Socia

The Election Process

A Grass Roots Call For Freedom

Helen P. Rogers

WELLINGTON PUBLICATIONS
CARMEL, CALIFORNIA

First Edition

Library of Congress Catalog Card No.: 87-051351

ISBN: 0-915915-05-7

Printed in the U.S.A.

To Honor

Nelson and Henrietta Poynter
Founders of Congressional Quarterly

They succeeded in their desire to further
a better understanding of our government.

"The only hope for democracy is the intelligence and public spirit of the citizenship as a whole, for in the nature of democracy, whatever teachers and leaders it pays heed to must be chosen by itself."

from *The Ethics of Competition*
(1935) by Frank H. Knight,
founder of the "Chicago School"
of economics

Contents

Section Four
The Watergate Legacy

Preface

Over the years there have been calls for every conceivable election reform. The reforms of the seventies were an attempt to make the nominating process more open and democratic and they have done that, but the price has been increased inefficiency and waste. Most recently Congress has considered bills to substitute direct elections for the electoral college, to provide public financing for campaigns and to limit contributions and spending—with various results. In *The Election Process* I argue against these proposals and discuss the pros and cons of extended or limited terms of office, Congressional pay, free television time, length and cost of campaigns, the advantages of incumbency and, most of all, the candidates our present system attracts and discourages.

Too many people of all ages have become disillusioned with our politicians and yet we are uncertain how to detect genuinely honorable statesmen. We have been deceived too many times before and do not wish to be considered gullible and na$_{82}$ve.

The Watergate tapes revealed the real man behind the public Richard Nixon. We discovered that Joe Biden didn't really think of the closing remarks to the Dubuque, Iowa, debate on the way to the event but had rehearsed the words borrowed from a British politician. It is hard to see through the flim-flam in order to distinguish the genuine from the fake. We cannot let our chief executive be elected on a manufactured image, but we no longer know whom to believe and cannot trust our heart and sense.

In 1888 Lord Bryce observed that "great men don't become presidents," and that's good because we don't know how to tell great men from con-artists. The good news is that all we need is decent men and women and apparently the office itself (*all* political offices) can make the man or the woman. Witness the 32-year-old porno star, apparently elected in jest, who sits in Italy's Parliament and is, to everyone's surprise, and some persons' indignation, taking her election and the job she won seriously.

Many of us are unhappy with *all* the candidates running for the presidential nomination in both parties in 1988, perhaps because we know so many people of higher caliber who are not running. It is true that the type of person who will conform to our present election requirements is not likely to be the type of person we would want as the head of the nation. We have an Alice-in-Wonderland scenario where the only candidate worth electing is one who refuses to run. As I write, California's Secretary of State, March Fong Eu, has withdrawn from the Senate race saying, "I am, to a significant degree, forced to choose between my marriage and my candidacy for the Senate." It seems her husband refused to make the financial disclosures required of candidates for federal offices and their spouses. Msrs. Laxalt and Rumsfeld refused to incur the large debts that are necessary in order to compete in the lengthy, expensive campaigns of today. Yet to curtail campaigning is not only impossible (where there's a will there's a way) it would be an abridgement of our guaranteed right to free speech. Try to imagine an America where it would be illegal for anyone to talk about running for office until three months before the election!

The challenge is to get the best people at the helm for the right reasons and, in my opinion, the most people. There are many fine people in our nation, not so great at tooting their own horns but who could rise magnificently to the occasion. We need to rotate public offices more frequently so that anyone who has a desire to serve can have an opportunity to do so—providing of course he or she can convince voters to give them that chance. And no, we're not quite back to the same dilemma. Limiting terms of federal offices, just as the president's term has been limited, would save us from professional politicians who have little experience in the real world and soon begin to hold an inflated opinion of themselves. In *The Election Process* I present evidence to refute the contention that a single term would make officials less accountable to constituents. One thing is certain; they would not be campaigning during their term of office if they could not run again.

Joe Biden pulled out of the race after the completion of this manuscript. I have, however, chosen to leave him in the book, as he played a part in the 1987-88 process and is an example of what is good and what is bad about the way we elect our officials.

I care that my views are not being represented by a political party or any individual candidate—that's why I wrote this book. I also know that I am not alone.

Helen P. Rogers
Carmel, California
November 3, 1987

Section One

Is This Any Way To Elect A President?

Is This Any Way To Elect A President

The Electoral College

According to a report presented by the American Bar Association (ABA) at a Judiciary Subcommittee in 1968,[1] "the electoral college method of electing a president of the United States is archaic, undemocratic, complex, ambiguous, indirect and dangerous." William Gossett, then ABA president, testified that "in fifteen elections a shift of less than one percent of the national vote would have made the popular vote loser president!"

When our founding fathers met in Philadelphia in 1787 they considered three methods of choosing the president: election by Congress, election by the various state governments and election by the people. The electoral college was a compromise measure, allowing each state to decide how its citizens would choose electors, who in turn would cast ballots for one state resident and one non-resident. Article II Section 1:2 provided that the candidate with the highest number of votes should be president and the runner up, vice president. If there was a majority the Senate would choose from the top five candidates. This provision was changed during the course of the Constitutional Convention and the House was substituted for the Senate, as it was thought to be more representative of the people. The House specified that members were to vote by states.

The best arguments for an electoral college were laid out by Alexander Hamilton in the *Federalist Papers Number 68*, but even they were not conclusive. From the start, certain problems were recognized as being indigenous to the system. The first major problem occurred in the election of 1796, which resulted in the election of John Adams a Federalist as president, and Thomas Jefferson a Republican as vice president. The 1796 election was marked by another first: a Federalist elector bolted and voted for Thomas Jefferson. In 1890, Thomas Jefferson and Aaron Burr wound up in a tie and the president had to be chosen by the House of Representatives. This led to passage of the 12th Amendment in 1804 which mandated that electors vote separately for president and vice president. It was decided that a candidate had to receive an absolute majority of electoral votes to be declared a winner. Today that means at least 270 votes. The same number of electors as congressional representatives are alloted to each state for a total of 535 with three added for the District of Columbia via the 23rd Amendment.

Election reform proposals have been around as long as the Constitution, but few have become amendments to the Constitution. In 1808 the proposal to choose the president by lot first surfaced, to reoccur unsuccessfully in 1844 and 1846 but in another form. Originally the candidates to be chosen by lot were to come from retiring senators; in the later proposals the states were each to elect a native-son candidate, one to be chosen by lot for the office of chief executive. In 1816 the first direct-vote plan was proposed by Senator Abner Lacock of Pennsylvania and was defeated 12 to 21. In 1820 the second faithless elector deprived James Monroe of an unanimous vote in the electoral college by giving John Quincy Adams, a non-candidate, his only electoral vote. In 1822 it was proposed that the president be chosen by regions (four regions) on a rotating basis. But despite the plethora of ideas the old electoral-college system continued.

In 1824 four candidates received electoral college votes, but none a majority: Andrew Jackson = 99, John Quincy Adams = 84, William Crawford = 41 and Henry Clay = 37.

The House awarded Adams 13 states and Jackson 7, which meant that although Jackson got more popular votes and a plurality of electoral college votes, Adams wound up with the presidency. Naturally Andrew Jackson became a strong opponent of the electoral college and, even though he was elected the next time around in 1828, he continued to call for its abolishment.

Although it is unusual, it is not unique to gain election to the presidency with less than a majority of the popular vote. James Garfield won the presidency by only 0.1 percent of the popular vote, which amounted to 9,457 votes in 1880. The following presidents received less than a majority of the popular vote:[2]

1844	J. Polk	49.6 percent	1888	B. Harrison	47.8 percent
1848	Z. Taylor	47.3 percent	1892	G. Cleveland	48.6 percent
1856	J. Buchanan	45.6 percent	1912	W. Wilson	42 percent
1860	A. Lincoln	39.8 percent	1916	W. Wilson	49 percent
1876	R. Hayes	47.9 percent	1948	H. Truman	49.5 percent
1880	J. Garfield	48.3 percent	1960	J. Kennedy	49.7 percent
1884	G. Cleveland	48.5 percent	1968	R. Nixon	43.4 percent

Five of the presidents who were unable to poll a majority are honored in the ranks of the nation's ten greatest presidents, while Ulysses S. Grant, who won a second term with 55.6 percent of the popular vote, and Warren Harding, who won with 60.3 percent, are numbered among the nation's worst presidents. Richard Nixon in 1972 received 60.69 percent of the popular vote, rivaling FDR's second win, yet he was forced to resign from office. The record doesn't say much about the people's judgment in choosing their Chief Executive. Many experts feel a plebiscitary presidency may encourage arrogance and remove an important political check.

George Meaney told the House Judiciary Committee during the course of the hearings mentioned earlier that "almost anything would be preferable to the present system."[3] The winner-take-all system, sometimes called the general-ticket system, gives a great deal of leverage to a few popular votes in low turnout states, small states and large pivotal states, which in turn gives ethnic minorities and others that tend to congregate in urban areas power beyond their numbers in presidential elections. This tends to influence candidates toward liberal domestic policies and makes them more internationalist in foreign policy—either good or bad depending on your point of view. Proponents claim direct elections would dilute this leverage, making fraud less of a possibility. Besides the possibility of fraud, the minority vote can be lost under our present winner-take-all system. Suppose A gets 40 percent, B gets 35 percent, C gets 25 percent. A ends up with everything and 60 percent of the voters are disenfranchised. In the past this has given the minority party little incentive to campaign in some areas knowing votes "won't count."

The winner-take-all system is used in every state but Maine. Maine in 1969 adopted a district plan whereby two electors are chosen on a statewide popular level and one is chosen from each of Maine's two congressional districts. Maine has four electoral votes, not many, but one more then Delaware.

In *Delaware v. New York* (385 US. 964 [1966]) plaintiffs declared that it was improbable that a resident of Delaware would ever be nominated for president under the current electoral process since there are too few votes to be won in a small home state. That seems to be less of a consideration today than it was 25 years ago—at least it didn't discourage Joe Biden or Pete du Pont from throwing their hats into the ring for the 1988 nomination.

Alternatives

Although results from the popular vote are known in November, according to Article II Section 1:3 of the Constitution, "The Congress may determine the time of choosing the electors, and the day on which they shall give their votes; which day shall be the same throughout the United States." That day has been set as the first Monday after the second Wednesday in December. In January the votes are counted before both Houses and the results are officially announced.

Everyone agrees the president should be elected by popular vote—the issue is how the popular vote should be aggregated. Existing electoral college and automatic plans say by states themselves; the district plan says by state subdivision; the proportional plan says by party vote by states and the direct-vote plan says by the entire nation.

In 1970 Senator Thomas Eagleton suggested it should not be enough to carry the popular vote, the candidate must also carry a majority of states or plurality in a group of states with more than 50 percent of the total vote. President Harrison in 1888 would have passed both tests as he carried twenty out of thirty-eight states.

Senator Birch Bayh pointed out under the present system it is theorectically possible for a candidate to capture eleven of the largest states and Washington, D.C., to win an electoral majority, leaving thirty-nine states without voice in the process—even if all thirty-nine states were unanimously against the candidate.

Other critics point to the distortions which occur because electoral votes are distributed among the states according to the decennial census which, because of our mobile society, quickly becomes outdated. Still others say the electoral college endangers the two-party system and encourages third-party strategy to win concessions from major candidates.

In 1968 Senator Birch Bayh advocated abandoning the electoral college and having the team with the most popular votes nationwide declared winners. He suggested a popular majority would not be necessary but that any majority of at least 40 percent should win. In case of a tie there would be a run-off between the two top pairs (pair and team refer to the office of President and Vice President). This would extend the one person one vote principle, and enhance the two-party system.

The American Institute of Public Opinion asked before the 1968 election and after, "Would you approve or disapprove of an amendment to the Constitution which would do away with the Electoral College and base the election of a president on the total vote cast throughout the nation?" Before the 1968 election, 66 percent approved; after, 81 percent approved.

If you will recall in 1968 Richard Nixon won the presidency with only 43.4 percent of the popular vote to Hubert Humphrey's 42.7 percent and George Wallace's 13.5 percent. But even with a direct vote Humphrey would have lost by 510,000 votes out of 73.2 million cast.

Advocates of direct elections claim such a system would always ensure that the candidate with the greatest popular vote would win the office of president, that it would give equal weight to every vote, it would do away with the faithless elector problem, would reduce the chance of fraud, would encourage greater participation and place the election more fully into the hands of the people where it belongs. Quite an impressive list to commend the direct-vote plan.

A direct plurality system is used in the states to elect the chief executive and they seem to have little trouble governing. This would seem to refute the argument used by those who claim that winning with a mere plurality of the votes, and especially winning after a run-off contest, would undermine or at least render more precarious the constituency base of the president.

An amendment to abolish the electoral college system, almost identical to the Bayh Plan, passed the House 339 to 70 and it looked as if the 91st Congress was going to resolve this on-going issue. However, the Senate failed to follow through and the furor over electoral reform continued throughout 1969. Opponents could not accept the unfavorable impact the direct-vote plan would have on the two-party system.

There is little doubt the direct vote would encourage minority parties as there would be a greater probability that two major parties would not receive a majority. The Bayh Plan would have made actual *voting* more important than *population* and, critics pointed out, would have given less voice to the poor non-voters represented by the weighted urban vote. A candidate, if elected on popular vote alone, could conceivably win on the votes of special interests; for example, on the labor vote, business vote, pro-life vote or, as Richard Nixon and Spiro Agnew did in 1968, on the law and order vote.

In their 1970 book *Voting For President*, William Sayre and Judith Parrish claim the direct vote would weaken the power of the states and strengthen the national government. State borders would be irrelevant in elections and probably federal standards of eligibility would eventually be determined to make the presidential choices uniform. Federal employees would end up tallying a national vote and all election officials would end up working for federal rather than state governments.[4]

On March 5, 1970, the Federal System Plan was introduced by Senator Thomas Eagleton of Missouri. It provided for direct-vote election of the plurality winner as long as he carried: (1) more than one-half the states; (2) a plurality in states with over one-half the voters; or (3) a majority of the electoral votes, awarded on a state general-ticket basis.

If there were no winner, votes won by minor candidates would be allocated to the top two contestants in proportion to their showing in each state, and the electoral vote majority winner would be declared President.

Also in 1970, Senator Joseph Tydings of Maryland and Senator Robert Griffin of Michigan presented a plan to do away with run-off elections. It provided that if there were no 40 percent popular plurality winner, then a majority of electoral votes would be sufficient to elect. These were compromise systems—not the first and surely not the last.

What would have been unthinkable years ago is at least "thinkable" today, thanks to television. It has been suggested that our national legislature (both houses of Congress) be elected directly by all the people, because a New York or Wyoming politician may be just as well known to a voter as is his local representative because of television; and, after all, what all congress people do on Capitol Hill affects the entire nation, not just local constituents.

Video Democracy, a recent book by television broadcaster Richard Hollander, envisions a time when local governments have given way to direct democracy via two-way communication channels and cable TV linked to computers in their homes. Ordinary politicians would no longer be needed, as people would vote directly on issues rather than trusting to representatives. The field of presidential candidates could be narrowed within a defined parameter of time and space. A special TV channel could be used only for election coverage and would be allowed for in the federal budget. The debates centering on the issues would be carried by private TV, radio and local papers as they saw fit. Not everyone would tune into the election channel just as not everyone tunes into beauty contests, Academy Awards, baseball or anything else. So what else is new? Maybe a lot of political hopefuls would end up eating less chicken and peas and have more time for things that would benefit themselves and society. The millions of freed dollars—? I thought that was what this country was short of anyway.

In 1826 the automatic plan whereby all of a state's electoral votes would automatically be cast for the candidate who received the highest popular vote was first introduced by Representative Charles Haynes of Georgia. The automatic plan keeps the winner-take-all provision of our present system but abrogates the office of presidential elector. All of a state's votes would automatically be awarded to the ticket that carried that state's popular vote. Most automatic plans have their own unique contingency election plans. The automatic plan is the most moderate of all reform proposals and is opposed mainly because the changes it calls for are so slight that many believe the reform is not worth the effort and cost required to get the necessary constitutional amendment. Another plan would keep the electoral college but eliminate the winner-take-all provision and its bias toward urban power and against minority parties. This plan would eliminate the electors themselves and just assign electoral votes to candidates on the basis of popular votes received.

The 1950s produced many ideas for reform. Senator Karl Mundt of South Dakota and Representative Frederic Coudert of New York presented the district plan, whereby electoral votes are allocated by districts within the various states. Proponents of the plan wanted to see less preference given to urban areas and hoped to fragment the power of the largest states. For instance, in 1968 California's forty electoral votes went to Nixon, under the winner-take-all plan. Under a district plan, other things being equal, Hubert Humphrey might have gotten seventeen of California's electoral votes and Nixon only twenty-three. California would have advanced Nixon by only six votes instead of forty. In 1968 Kansas gave all seven of its votes to Nixon, which would have made Kansas politically more important to Nixon than California under the district plan. The district plan would encourage minor party candidates, giving them a chance to get at least a few electoral votes, and would elevate local leaders at the expense of national party officials. The emphasis on local constituencies, on bringing government "home to the people" and giving a greater sense of worth to individual citizens is either a plus or a minus depending on where you stand. The biggest problem lies with the increased incentive to gerrymandering. District lines would become more important than ever, opening areas of potential contention. In 1970, Sayre and Parrish feared the district plan would reverse the system which has always ensured that the winner in our presidential contests has received a greater margin in electoral than in popular votes, and that it would make presidential races closer, possibly throwing more decisions to Congress and thus undermining the presidency.[5] They warned that a vote for the district plan would be a vote against the balance of power then prevailing in the country.

In 1848 Representative William Lawrence of New York introduced the proportional plan which called for a division of each state's electoral college votes according to the popular vote received by each party. Under the proportional plan, urban areas lose power, as they would with any plan other than the current winner-take-all system, and third parties are encouraged. The proportional plan was raised again by Henry Cabot Lodge of Massachusetts in 1941 but didn't go anywhere until 1948 when Ed Gossett of Texas joined with the Massachusetts senator as co-sponsor. In 1950 the Senate approved the plan 64 to 27 but it couldn't get by the House. A few years later Senators Estes Kefauver of Tennessee and Price Daniel of Texas proposed another version of the proportional plan which was loudly opposed by Senator John F. Kennedy who had ousted Senator Lodge in 1952. Proponents say this plan

> is the only electoral reform measure that would preserve the existing national-state relationship and at the same time reflect the popular vote outcome more closely. They are correct about the federal system but wrong in saying that the plan would assure victory to the popular vote winner.[4]

Sayre and Parrish claim under the proportional plan, for instance, Richard Nixon in 1960 would have received 1.759 of Vermont's three electoral votes and John F. Kennedy would have received 1.240 of Vermont's three electoral votes, giving Nixon an edge of only 0.519 in Vermont. In New York, Nixon would have received 22.3 and John F. Kennedy would have received 22.7, thus giving Kennedy an edge of 0.4 in New York. Sayre and Parrish's point is that under the proportional plan, a small homogeneous state could yield more to a candidate than could a large diverse state. A proportional plan would distort the nationwide popular vote total. Under the proportional plan, the margin of victory of every president would have been decreased between 1864 and 1968 with the exception of Woodrow Wilson, whose margin would have been increased. The trouble with the proportional plan is that it doesn't satisfy any group; The direct-vote plan goes further, the district plan satisfies conservatives better and our present system already occupies the middle ground.

In 1956 a proposal was offered in the Senate which would have permitted each state to choose between a district plan and a proportional plan. The proposal was rejected on the grounds that it would have enhanced the power of the states and generally been too complicated. The second objection has not stopped our legislatures from enacting tax law—if you want complications, look no further than the Internal Revenue Code.

The Case For The Electoral College

Judith Best in her 1971 book, *The Case Against Direct Election of The President*, says:

> The prospect of winning the popular but not the electoral vote spurs those parties to seek the support of broad cross sections of the nation. The risk of a runner-up presidency may not be too great a price to pay for a system which minimizes conflicts, promises stability, suppresses factions, promotes moderation, and requires a broad base of support.[7]

Besides, with only two major parties, a majority is almost assured. The House only had to choose the president in 1800 and 1825 and the Senate was called upon only once, in 1837 when, by a vote of 22 to 16, they selected Richard Johnson as Martin Van Buren's vice president.

In 1948 one of Tennessee's electors bolted and voted for Stom Thurmond, as did electors from Alabama, but, as in 1796 and 1820, it didnt' affect the outcome of the election and the Alabama State Supreme Court ruled national parties could not control the vote of electors. In 1956 another Alabama elector bolted and cast his vote for Alabama Judge Walter Jones and Senator Herman Talmadge of Georgia, but again, since Eisenhower won 457 out of 531 electoral votes, the Alabama defection had no bearing on the election's ultimate outcome. In 1960 a Republican elector from Oklahoma refused to cast his vote for Nixon and, like the others, his defection did not distort election results. Most recently, in 1972, a Virginia elector defected to the Libertarian candidate.

The electoral-vote system conveys an aura of legitimacy to the popular vote mandate, and many believe it is responsible for the political stability the United States enjoys in its government. No one denies the inequality in individual voting power that it creates, but that may not be all bad. Extreme views are purged by the system, which overall does a good job of balancing power between urban and rural areas and in general nurtures our moderate two-party system. It should be remembered that the executive is only one branch of government and that the legislative branch tends to overrepresent rural at the expense of urban populations. As Judith Best points out on page 159 of *The Case Against Direct Election of the President,*

> The power system is federal, decentralized, Madisonian and, to a degree usually unrecognized, approaches a system of unanimous consent. The nation has sought and largely achieved a system that reflects the views and interests of broad cross sections of the polity.

Ms. Best suggests that a "Madisonian system of concurrent majorities" is best judged on its results.

Concurrent majorities are typically American; they intentionally counter the majoritarian principle of assigning equal weight to every vote. No one denies political equality is a goal under the constitution, but it is not the *only* goal. The present system has been designed to reflect broad interests, not to merge minority interests into the vast majority. It depends on what is meant by "the will of the people." The majority is one segment of "the people" and not the whole. America is not a pure democracy, a nation of majority rule, but a democratic republic, a representative government with an elaborate system of checks and balances.

Judith Best points out that three-quarters of states required for ratification means one-quarter plus one man weigh more than the votes in three-quarters of the states minus one. Think about it. She says

> The list of constitutional limitations on the majority is a long one, including the Supreme Court, the Senate, the guarantee of at least one congressman to each state and the extraordinary majorities required for the Senate to convict those impeached by the House, for Congress to expel one of its members and for Congress to override a presidential veto. In addition, the Constitution places certain limitations on even a unanimous Congress, restrictions designed to protect

individuals and minorities, such as the provisions respecting the writ of *habeas corpus*, the bill of attainder and *ex post facto* laws. Other restrictions are placed directly on the states.[8]

Our forefathers realized the dangers inherent in pluralistic democracy—tyranny by the majority—and developed our elaborate system of checks and balances to forestall it.

At the invitation of the Brookings Institution in Washington, D.C., sixteen experts gathered on February 6, 1969, to discuss the ideal system of electing the president. They agreed on the following points: (1) the need for a quick decision and clear-cut winner; (2) the victor should be the peoples' choice—winner of the most popular votes; (3) the president-elect should have a mandate to govern, a legitimacy which comes from a good margin of victory; and (4) the ideal system should not undermine the two-party system. All agreed that the method of electing the president holds broad implications for the political system as a whole.

Senator Howell Heflin of Alabama told the Judiciary Center on October 1987, when explaining his reason for deciding to vote against Judge Bork's confirmation to the Supreme Court, "When in doubt, don't." That may or may not be good advice, but so far it is being followed regarding election reform. The electoral college and the winner-take-all system continues to be criticized but not changed.

Who Votes

Presidential elections always draw more voters than other elections, and the closer the race the greater the participation, as people feel their vote has more of a chance of making a difference. But even so, voter participation has fallen over the past 25-30 years. In the non-presidential election year 1958, only 43 percent of those eligible bothered to vote for members of Congress, and that percentage had fallen to 37 percent in 1982 and 1986. In the presidential election years, the same trend is evident, with 62.8 percent turning out for the Kennedy-Nixon battle in 1960 versus only 53 percent for the 1984 Reagan-Mondale contest. From another perspective, however, one could say that more citizens voted in 1984 than ever before in American history: 92,652,793 versus the 68,838,000 who voted in the 1960 battle between John F. Kennedy and Richard Nixon. Part of the increase can be attributed to a broadening of the franchise by the 23rd amendment to residents of the District of Columbia (1961), by the 24th amendment banning poll taxes on federal elections (1964) and the 26th amendment expanding the vote to eighteen-year-olds (1972).

Sayre and Parrish claim that uneven exposure of candidates to the fifty states does not necessarily encourage apathy among the voters who are slighted. They feel that television means all voters have an opportunity to familiarize themselves with the candidates. They suggest:

> Human voting motivations are complex, involving both what has been termed the "sense of political efficiency"—the belief that one's efforts make some difference—and the "sense of citizen duty"—the belief that one ought to be politically active in order to be a good citizen.[9]

Education makes politics and voting easier to understand and is the single most important variable in increasing citizen participation in the election process. A well-informed and responsible electorate is the underlying basis for the American system. In a recent column, Carl Rowen informed us that a "well-informed electorate ... doesn't exist in this country" and cited a June 1987 survey by Market Facts, Inc. which reportedly showed that

> Ninety-two percent of Americans could not name the Chief Justice of the United States, William Rehnquist. Only 7 percent could name Alan Greenspan, the newly-appointed head of the Federal Reserve. And 25 percent could not even name the vice president of the United States, George Bush ... 54 percent could name Mikhail Gorbachev as "the head of the Soviet Union" and 30 percent identified Fawn Hall as "Lt. Col. Oliver North's secretary," but only 8 percent knew the chief justice ...[10]

But more formal education isn't necessarily the answer. Professors Raymond Wolfinger of U.C. Berkeley and Steven Rosenstone of Yale soften Mr. Rowen's comments by pointing out that an individual's life experiences are a substitute for education and that although students tend to vote more often than their non-student counterparts, there is a distinct correlation between a rise in age and a rise in voter turnout. Their studies tended to debunk the theory that young people are encouraged to vote as they assume adult roles. The professors found, if anything, young marrieds voted less often than their single student counterparts. The professors also found that people with lots of free time do not vote in greater percentage than the rest of society. Rather, the unemployed tended to vote less, distracted, no doubt, by other concerns. There was no evidence that low voter turnout is related to disaffection with our political system. It was found that people who expressed alienation voted in the same numbers as the general population. On the other hand, it appeared that those with a stake in the patronage system, where political issues were likely to affect their own jobs, had above average voter turnouts.

The professors were able to determine how much each group's electoral strength was deflated or inflated by its voting rate. They discovered that

> The young, the unmarried, Southerners, the unemployed, minorities, and people who moved within two years of the 1974 election all comprise a smaller share of voters than the population as a whole.[11]

Those without a high school diploma, below the median income, youngest, oldest, unemployed, single and blacks shared a reduction in voter strength also. However, those with college degrees, higher incomes, government employees and those that stayed put over three years all had greater strength at the polls than their share of the population would indicate.

According to the *1972 National Election Study of the University of Michigan Center for Political Studies*, 51.4 percent of all citizens and 51.3 percent of all voters identify with the Democratic Party, whereas 36 percent of all citizens and 39.7 percent of all voters identify with the Republicans. In general, voters are amazingly close to representing the views of the non-voter population.

> Those most likely to be underrepresented are people who lack opinions ... Both self-described liberals and conservatives are slightly overrepresented at the polls at the expense of moderates and people who say they have no ideological tendency ... As long as attitudes on issues are so weakly related to social class and race, the poor and minorities will find enough allies to avoid political weakness in proportion to their own voting rates.[12]

The Role Of Government

For over 200 years the role of government has been debated in this country. Most recently the Democratic Party has been emphasizing what government can do for citizens, indirectly encouraging dependence. On the other hand the Republicans, most recently in the person of Ronald Reagan, have been emphasizing what government can do *to* citizens. You've probably heard that you can't love your country and hate your government, a statement which has caused contention between the two parties. We are all in this together is the Democrats' message and what we need now is leadership. In contrast, the Republicans claim citizens want to stand on their own two feet and their call has been to get government off the backs of the people.

One of the main problems facing the Republicans is how to make the so-called party of big business and wealth appeal to a majority of Americans.

An activist government manages and regulates the economy and endorses specific social values. Republicans generally claim that in a pluralistic society with no official ideology it is important for the state to remain neutral in such matters. Always, and in every society, those who feel threatened by change gravitate to government for protection. In our country the Progressives used government to attack private power, and in the 1920s it wasn't much of a step from there for the New Dealers to use government not so much to attack but rather to defend citizens against the economic perils of the thirties. Democrats, especially when the economy looks a little shaky, tend to look to government for protection and solutions. When the economy is humming along they turn to government-business partnerships and just about anything else that works. After the second world war, government continued its role of social protector and reformer. Thus the laissez-faire government of a capitalist society was turned into an entity whose purpose became not to see that people are left alone but to see that social and economic justice are promoted.

Democrats in 1987 agreed overwhelmingly that government cutbacks in social spending are undesirable and that spending on the poor should rise even if it means higher taxes. The Republicans are split about evenly on that issue. Democrats believe that government has a definite role to play in the economy and social life of this nation—here, also, Republicans are divided. Kevin Phillips, an expert on Republican politics, says that two-thirds of the Party in 1987 "dissent from the Reagan administration's efforts to reduce federal involvement in health, poverty, housing and education."[13]

With growth comes diversity of opinion. Not a bad thing for a society but rather a hindrance for a political party trying to win a national election. The anti-government fervor that brought the Republican party into prominence in the eighties began twenty years ago and may have worn itself out.

Political analysts tell us that the American voter shuns ideologues in favor of pragmatists; their concern is not whether a proposal is consistent or right, but on the contrary, the concern is whether a proposal works. The way to the popularity of both parties is their appeal to moderates and their association with ideas that work.

More than any campaign in recent memory, the 1980 campaign was the campaign of two ideologues. Ronald Reagan attracted those with a distaste for taxes, regulation and all the trappings of big government. He made middle class voters see themselves as the source of funds for the programs they used to clamor for. They came to recognize that the pocket Uncle Sam would have to pick to finance compassionate programs was their own. Under Ronald Reagan they became aware of costs, although critics, in order to invoke shame and gain support for their own point of view, prefer to say the middle class became selfish and hard. Candidate Reagan gathered a constituency with a common enemy—the redistributionist, anti-defense liberal—and a common interest—restricting the federal government. All had a desire to see a transfer of power from the federal to state and local governments.

But candidate Reagan had a record of pragmatism; his method of governing was moderate, circumspect and, above all, pragmatic. Jimmy Carter focused on ideology all the way, trying to attract votes by claiming a vote in 1980 was a referendum on conflicting ideas, whereas his opponent asked the now famous pragmatic question, "Are you better off than you were four years ago?"

Those who point to Mr. Reagan's experience as an actor and try to attribute his success to his professionalism on camera miss the point of his achievement. William Schneider, journalist and political analyst for the American Enterprise Institute, put his finger on the role communication plays in Ronald Reagan's ability to attract support in an article for the *Atlantic Monthly*, January 1987.

> Reagan's relaxed, reassuring television style is important because his ideological image is neither relaxed nor reassuring. He used television in 1980 to persuade the voters—during the last week of the campaign—that he was not dangerous or extreme, despite the dangerous and extreme things he was on record as having said. Millions of angry, dissatisfied voters felt it was safe to replace Carter with Reagan. A man with such a nice, avuncular personality would not blow up the world.[14]

Ronald Reagan was able to convince voters that he was not as advertised by his opponents. I have elsewhere[15] referred to Ronald Reagan as the "do as I say, not as I do" president. This is his genius. His words are defiant and uncompromising but his actions are shrewd and conciliatory. To true ideologues it often seems that he has abandoned his principles.

Californians already knew this about Ronald Reagan. As governor (1967-75) he denounced welfare fraud, high taxes and was anti-abortion all the while increasing welfare benefits, raising taxes and liberalizing California's abortion law. How was the sale of arms to Iran any different? All the while Ronald Reagan was telling the world there could be no negotiations with terrorists, those in his administration were making deals. They, too, knew the man and his desire to get things done, to maneuver for the best deal possible. But Ronald Reagan knows the American people, as any successful politician must, and is well aware of the American tendency to overlook just about anything as long as it works.

Ideologues believe that if something is contrary to principle it cannot work, even if appearances show otherwise. William Schneider gave the Republicans and their reaction to FDR's New Deal as an example in his article for the January 1987 *Atlantic Monthly*.

> They claimed that the New Deal could not work because it was wrong; it entailed an unprecedented growth of government and threatened tremendous inflation. Those warnings proved right—fifty years later. It took the hyperinflation of the 1970s to make the Republicans' case.[16]

The strategy the Democrats used in 1986 was, according to Mr. Schneider, a focus on local candidates and issues and near inviability of the national party. But he explained that "Democrats cannot have it both ways: after avoiding national themes in the campaign, they can hardly claim that the election was a repudiation of the Reagan revolution."[17]

If the economy remains healthy the Democrats will have little to attack during the 1988 campaign. Discussing the deficit is risky because they must mention cuts in social programs, a rise in taxes and defense—all political hot seats. The Democrats might take heart from polls conducted by the University of Michigan, which in 1987 found that resentment against income taxes, which have been lower lately, and even social security taxes, which have been higher lately, has declined. The same polls showed that the percentage of Americans who could trust the federal government to do what is right has been steadily declining: 76 percent in 1964, 54 percent in 1970, 33 percent in 1976 and 25 percent in 1980. On the other hand the percentage of Americans who believe government is run by large special interests looking out for their own welfare has been rising: 29 percent in 1964, 50 percent in 1970 and 69 percent in 1980. This provides ammunition for those who would campaign against selfishness, what they see as the mean-spirited survival of the fittest legacy of Reaganism. (Joe Biden had mastered this theme.)

Professor Robert Bellah of U.C. Berkeley, a co-author of the recent book *Habits of the Heart*, spoke before the Commonwealth Club in San Francisco on August 21, 1987. At an earlier time, parts of his speech would no doubt have made their way into the Biden campaign as the theme was relevant.

> As the dangers of radical individualism become increasingly evident, these groups give us reason to hope that we can counter our individualism with a renewed emphasis on community obligation and public responsibility.

Ronald Reagan has called the eighties the age of the individual and the entrepreneur. His critics have called the Reagan years the age of egoism and selfishness. Walter Mondale tried to make the nation view the 1984 election as a decision to be a generous nation versus a vote for greed and selfishness. Alexis de Tocqueville distinguished individualism from selfishness, claiming that selfishness is endemic to all societies and all forms of government but individualism is a product of America's unique brand of democracy. "Individualism is a novel expression to which a novel idea has given birth."

In Part I of his treatise, de Tocqueville attributes

> the small number of distinguished men in political life to the ever, increasing despotism of the majority in the United States . . . I have found very few men who displayed that manly candor and masculine independence of opinion which frequently distinguished the Americans in former times and which constitutes the leading feature in distinguished characters wheresoever they may be found.[18]

Professor Bellah told his Commonwealth Club audience that

> Middle-class Americans share Emerson's emphasis on self-reliance and belief that help comes only from our own bosom. They also tend to share his view that society is inimical to the individual and that the quest for the self involves freeing ourselves from society. Thus the quest for the self is a quest for autonomy, for leaving the past and the social structures that have previously enveloped us, for stripping off obligations and constraints imposed by others, until at last we find our true self which is unique and individual.[19]

Professor Bellah believes that individualism can be harmful to society. Rather than advocate special interests, government should stimulate innovations. It's not enough for politicians to point out the things that are wrong in our society, to sympathize with interest groups; they should be laying out strategies to right the wrongs they love to rant and rave about.

What We're Looking For In A President

The 1987-88 campaign season started out with a heightened awareness of character and attention to decorum. The Democratic candidates who were caught in the spotlight were harmed in each instance not by their discovered deeds as much as by their handling of the situation once they were put on the hot seat. Gary Hart and Joseph Biden were ousted because of poor judgment and knee-jerk denials. Michael Dukakis saw his decisive super-manager image tarnished when he claimed no knowledge of the Neil Kinnock video tapes which were the catalyst to Mr. Biden's downfall. The governor's refusal first to accept the resignation of his campaign manager and the later change of mind gave the wishy-washy label credence. As political analyst Robert Squier pointed out, "His (Dukakis') biggest asset was management, and here's an unmanaged situation; and his appeal was innocence, and his campaign was guilty."[20]

Ellen Goodman summed up what a lot of us thought in early October 1987:

> If I had to triage the mistakes of Hart, Biden and Dukakis, which plugs would I pull? Hart? Yes. Biden? Maybe. Dukakis? No. But today, every trouble draws blood. We used to talk about winners in politics. We used to focus on Election Day. This year, this brutal year, we talk about survivors. Can anyone make it to Election Day?[21]

By itself, Senator Biden's plagiarism would not be enough to ruffle American voters or political colleagues. No one has a patent on thoughts and there are only so many ways to express them. The much loved and greatly respected late Senator Sam Ervin once said, "If men and women of capacity refuse to take part in politics and government, they condemn themselves, as well as the people, to the punishment of living under bad government." It reminded me of one of my favorite quotations: "The punishment which the wise suffer, who refuse to take part in the government, is to live under the government of worse men." (Plato, 4th century BC.) There's nothing new under the sun. (Who said that?)

In the *American Commonwealth*, written in 1896, Lord Bryce noted that when it comes to a choice between a meritorious candidate or a meritorious president, the former would always win out. Lord Bryce thought that meant Americans were doomed to suffer under second rate leaders. He observed that obscure men tend to make fewer enemies and for that reason make better candidates.

William Schneider and other political analysts have told us that Mario Cuomo is sensitive and easily provoked. Sensitivity to the issues and desires of the people is an asset but sensitivity to criticism is apparently a sign of instability in 1988. The governor may have been well advised in his decision to pass on the 1988 race for the Democratic presidential nomination. In fact, if a warning were televised stating that only those with hides at least as thick as a rhinoceros need apply for the job of presidential candidate, it might save not only the feelings of potential candidates but also the country. According to Mr. Schneider

> The greatest tragedies as Presidents—Lyndon Johnson, Richard Nixon, Jimmy Carter—were all deeply insecure men, who worried incessantly about their reputations, made lists of enemies and carried polls around in their pockets. Psychological security may be the most important characteristic to look for in a presidential candidate.[22]

On the eve of his withdrawal from the presidential race, Gary Hart told the nation that press scrutiny was responsible for many qualified and talented people deciding against a career in public service. Mr. Schneider puts it this way:

> Candidates for president these days must sacrifice dignity as well as privacy. They have to spend their time suffering fools gladly and being badgered by arrogant twenty-year-olds with questionnaires. We have reached the point at which politicians like Cuomo and Nunn would actually diminish their stature by running for President.[23]

Ellen Goodman reminded us in one of her columns that "qualifications on paper don't always translate into votes. . . ." Fund raisers have to sell a winner and qualifications are only part of it. Pat Schroeder, the subject of Ms. Goodman's June 12, 1987, column, already had more national name recognition than most of the candidates, especially among women. She has been in Congress for fifteen years and is one of the most outspoken women in politics, which gives her a uniqueness second only to Jesse Jackson's among the candidates for the 1988 presidential nomination. A campaign chest of $10 million is the figure generally recommended to the 1988 candidates. Ms. Goodman reported the head of a fund-raising organization called "The Emily List (Emily as in 'Early Money Is Like Yeast')" seemed skeptical of the Schroeder candidacy and would only recommend viable candidates in their solicitations. To raise the money necessary to finance a campaign a candidate must not only have experience and something important to say, he or she must have charisma and photograph well on television. In explaining Ms. Schroeder's decision not to run in her October 2, 1987, column,

Ellen Goodman said, "... it wasn't just money that stumped and stopped the senior woman in Congress. It was the method of presidential politics." She quoted Ms. Schroeder: "I could not bear to turn every human contact into a photo opportunity. I would shrivel."

1988 is a prime example of the folly of our nominating system. Candidates "select themselves and then try to secure nomination through one to four years of shallow, demeaning hucksterism," says political writer Alan Ehrenhalt. "We have a system that is capable of producing good presidents only by accident, and we have a right to object to it."[24]

We lost a good man with business acumen and both political and international experience when Donald Rumsfeld withdrew from the 1988 presidential race long before it should ever have begun back in April 1987. Actually, the race began for Mr. Rumsfeld in the summer of 1985, more than three years before the presidential election. It took time to collect a war chest of $4 million and promises of more, but in the end that sum appeared inadequate to the job. Few knew better than Mr. Rumsfeld himself what he as an outsider (not current office holder) would be up against when it came to raising money because he is active in *Citizens For American Values*, an organization to help non-incumbent Republicans run for office and to keep the system open.

In his April 2, 1987, letter notifying supporters of his decision not to run for the 1988 Republican nomination, Mr. Rumsfeld, a former congressman, former director of the Office of Economic Opportunity, ex-Ambassador to NATO, former White House chief of staff, one time Defense Secretary and Chairman of one of America's largest companies, provided evidence of the nation's loss in his verdict. He had considered the race because of

> a desire to see our country and our people realize our true potential as a humane and positive force in the world, and my conviction that values have consequences for our country's future.

He aired his misgivings about our current federal election laws:

> The cost of a Presidential campaign is enormous ... In the past, funds could be raised far along in a campaign, as a candidate gained

visibility and public interest heightened. Today, the money must come heavily "up front."

Non-candidates, like Senator ~~Tom~~ Bill Bradley of New Jersey and Bill Clinton of Arkansas, basked in the publicity that resulted from their pondering and then rejecting the thought of entering the 1988 race, publicity that could only enhance name recognition for the future.

Laurence Barrett talks about

> the Shrinkage Phenomenon, a mysterious effect that diminishes prospects' stature as soon as they enter the race . . . There is also the obverse effect, an optical illusion called the Sidelines Magnifier. When the Cuomos and Bradleys and Nunns stay out wrapped in the dignity of duty or humility, they seem so much grander than those scurrying after votes and donations.[25]

Senators Sam Nunn of Georgia and Dale Bumpers of Arkansas decided the pressures of the Senate and their families would not allow them to take on the added obligations that a presidential race would entail. Governors Cuomo and Clinton felt the same way, whereas Paul Laxalt and Donald Rumsfeld pleaded lack of funds for their decision not to enter the race. As journalist Laurence Barrett put it: "To hear the defectors tell it, you have to be an unemployed monk with rich friends to run comfortably." And he intimated it would help to be a thick-skinned workaholic, unconcerned about the privacy of family and with enough ambition to make it through hundreds of fund raisers and over thirty primaries.[26]

Many have speculated that Senators Bradley and Nunn, Governors Robb, Cuomo and others, may have opted to stay out of the 1988 presidential race realizing that the nation has gone through the longest economic expansion in history and a recession is overdue. The huge trade and budget deficits almost ensure that when a break comes it will not be a mild recession, and who wants to preside over a catastrophe? If that is indeed their thinking, then the 1988 non-candidates have failed to consult their history books. Crisis is opportunity; it fosters great leaders. Lincoln, who won the presidency with the lowest popular vote ever, earned his place as one of the nation's greatest leaders by presiding over total chaos. FDR can thank the economic turmoil of his presidency for his reputation. Besides, the greatest catastrophe for the Democratic Party would be to lose yet another presidential election.

According to political expert William Schneider, the turnout in Southern primaries dropped from 18 percent of those eligible to vote in 1980 to 14 percent in 1984. Blacks make up 25 percent of southern Democrats yet in the 1984 election accounted for 30 percent of the voters. Those 14 percent who bothered to vote were more liberal than those who decided to sit the election out, thus creating a liberal bias within the party. If Southern conservatives refuse to participate in the Democrats' primary, they will be giving up their opportunity to influence the party platform and have a say in who is to be the party's standard bearer in 1988.

The Democratic Leadership Council (DLC) took shape in 1985 and counted among its illustrious founders non-candidates Charles Robb and Sam Nunn and candidates Richard Gephardt and Bruce Babbitt. The DLC was, in the words of its founders, an attempt to give the party a centrist image.

> Centrists define their program in terms of *consensual* values, values shared by the whole society—peace, prosperity, growth, national security, freedom. An ideological program bases its strategy on *conflicting* values, issues that pit "us" against "them" . . . the key element in . . . the DLC's political thinking is resistance to conflict and division, to the ideological style of politics.[27]

Of course it is as important as ever before that Democrats talk about justice and compassion, women's rights and affirmative action, just as bona fide Republicans must take stands against tax hikes and big government.

Super Tuesday, the brainchild of the DLC, could backfire on those who conceived it with the idea that the importance of Iowa and New Hampshire should be minimized. Governor Robb has legitimate complaints beyond the fact that two small unrepresentative states have too much influence over which candidates will filter down to the rest of the nation. Many agree that those who campaign in Iowa and New Hampshire don't even attempt to present a broad national agenda.

In a phone call made to columnist David Broder after Senator Sam Nunn announced his non-candidacy, Governor

Mario Cuomo of New York declared that he would endorse his favorite Democratic candidate in February—before Super Tuesday (March 8). Mr. Broder believes the AFL-CIO is also likely to make an endorsement decision based on the New Hampshire primary. Instead of diminishing the influence of Iowa and New Hampshire, the Super Tuesday event may only serve to glorify an earlier successful candidate even more, or even worse, to drive the disenchanted moderate Southerners to the Republican Party in search of a middle-of-the-road candidate. This will leave representing the South largely to the black liberal voters, who are likely to turn out in numbers beyond their representation in the society as a whole. In that case, the beneficiary of Super Tuesday will most likely be Jesse Jackson.

Jesse Jackson has a core of supporters waiting to be called into action left over from his 1984 campaign. When Jesse Jackson enters a state, his network does much of the advance work that is so troublesome for other campaigns—like choosing suitable locations for meetings and getting people to answer phones, distribute flyers and so forth.

Jesse Jackson appeals to the discontented, but not so much those discontented with the lot of others as with their own situations. Californians are used to saying "I'm okay and you *might* be okay *but* . . ." Mr. Jackson pulls his support from those who say "I'm not okay." Nevertheless, a Mervin Field poll conducted in the summer of 1987 showed Mario Cuomo, a non-candidate, the favorite of 29 percent of Californians polled, followed by Jesse Jackson at 13 percent. The Republicans showed George Bush (30 percent) polling about the same as Governor Cuomo, followed by another non-candidate favorite of Californians, Howard Baker, who led Robert Dole 18 percent to 12 percent.

Californians have been described as self-satisfied and unconcerned with the rest of the nation. In his *Atlantic* piece, William Schneider discussed the views of two astute political scientists who were familiar with the *California experience*. James Q. Wilson in an article for *Commentary* in 1967 tried to describe the support that emerged in the Golden State for Goldwater as a protest movement against the ignorance of the rest of the nation. Wilson wrote that their discontent was not with themselves but with the rest of society:

> The very virtues they have and practice are, in their eyes, conspicuously absent from society as a whole.[28]

Mr. Schneider pointed out that Richard Todd said almost the same thing in the same year when discussing what went on in Berkeley.

> The Berkeley life-style was tolerant, expressive, open, non-violent, permissive and, above all, contented. No one wanted to leave. Then why were the students angry? Because the outside world was racist, uptight, elitist, violent and repressive. The very virtues that Berkeley students had and practiced were, in their eyes, conspicuously absent from society as a whole.[29]

These observations took place twenty years ago, and as one who was there (in Berkeley) I can attest to their insightfulness. What was true in 1967 was true, I believe in 1957, '47 and '37, but the question before us today is the relevance of these observations to 1987.

In 1980 Jimmy Carter conceded the election before the polls had closed in the West. (No wonder many Californians feel they can't make a difference in the political process!) As a result, there were proposals for twenty-four hours' voting or uniform poll closings, which were not taken seriously at the time mainly due to cost. The continual rise in the debt ceiling bears witness to the fact that those on Capitol Hill don't take *cost* seriously and so the recent sponsorship of HR435 by Al Swift (Democrat, Washington) and William Thomas (Republican, California) comes as no surprise. The bill would require every state in the union, except Arkansas and Hawaii, to close polls at 9:00 p.m. Eastern Standard Time. Daylight savings would be extended for two weeks past normal (the last Sunday in October) in the Pacific Time Zone so that closing would be 7:00 p.m. Pacific *Daylight* time. The airlines oppose the measure because of the havoc extending daylight savings will work with their schedules.

But it is more than poll closings. The politicians themselves have made many Californians feel like the forgotten people when it comes to choosing presidential candidates. As columnist Dan Walters said on August 7, 1987:

> So far, the candidates have acted as if California consists of two large reservoirs of cash, one in West Los Angeles and the other in San Francisco. They have jetted in, staged their fund-raising events

and then left as rapidly as possible for Des Moines or Manchester to spend the proceeds.

If there's a presidential selection process under way in the United States, it is one that is disconnected, at least so far, from California.

Once in a while they alight in Carmel, as Senator Robert Dole did recently in pursuit of an endorsement by our colorful mayor Clint Eastwood.

Gary Hart was clearly the choice of a majority of California's Democrats, and with his withdrawal from the pack, many Democrats in the Golden State lost interest, at least temporarily. Mr. Hart was as direct in his social policies as he was indirect in his personal life. He won favor with many Westerners by declaring that using the tax code to direct social policy is a sign that our legislators don't have the courage to make a case for their policies above board and directly to the American people. Gary Hart criticized the practice of obtaining low-income housing by offering tax-incentives to developers as a typical example of the lack of courage we are talking about:

> The hand that can give the housing developers a tax incentive is also the hand that can slip something in for an individual company or special interest. Government is going to require a kind of intellectual honesty of politicians in the future. If it is good for the society to do something, then take the case to the American people.[30]

Gary Hart was an early advocate of the president's role as a broker between labor, management and private capital. The idea is neither new nor unique but, like the ideas of technocrat Michael Dukakis, it appeals to California's yuppie voters.

Peter Hart, a political strategist who appeared on a panel September 7, 1987 (C-SPAN), spoke of the advantage Democrats have over Republicans going into the 1987-88 campaign.[31] Mr. Hart told his audience that by a 5 to 3 margin (poll) Americans would prefer a president in his forties with ten to fifteen years' experience. The Democrats reportedly have a twenty-eight point advantage with female and older voters and 30-39 percent of Americans would prefer to switch from the Republican to the Democratic party. The Democrats have been doing something mighty wrong to have so many voters overcome their natural inclinations and join with the Republicans. The Democrats hope to find and eliminate their error before November 1988.

Most people are too busy with their work, family and friends to stop and on their own analyze where America as a nation is headed and whether or not they approve. But because politicians are notoriously short-sighted, seeing only from one election to the next, it is up to the people to take that long-range view to see that the America they envision is preserved for future generations.

Adlai Stevenson once said, "I'm not an old experienced hand at politics. But I am seasoned enough to have learned that the hardest thing about any political campaign is how to win without proving that you are unworthy of winning."

Voters should ask the 1988 presidential candidates for their game plans issue by issue. What we need is an election based not on charisma as much as character, not on rhetoric as much as research, not on promises as much as policies. (The preceding sentence is proof that political rhetoric rubs off as well as wears thin.)

A biographical sketch follows of thirteen of the more than two hundred declared candidates for the 1988 presidential nomination. Already, in the fall of 1987, Joe Biden has quit the race and the list will narrow even more after March 8, 1988. Sections II and III analyze what is being said on the 1988 campaign circuit and cut beneath the rhetoric to reveal the candidates' stand on various issues.

"Meanwhile," as Alan Ehrenhalt suggests, "other political leaders who might make good presidents are confined to the sidelines. They are unwilling to participate in an undignified process in order to be considered for the job."[32]

Section Two

Democratic Presidential Hopefuls

Bruce Babbitt

Forty-nine-year-old Bruce Babbitt is many things: an accomplished outdoorsman, an attorney and an ex-attorney general who, by the process of succession, became Governor of Arizona and was later elected and reelected in his own right. He has been married for almost twenty years (August 1969) to a former Texan, now a practicing trial attorney in Phoenix, and has two lively young sons. Although Bruce Babbitt was born in Los Angeles, he is a third generation member of an Arizona pioneer family and was raised in that state. He has the intensity and drive required to run a hard political fight. His ambition and stamina were evidenced by his 397-mile bicycle ride across Iowa in an attempt to draw media attention to his campaign.

In 1960 Bruce Babbitt received a degree in geology from Notre Dame and immediately began working on a graduate degree in geophysics by doing field work in Bolivia. However, in 1962 he decided his destiny lay in public service and he left the pursuit of science and entered Harvard Law School, paying his room and board by working as a freshman dorm master in Harvard College. He spent his summers as an accíon volunteer in Latin America and directing an international student workcamp in Peru. He is proud of his participation in the Selma civil rights marches which led directly to his involvement in several antipoverty programs after he received his J.D. in 1965. As an attorney with the U.S. Office of Economic Opportunity (1965-67) he worked on migrant workers programs in the Rio Grande Valley, school desegregation programs and the creation of legal service programs for Native Americans.

Between 1967-75, Mr. Babbitt practiced law in a private firm in Phoenix, Arizona. In 1974 he was elected Attorney General of Arizona and upon the death of former Governor Wesley Bolin became governor in March 1978 through constitutional succession. Later that year he was elected governor in his own right and received 62.5 percent of the vote to win reelection in 1982. When his term expired on January 5, 1987, he became affiliated with the law firm of Steptoe and Johnson, which has offices in Washington, D.C., as well as Phoenix. Since then he has been constantly on the campaign trail—mostly in Iowa and New Hampshire.

There is little doubt that Bruce Babbitt supports an activist's role for government. He has said, "We can use government to create a more just society" and has ridiculed the Reagan administration's contention that what this country needs is for government to take a holiday. He wants to see government chart a course for the nation and envisions the President of the United States as the captain steering the country by that course. In his statement of candidacy Mr. Babbitt showed a certain naiveté by declaring, "I want to see an America in charge again. All it will take is leadership." Unfortunately it will take a great deal more than leadership to keep America number one in the world. Number one is, of course, the stated goal of every presidential aspirant who also professes to have what it takes to achieve the goal.

Mr. Babbitt claims that seeing that America is in charge again is the cause of a lifetime. Although he never specifies what he means by "in charge again," one is not really interested, assuming it is merely candidates' rhetoric. But Bruce Babbitt, unlike many of his challengers, offers more than platitudes.

Trade

Regarding trade, ex-Governor Babbitt rejects the Gephardt amendment but offers some innovative and concrete strategies of his own in its stead. He suggests that any nation running an overall multilateral trade surplus be required to reduce that surplus by a third each year or face across the board tariffs. He envisions an international agreement for balanced trade which says a nation must import and export in equal measure. If a nation sells too much it must see that it buys the same amount—not of the same goods, of course, but nevertheless this may be an artificial mindless non-market-oriented solution which can hardly be good for the world's consumers. Making people buy what they don't want is like trying to fit a square peg in a round hole in order to satisfy some leader's grandiose scheme. Ridiculous!

Workplace Democracy

Mr. Babbitt thinks not only in specifics but he thinks big when he considers national goals. He wants the nation to set a goal of cooperation whereby American workers will share in the profits and losses of business (workplace-democracy). Of course if workers have little capital to lose it is a one-sided arrangement where the potential risk is no match for the potential gain. As things stand now, if a company fails to make a profit the owners stand to lose their capital, and in many instances time and energy, whereas workers stand to lose a job. Workers get their time and energy compensated as they go, by wages that have been negotiated and agreed upon. Owners are compensated from the potential profits. For workers to share in those profits without the risk is nonsense.

Mr. Babbitt spouts more nonsense when he declares that after two terms of his presidency "1996 will signal the end of trickle down economics and the arrival of an economy built from the bottom up." Mr. Babbitt seems to assume that workers are always responsible for greater productivity when he says that if he has his way "no American company will be permitted to deduct an executive bonus as a business expense unless it offers productivity pay for all of its employees." He forgets that it is often creative approaches to management and capital expenditures that are reponsible for greater business productivity. On the other hand his idea that bonuses given for performance should not be taxed away would probably meet with universal approval. He would like to see a tax-exempt account set up for bonuses. The rest of us can no doubt give the ex-governor a myriad of suggestions for other such tax-exempt accounts. How about exempting savings for education or for self-improvement in general, for future health care needs, for money set aside toward achieving the American dream of home ownership? Please, Mr. Babbitt—why one without the other? How about an account for receiving withholdings that offers the taxpayer interest while the government waits at its turn to get at their money?

During a debate against Republican presidential hopeful Pete du Pont held at Drake University in Des Moines, Iowa, in May 1987, Mr. Babbitt told his audience that managers ask workers to take wage cuts and then give themselves bonuses for solving the problems. Bruce Babbitt wants to enact a law which forces managers and workers to have equal cuts and bonuses. Perhaps there ought to be a law against a politician rewriting the economy according to his own dictates.

Surely it is not too much to ask that politicians back up their facts. (No more Gary Hart-style vagueness even about his own birthdate.) Mr. Babbitt claims "... our productivity is growing at half the rate of Germany, one third the rate of France, one fourth the rate of Japan." What he failed to mention is that America is still the most productive nation on earth and that other nations have been extremely inefficient in the past and are now catching up. According to the Bureau of Labor Statistics the following are international productivity levels given as gross domestic product per employee for 1985: USA—100, Germany—81.5, France—82 and Japan—68.7. As for growth (the average annual change in gross domestic product per employee) for the period 1983-86: USA—1.5, Germany—2.2, France—1.7 and Japan—2.8.[1] Even with TEFRA (the 1982 tax reform) which repealed ERTA's (the 1981 tax reform) deductions for equipment and machinery, manufacturing productivity grew faster in this country under the Reagan administration than during the average postwar expansion. According to the 1987 report of the Council of Economic Advisers, output per hour rose an average of 3.8 percent per year in the manufacturing sector between the third quarter of 1981 and 1986; more than double the average 1.5 percent rate reported for the 1973 to 1981 time period. That meant that labor costs (wages and productivity) had been rising, but at only a relatively small fraction of the average rise between 1946 and 1981. It is hard, therefore, to understand Mr. Babbitt's claim that for the last six years we've been standing still in this nation. Perhaps he and other presidential candidates should be asked to produce citations for their "facts."

In August 1987 he told his audience at the Southern Legislative Conference in Little Rock, Arkansas, this his workplace-democracy would encourage profit sharing, employee ownership and cooperation in the workplace. It would also eliminate greed and speculation and outlaw "greenmail" and "golden parachutes."

Taxes

Mr. Babbitt proposes a combination of new revenues while opposing oil-import fees as injurious to any concept of free open international markets and claiming also that excise taxes unfairly burden lower-income taxpayers. Progressiveness is all important to Mr. Babbitt. He has proposed a 5 percent federal sales tax which he estimates might bring in about $40 billion per year but he is not specific in his thoughts on how to ensure that it is progressive. He suggests there are many ways to do so as in exempting necessities such as food, shelter and medicine or, as another means, offering personal tax exemptions as an offset. He wants to broaden the tax base by eliminating all mortgage deductions on second homes and restricting the deduction allowed on expensive first homes (limit deductions to $20,000 for joint filers).

Education

Let's examine Mr. Babbitt's proposal that the federal government take over the state's funding of Medicaid and put the savings toward education. Medicaid, according to the 107th edition of the Statistical Abstract of the United States (1987) cost the states and the federal government approximately $25 billion each in 1986, whereas federal funds to public schools was just under $17 billion. This then is what Mr. Babbitt calls a fair exchange. Not even exchanging a $25 billion obligation for a $17 billion obligation because it was not even suggested that the federal government be relieved of the $17 billion obligation. No—the states are to be relieved of the obligation to provide $25 billion in Medicare (Mr. Babbitt refers to $20 billion) in exchange for doing something they were supposed to do in the first place—fund education!

Education has always been the prerogative of the states with the federal government providing, in recent years, a mere 7 percent of educational funding. Under Mr. Babbitt's plan the states must apply the windfall "directly into teacher salaries and education programs." Mr. Babbitt says:

> Strengthening our educational system must be one of the nation's top priorities for the 1990s and beyond. Of all the investments we make in our future, none is more important than education. The federal government has a responsibility to help state and local governments make the investment we need to give our children the best education in the world ... (the federal government should provide) guaranteed access to educational programs and student financial assistance, including Pell grants and guaranteed student loans, help for special groups that are at risk in standard educational programs and training programs for the workforce ... The Department of Education should fund research and development, develop model programs and establish educational objectives—based upon concrete measures of student achievement that challenge every school in the country to be the best."

During his governorship, Arizona's constitutional spending limit for education was raised and he was responsible for the largest teacher pay package in Arizona history. What we as taxpayers really need is a guarantee that more money will buy a system that gets results!

Mr. Babbitt claims that states are already spending nearly $70 billion on education and local governments provide another $60 billion, but that is not enough. In his 1983 State of the State address, then-Governor Babbitt said: "Throughout the history of our nation, the public schools have been the driving force behind our economic growth, the source of much of our social progress and one of the great foundations of our democratic traditions." Mr. Babbitt believes that local communities, as opposed to Washington, D.C., are responsible for excellent schools. He would like to see poorer communities have the same amount to spend on education as more wealthy communities and suggests that federal subsidies and funds be allocated on a per student basis not according to property values. I would argue that an even more democratic answer to our education problems is the universal voucher whereby every youngster in the nation is given the same amount of credit to spend on private or public education as his/her family sees fit. This would have the added benefit of making certain the schools compete against one another for students and ensure that parents can get what they seem unable to get today—that is a quality education for their children.

At the Southern Legislative Conference in Little Rock, Arkansas, in August 1987, Mr. Babbitt told his audience that:

> We must end the neglect of our children. Thirty percent don't graduate from high school ... There is a federal role in education ... we must get rid of (Secretary of Education William) Bennett, provide day-care, universal pre-school and more access to college.

There is no doubt that many of his achievements in Arizona deserve to be recognized. Mr. Babbitt takes credit for Arizona's policy of allowing employees of high-technology firms to double as math and science teachers and for doubling the math and science requirements for high school graduation in the state.

Child Care

During the debate between the seven Democratic candidates for the presidential nomination held in Dubuque, Iowa, on August 22, 1987, Mr. Babbitt insisted that child-care is an issue of workplace democracy. He was incensed that single parents go out and take a low paying job and then are burdened with child-care payments. He claimed day-care is a moral issue and what is needed is a uniform day-care voucher.

While governor of Arizona, Bruce Babbitt fought for the right to use public facilities as child-care centers during their off-hours.

At one time there was a law prohibiting school districts from using public schools for custodial care, probably because government would be in direct competition with private custodial care facilities (those things used to matter) and probably because of liability insurance (something which along with government regulations keeps down the number of private care centers available to working parents).

Although Mr. Babbitt does not support a national education voucher he has gone on record as claiming that, "It's time nationally to create a uniform federal state voucher based day-care entitlement system for every child in this country." When confronted by those who would label such a voucher system as one more welfare scheme he responds that it is an entitlement. But Mr. Babbitt goes even further in justifying day-care vouchers—he claims they are the opposite of welfare and that they are rather an inducement for parents to be responsible.

Welfare, if you ask the ordinary man on the street, is acceptance of help from society at large. The opposite would seem to be the giving of aid to society at large. Perhaps Mr. Babbitt assumes society is helped by parents being responsible—a not uncommon view of things now days. Over and over an already responsible majority submits to blackmail (Pay for this or else!) They are told that they must spend more on schools now to avoid spending more on prisons later. Paying a minority to do what the majority already does responsibly is ridiculous and I wonder how long and why a responsible majority will continue to acquiesce.

Mr. Babbitt refuses to call a spade a spade—or in this case, day-care vouchers welfare. They may well be an inducement for parents who might otherwise be tempted to leave their children unsupervised to be more responsible and are in that sense a benefit to children as Mr. Babbitt claims. But there are many other ways society might achieve the goal of responsible parenting and supervised children.

Children come into this world neither rich nor poor on their own merit, yet it is fashionable to decry the poverty of children. Children suffer or rejoice in the irresponsibility or responsibility, the neglect or the care, of their parents. And don't tell me poverty negates opportunity when Charles Kuralt showed us all the wonderful example of Alex and Mary Chandler who raised nine children in a sharecropper's cabin on the poorest farm in the poorest state. With often nothing to wear and nothing to eat, all nine children managed to put themselves through college, many obtaining advanced degrees. It is love and care, not money, that determine success.

All societies adopt a particular role toward children. At

one time, even in this country, children, as well as women and slaves, were considered chattel. A man could do with them as he pleased—PERIOD! The other extreme is a state which takes total responsibility for the welfare of the young—a kibutz situation as illustrated in George Orwell's *1984*—where all children are cared for by the state as to food, shelter, health and education. America today is vague on government's responsibilities to the young, with the rights of the child as a distinct human being often clashing with the rights of the parents to act as they see fit. The state towers over both omnipotently deciding whether it will tolerate certain actions (or lack thereof) and their results. Clashes can be seen in the ongoing battles over abortion rights, Baby Doe cases where medical care is mandated for a child contrary to a parent's judgment and in the pleas to provide children from poor and often uncaring families (and by no means do the two always go together as evidenced by the Chandler family) with services (health care—school lunch programs) or their families with money (often the child never sees any benefit from those dollars) to bring them more nearly up to the level of their more fortunate peers.

Bruce Babbitt tells heart wrenching stories and asks, "Who are we as a society if we are housing a generation of children too hungry to learn and too sick to dream of a better future." He backs that up by claiming that one quarter of our children live in poverty (should we take them away from their poor parents—no? Should we then let hardworking, self-sacrificing responsible non-poor parents give these poor parents some of *their* money?) and half don't have access to health care.

Figures for "children in poverty" were first calculated in 1929. In 1959 the figures stood at 26.9 percent and in 1985 at 20.1 percent; more like one-fifth rather than the one-quarter claimed by Mr. Babbitt. But when it comes to such statistics there is little accuracy at any rate. Poverty was one of those subjective words until policy-makers stepped in and gave it their own concrete meaning. Actually many people are counted as poor who are not deprived by any objective standard, because there is considerable disagreement as to what should be considered in determining poverty.

AFDC (Aid to Families With Dependent Children) benefits vary from state to state. Monthly AFDC benefits for a family of three are $118 in Alabama versus $389 in Maine even though per capita incomes in the two states are approximately the same. But no matter what is wrenched from a compassionate and responsible public it will never be enough.[2] It is the philosophy itself that is bankrupt.

Social Security

Mr. Babbitt believes firmly in means testing. He would like to see all government support—Social Security and Medicare benefits, farm, trade and education subsidies and all tax deductions and credits, targeted on the basis of need. He advocates this policy despite the Democrats' long-standing principle first articulated by Franklin Delano Roosevelt that in order to win support for welfare programs one must appeal to the self-interest of the nation's large middle class. The original purpose of Social Security was to maintain customary standards of living for retirees while waging a more general war against poverty. In 1935, President Roosevelt committed the country to payroll financing and convinced policy-makers that general revenue should not be used as a source of funds. He was shrewd enough to realize that it was the payroll that lent a legal, moral and political justification to the beneficiaries' claims. Even though those close to him pointed to the fact that since employers would pass their share of the taxes through to the consumer, making the payroll tax a form of sales tax falling hardest on those least able to afford it, FDR obstinately stuck to his guns.

> I guess you're right on the economics . . . but those taxes were never a problem of economics. They are politics all the way through. We put those payroll contributions there so as to give the contributors a legal, moral and political right to collect their pensions and their unemployment benefits. With those taxes in there, no damn politician can ever scrap my social security program.[3]

In a column which appeared in the *San Francisco Examiner* on December 31, 1986, Mr. Babbitt showed himself to be a politician somewhat less shrewd than his mentor, FDR, when he wrote under the heading "Don't Scuttle Social Security":

> Some say that relating benefits to income represents heresy. But I've

never understood why the Mellons, Hunts (and even Babbitts) should get the same federal entitlement as a widow living in a cold water flat.

Aside from the strange imagery from an Arizona native (the only people I was able to find who had any inkling of the term "cold water flat" were either over age sixty or from the East Coast), Mr. Babbitt expressed his ignorance of the conflict between those who would refer to Social Security as insurance and those who would call it welfare which surrounded the birth of that program in the thirties and continued in the ensuing years. To be sure, in the *Examiner* Mr. Babbitt cautions that,

> Neither can we turn Social Security into welfare. The advantage of universal participation in the system is that everyone can feel they are part of a national community that looks to the care of those in need.

Unfortunately that is not the advantage at all—self interest, not philanthropy was what was argued in behalf of universal Social Security, as well as concrete acturial benefits, of course.

There's no denying the real psychological differences, at least in the minds of the recipients, in thinking of Social Security as insurance rather than assistance even though it is admittedly a combination of the two. In an insurance contract, the insured demonstrates that he has earned the benefits; in an assistance program that he has a need. Anything which might supplement that need, such as savings and earnings, are deducted from assistance, effectively reducing all recipients to the same low level. The insurance concept, on the other hand, encourages variation. Savings and private insurance don't detract from the government's liability but instead supplement Social Security benefits.

Not surprisingly Mr. Babbitt sees,

> Opting out of the Social Security system is no option: we cannot turn the fate of elderly Americans over to a capricious generational struggle of the fittest.

In 1982, the National Taxpayers Legal Fund suggested splitting the insurance and welfare elements of Social Security. It is an idea that, in one form or another, was promoted even earlier by such notables as William Simon, Milton Friedman, Barry Goldwater, Pete Wilson and James Buchanan. The welfare portion might be financed under SSI (Supplemental Security Income) from general revenue. That would leave the insurance segment of Social Security to accumulate and be invested in private sector IRAs. Benefits derived from their own investment choices would, in most cases, more than compensate citizens for any lost Social Security benefits. For example, if a thirty-five-year-old worker made an average of $25,000 per year, his combined tax, i.e. the amount withheld annually from his paycheck and matched by his employer, would amount to $3,500. If that money was invested at a currently conservative 8 percent, by the time the worker was ready to retire at age 65 he would have an accumulation in the neighborhood of $400,000. There's a good chance (depending on future economic conditions) that our worker could live comfortably on the interest and, if he wished, could leave the untouched principal as an inheritance for his children; something that, for many, makes working worthwhile. It can be a great feeling to leave a legacy, material as well as spiritual, to the younger generation. And, on the other hand, if the retiree has no family, upon retirement that $400,000 could be used to purchase a lifetime annuity that would yield enough to make retirement dreams come true.

The decision to tax certain Social Security benefits made as part of the 1983 Reform package was not a popular or welcome reform. The reason for the new tax was quite simple—the system needed money. The superficial justification for taxing Social Security benefits was that they should be treated in the same manner as private pension plans. For IRS purposes, the employee's contribution was already taxed when paid because the amount paid in payroll tax is included as part of the employee's income even though never actually received by him. But to follow through in a logical manner on the theory that Social Security benefits should be exempt from taxation only for the value of the beneficiaries' contributions means that on the average, since early contributions were so small, 20 percent of today's benefits would be exempt and approximately 80 percent taxable, not 50 percent! That would probably be agreeable to Mr. Babbitt providing

> the revenues can be used to finance the health care and income needs of the elderly, to scale back the regressive FICA payroll tax and to achieve greater equity for women.[4]

As for targeting society's limited resources, I agree with Mr. Babbitt that it must be done better and soon. In 1981, certain members of the Greenspan Commission, which was formed to make recommendations concerning Social Security, argued that cutting the $122 minimum Social Security benefit could be defended on grounds the truly needy would be eligible for that much or more from the means tested programs already functioning, such as SSI. In response, a reader wrote a letter to the *New York Times* claiming SSI could never adequately replace the minimum benefit because many people would be reluctant to apply for SSI since it carried the stigma of a welfare program. Because of their reluctance does it make sense to collect a lot of taxes and deal them out again without regard to need? Overkill? You bet!

Among its many recommendations for Social Security reform the Greenspan Commission called for full catastrophic hospital coverage for long-term illness in exchange for the insured's shouldering more of the cost for shorter hospital stays. (David Stockman when he was head of the Office of Management and Budget and Dr. Otis Bowen as Secretary of Health and Human Services made essentially the same recommendation.) This is, in my opinion, always a good trade-off when it comes to insurance of any type. Currently, however, Medicare stresses the opposite priorities. Co-payments (the amount the insured must pay) increase the longer the hospital stay.

But Mr. Babbitt wants to have his cake and eat it, too. In the January 19, 1986, edition of the *Los Angeles Times* he said,

> The Stockman and Bowen proposals have the right objective but the wrong approach. Medicare should be reformed to provide catastrophic coverage, but without imposing more hardship on those who cannot afford higher charges. ... All enrollees would be fully protected (under Mr. Babbitt's proposal) against all hospital costs after the first-day deductible, *no matter how large the bills become*, and against physician's costs above $225. [Italics are mine.]

Energy

As an environmentalist, a respected geologist and a member of the President's Commission on the Accident at Three Mile Island (the Kennedy Commission), Mr. Babbitt's opinion on nuclear power deserves attention:

> Anyone who thinks a utility company can plan the evacuation of thousands of citizens—coordinating resources from the private sector and from dozens of agencies of state and local government—has simply not considered the problem. Experience suggests that many nuclear power plants cannot even plan routine operations within their own four walls. Asking them to take responsibility for dealing with a disaster on the scale of Chernobyl, or worse, is nothing more than preposterous.

Mr. Babbitt takes the stand that no nuclear power plant—including Seabrook in New Hampshire—should be allowed to operate until state and local governments have developed emergency response plans. He is against the development of a second high-level waste repository in the East. "It doesn't make economic, environmental or geological sense. There is plenty of room to expand the existing western facilities." He would like to see Senator Moynihan's bill, which seeks to hold utilities fully liable in the event of an accident, replace the Price Anderson Act which expires in 1987. However he believes it should hold contractors accountable as well as utilities. He would like to see the Nuclear Regulatory Commission replaced by a single accountable administrator.

Agriculture

As for the farm crisis, Mr. Babbitt expressed several views during the debate held at Drake University, Des Moines, against Mr. du Pont in May 1987 and during the August 1987 Dubuque debate, which included all seven Democratic candidates. Mr. Babbitt berated Mr. Gephardt's mandatory production controls claiming they would only drive up prices and isolate us from the rest of the world. He again berated the present policy of sending $10,000 checks to large farmers and declared that his policy would be to concentrate on the small family farms. He critized Ronald Reagan for wanting to get rid of deficiency payments and Pete du Pont whom he claims said, "Let's terminate all government programs." Bruce Babbitt says we'll make the midwest a corporate farm by driving off all family farmers. He wants corporate agribusiness out of the farm program, no more checks for them—"Family farms in the tradition of compassion and common sense." He reiterated that as a nation we must ask,

> Is this program necessary and targeted? . . . We must get rid of agribusiness subsidies and focus on family farmers . . . Mortgage subsidies are simply not needed for ski cabins . . . we must focus on first-home owners.

Priorities

Mr. Babbitt outlined three priorities he would have if elected president. The first was in reference to workplace-democracy and involved mandatory regulations designed to bring labor and management together. The second related to the necessity for implementing a universal needs test. He said that a question must be asked of each and every item in the budget—"Is it really needed and really focused?" His third priority would be children. He would end the neglect of our children by providing day-care and education. He went on to say:

> We are picking the pockets of our children by cutting taxes. Raising revenue is the only answer. Every $1 cut will raise $1. We must ask, "Do we really need that program and is it targeted?"

Mr. Babbitt left his audience in Dubuque with the thought that the major issue in 1988 is whether we, as a nation, can find the leadership to take charge of our economic future.

The April 1987 issue of the *Atlantic Monthly* presented Mr. Babbitt's philosophy simply:

> We, as a society, cannot afford to continue buying off the middle class in order to retain government subsidies for the "truly needy." . . . Targeting benefits allows us to move away from the notion that the only way you can expand the safety net is by buying everybody off in equal measure . . . As we have progressive taxation we will also have progressive benefits in society.

Bruce Babbitt appears to be a compassionate man with an ambition as big as his heart. He is a man of ideas, not merely rhetoric and that is assuredly in his favor except that his ideas would bankrupt the nation and forever change its character.

Joe Biden

It is impossible to run for the nomination for President of the United States without having an enormous amount of ambition—moxie, if you will. All candidates of both parties showed an extraordinary amount of ambition at an early age but none more than Joseph Robinette Biden, Jr. Even while still a college student Joe Biden had his heart and mind set on becoming a United States Senator.

In studying the candidates I find many have several traits in common and to a greater degree than the traits or circumstances are found throughout the population at large. First, the extraordinary ambition I have been discussing; second, a strong and supportive wife (a surprising number of wives are attorneys); and third, a handicap or personal tragedy to overcome and in some cases an almost pathological need to prove themselves. Then, of course, there are the obvious accoutrements which all politicians share—the vision for the nation, charisma and even, in some instances, intelligence and more likely than not, legal training.

Joe Biden was born in Scranton, Pennsylvania, on November 2, 1942, the oldest of four children (three boys and one girl), and moved with his family to Delaware when he was ten years old. He stuttered as a child and, like fellow presidential hopeful Jesse Jackson[5], he worked so hard to overcome his impediment that he emerged as one of the Democrats' most commanding and persuasive speakers. Senator Biden earned his B.A. degree from the University of Delaware in 1965 and enrolled in law school at Syracuse University because his future wife, Neilia Hunter of Skaneateles, New York, was enrolled at that institution. The Senator received his J.D. degree from Syracuse in 1968, was admitted to the Delaware bar and began to practice criminal law, first as a public defender in Wilmington and then in his own firm. His opponents might want me to mention his one brief digression from the Party when, as a new lawyer, he clerked for six or seven months for a GOP law firm before turning to more stimulating work as an assistant to a Democratic activist.

By the time he won his first election in 1970 to the New Castle County Council, he was married and the father of two sons, Beau and Hunter. No sooner did Joe Biden have his first political victory under his belt than he began planning for his second. The stakes were far bigger this time. This inexperienced 28-year-old had the chutzpah to aspire to the United States Senate and no one in the Democratic Party had any inclination to stop him. In fact no Democrat in Delaware thought it was possible to defeat the popular incumbent, Senator J. Caleb Boggs, who would be defending his seat in 1972. However, Senator Boggs had already served two terms as Delaware's governor and three terms as its at-large member of the House of Representatives and had agreed to run again for the Senate only at the urging of President Richard Nixon. Perhaps that reluctance worked subconsciously in Joe Biden's favor. At any rate, with raw ambition and the love and energy of his close family members (his sister was his campaign manager) and any others he could entice, the Biden for Senator campaign was launched in 1970. Really it had taken shape in Joe Biden's mind back in the sixties during his college years, as I mentioned earlier. In order to achieve name recognition Councilman Biden from New Castle County attended five to seven coffee hours, or teas, a day. "Biden's mother organized the thirty to forty coffee hours that her son attended each week."[6] Name recognition could never be achieved without a campaign chest for advertising costs in most states, but then Delaware is not California and Joe Biden was able to avoid the cost of postage and reach his constituents with the help of teenagers who distributed leaflets by hand. The victory was narrow, with Biden winning 116,006 votes to Boggs' 112,844. At the time Joe Biden was only 29 years old and did not reach the required age of 30 until November 20, which was, of course, well before he took the oath of office.

Joe Biden has had more than his share of personal tragedy. The teasing over his speech impediment that he endured as a youngster only made him determined to succeed and have the last laugh on his tormentors—a classic example of turning lemons into lemonade. However the tragedy which occurred on December 18, 1972, in Ockessin, Delaware, was enough to swamp any ordinary man. His wife, 27-year-old Neilia, sons 3-year-old Beau and 2-year-old Hunter and daughter, 13-month-old Naomi, were bringing home a Christmas tree in the family station wagon when it collided with a tractor-trailer. His wife and daughter were killed instantly and the two boys were critically injured. It was no doubt the hardest decision of Senator Biden's life to take the oath of office required to serve in the United States Senate, which with considerable urging, support and love from his family he did in his sons' hospital room. His sister and her husband moved into the Senator's house in order to care for the boys and the Senator began commuting daily between Wilmington and Washington—a ninety-minute train ride each way. Again, if he had been elected to the Senate from California the decision would perhaps have been impossible to make. Luck—if there really is such a thing—seems to play a very large role in Joseph Robinette Biden, Jr.'s life—luck intensely good and intensely bad. But then Joe Biden is an intense man. He was subdued somewhat for about three years until 1975 when he met Jill Jacobs, his second wife-to-be, and began at the same time eyeing the White House.

Joe Biden received some help in his 1970-72 campaign for the Senate from Patrick Caddell who was handling polling for George McGovern, the Democratic presidential candidate. The two (Joe and Pat) have remained fast friends over the ensuing years, with the *Washington Post* claiming that Biden once blurted that, "Sometimes I don't know where Pat's thinking stops and mine begins." *Time* magazine quotes a former Biden ally as saying, "In political terms Joe and Pat are really one candidate."[7] Patrick Caddell tried to get Joe Biden to run for the presidency in 1984, but the Senator decided he probably was not "lucky" enough to repeat his win against Senator Boggs in a second successful run against a popular incumbent—this time Ronald Reagan. Mr. Caddell then offered his not inconsequential services to Gary Hart who, we remember, came within a hair's breadth of capturing the Democratic nomination. Biden and Caddell could well prove to be a formidable team.

What has come to be known as "The Biden Speech" was actually drafted under the guidance of Mr. Caddell and first delivered to a group of New Jersey Democrats in the fall of 1983. On paper it's not bad if you like imagery, symbolism, demagoguery and what many call "lots of hot air." But when Senator Biden breathes life into it, it becomes pure poetry—with the cadence and gestures guaranteed to evoke the emotions of any audience and leave a good many of them weeping. The following is one of his best lines reputed to bring the house down: "Just because our political heroes were murdered does not mean that the dream does not still live, buried deep within the broken hearts of tens of millions of Americans." He loves to invoke the memory of Jack and Robert Kennedy and Martin Luther King, Jr., and wraps himself too closely in their cloak for some tastes. But it works for those who like their politics with theatrics. Michael Barone, a columnist for the Washington Post, has said that "... the intensity of his (Senator Biden's) speaking seems not contrived or cynical ..." I do not agree, but that is perhaps because I have heard the same speech over and over and find it hard to believe that each time it comes from the heart. But repetition is what is demanded of those running for office and it is beyond me how they can get up the enthusiasm and present as much sincerity as they do day after day—for years! Is it possible? Five to seven coffee hours a day for two years in the campaign against Senator Boggs? No wonder so many of us would never dream of running for office. Masochistic!

Senator Biden has been referred to as the Democrats' answer to Ronald Reagan—he is their own "Great Communicator" with the same ability to inspire and motivate. The speeches, whether or not they are masterminded by Pat Caddell, are carefully orchestrated to convey a "national message" saying nothing concrete as to specific issues but structured to convey a feeling. Such a talent to persuade can be dangerous. Some of history's best motivators led their followers into chaos.

No one would deny the Biden campaign has charisma and is long on strategy. In an appeal to the largest segment of potential voters, the Baby Boomers: ". . . a young generation is waiting to be summoned to great deeds." Or for a real blast of hot air how about this: "In the spirit of another time let us pledge that our generation of Americans will pay any price, bear any burden, accept any challenge, meet any hardship to secure the blessings of prosperity and the promise of America for our children."

Even Senator Biden's attempt to palm himself off to the Baby Boomers as one of them is false and contrived. Baby Boomers are generally considered to include those born between 1946-1957 which would ordinarily disqualify Joe Biden leaving the field to genuine Baby Boomer Al Gore (born in 1948).

Many of Joe Biden's big name political managers and consultants worked for Walter Mondale. (Remember they got "big names" not because they pick losers. On the other hand no one picks winners all the time!) Some of Senator Biden's good luck is evidenced by having an illustrious team on his side while his bad luck is in having them feuding among themselves. Pat Caddell, David Doak and Robert Shrum used to have a consulting business together but had a falling out last year which may or may not have been resolved to everyone's satisfaction. In spite of, or because of, is uncertain but nevertheless by the time Joe Biden formally announced his candidacy for the Democratic presidential nomination early in June 1987 he had already amassed a war chest of more than $2 million, a formidable campaign machine and a treasury of speeches guaranteed to mobilize the Baby Boomers and invoke the spirit of the 1960s. Senator Biden's stated goal is to inspire (pure poetry) ". . . untapped legions, whose success in other fields prepares them by disposition, experience, confidence and creativity to transfuse the tired blood of our politics with new ideas, new approaches and new energy."

The Senator's speech before the winter meeting of the Industrial Unions of the AFL-CIO held early in 1987 in Bal Harbour, Florida, illustrates the cursory approach given "new ideas and substantive issues."

He began claiming that in Ronald Reagan's America, Americans aren't idealistic anymore! Americans have supposedly lost their sense of compassion and their hearts. No, not their hearts, they've simply lost their leader. "America is at a crossroads," he pontificated and began talking about making fundamental changes in foreign policy, education, civil rights, labor and management and in determining the rightful role for economic policy in this country. "This is about breaking your back," he told his labor audience. "The question is whether you're going to share in the economic bounty." He then took a few minutes to denounce Star Wars and told his audience that it was up to them to decide whether we'll have two societies—one for the wealthy and brightest among us and one for all the rest. The way to prevent such an occurrence, he said, was via education. Again, no specifics. He claimed that every day 70 percent of our jobs are on the line to foreign competition. (No cite offered for this figure.) As for the debate between free traders and protectionists he affirmed the fact that there is no pure free trade practiced anywhere in the world, but if we accept our fate as pre-ordained and beyond our control our competitors will get the best of us. He informed his audience that more than half the jobs created during the Reagan Administration pay less than $7,000 per year. We have, he said, $16 per hour steel workers reduced to making hamburgers at $3.50 per hour. In perfect cadence and with just the right amount of imagery the Senator informed his audience that, "We don't have to resign ourselves to being the world's largest McDonald's outlet!" However, he offered no substantive plan to avoid such a fate.

Those who promote the all-too-popular image of America becoming a nation of hamburger flippers should check their facts. The stereotype of service work as menial and low-paying is simply misleading. Of course there are fast-food and janitorial jobs which fit into that category but so do the jobs held by physicians, government officials, professors and lawyers.

From 1983 to 1987, 75 percent of all new jobs were in the professions, in management, technical sales, precision repair or skilled production. Only 10 percent of the new jobs were menial minimum wage.

Labor Department statistics show America is upgrading her workers at the same time Labor Unions are losing membership. Special interests may distort the facts. The ways are infinite: for instance, using the CPI (Consumer Price Index) instead of the more accurate PCE (Personal Expenditure Index) and picking atypical years has been known to make the incredible credible.

Janet Norwood, Commissioner of Labor Statistics, issued a warning: an old-fashioned *caveat emptor* to concerned citizens attempting to ascertain the true state of affairs amid the conflicting information being pushed on us from all sides: "... the findings (supposed proliferation of low-paying jobs at the expense of high-paying) are extremely sensitive to the particular set of data used (as well as) the years chosen for analysis." For example, a report released in December 1986 by Congress's Joint Economic Committee found from 1979 through 1984 nearly three-fifths of all jobs created in this country were in the lowest wage category and that a startling 97 percent of new jobs recently acquired by white males paid $7,000 or less. The report was authored by Barry Bluestone and Bennett Harrison, who for many years have been arguing that the middle class was on the decline in this country.

On March 15, 1987, a labor lawyer argued that 44 percent of the new jobs created during the Reagan Administration paid $7,400 or less, and Senator James Sasser of Tennessee picked that comment up and embellished it a little more and it came out before the March 23, 1987, meeting of the Economic Competitiveness Senate Government Affairs Committee as: "Sixty-four percent of the jobs created since 1979 pay less than $7,500/year; we're witnessing the deindustrialization of America." Unfortunately the questionable information was echoed by countless other politicians wishing to advance their own political agendas—Joe Biden being one.

Actually there are approximately the same mix of high- and low-paying jobs as we had in this country a decade ago. You don't suppose anyone might wish to mislead the public on this score now do you? Citizens might well figure out the truth on their own, anyway—after all, excessive borrowing couldn't account for the entire rise in real (after inflation) per-capita disposable income.

Brian Motley, writing for the newsletter of the Federal Reserve Bank in San Francisco in January 1987, expressed an interesting view. He said that the rising share of service jobs may be beneficial because a more service-oriented economy is bound to be less affected by the cyclical ups and downs which are the hallmark of a manufacturing oriented society. "Because goods are durable and can be stored, producers tend to add to their inventories when business is strong and to draw them down when business is weak. Similarly, households tend to accelerate or delay purchases of durable goods in response to changes in current economic conditions." Employees are more readily expanded and contracted which means more flexibility within the economy. Where it would be unthinkable to build or dismantle plants and machinery, it is now possible to move workers to meet changing demand. Mr. Motley sees the trend to a more service-oriented society as a sign of America's strength rather than a cause for concern.

Mr. Biden has spoken of the need to eliminate greenmail, change anti-trust laws and education and encourage labor participation, but generally fails to mention how to go about it. He favors the idea that bankers should be made to write off the interest they're not going to collect anyway and stretch out principal payments so that the lesser-developed countries can buy our goods again. (But would they with increased world competition?) He has suggested raising teachers' pay but it came out melodiously as "(Let us) reward the producers of real wealth, the teachers of our children."

In deference to his labor audience, the Senator attempted to compliment American workers. (So what politician could have resisted?)

> Fifteen years ago there was a joke—never buy a car made on a Monday. Not now—now there is excellence every day . . . It is up to the people to use wisdom, resolve and courage to meet the challenge.

He then went into his pitch to the Baby Boomers, reiterating his belief that they had surely not forgotten about commitment, compassion and willingness to make sacrifices. He evoked the memories of the Kennedy era that I told you about ("Let the torch be passed") and touched on spiritual soaring sensations, (sorry, I've heard it too many times) and crescendoed to the thundering conclusion that, "It's time to restore America's soul!"

I am dwelling so extensively on Senator Biden's speeches

because that is what he does best—he's hardly a detailed issues man. He's more of a media event with a lovely (luckily) photogenic family, all of whom you would love to hug and can hardly help but wish well. And to be fair, he *has* addressed some issues.

According to the March 30, 1987, issue of *Business Week,* regarding trade Senator Biden eschews quotas and would rather prevail upon America's trading partners to open their markets. On the other hand, the June 29, 1987, issue of the *Wall Street Journal* portrays his stand: "Mr. Biden . . . envisions temporary import protection for industries in the form of tariffs not quotas; he proposes to use the estimated $10 billion that such a plan would raise to train and relocate workers injured by unfair trade practices." Although he opposes the Gephardt amendment, he nevertheless favors automatic retaliation against countries with excessive (who's to judge?) trade surpluses and those that "fix" exchange rates, like the Taiwanese and South Koreans. Perhaps his political advisers have warned him that despite all the foreign cars out there on America's highways and TVs and VCRs in her living rooms, Americans wish they had the courage to restrict foreign goods. They feel in their hearts, bones, or whatever, that it is the morally right thing to do. Although they may personally be too weak to follow through with any resolve, they will nevertheless admire and perhaps elect a leader who comes out on the side of "right" as they—according to polls—see "right."

The *Atlantic Monthly* (April 1987) gave a brief rundown of Senator Biden on the issues thus:

> He is a leading critic of school busing for purposes of racial integration. He supports freedom of choice on abortion but opposes federal funding of abortions for poor women . . . he has supported a crackdown on crime, a line-item veto for the President, an across-the-board freeze in federal spending and the Gramm-Rudman-Hollings automatic deficit-reduction plan.

He has come out against a constitutional amendment for a balanced budget and, not surprisingly, is against eliminating federal subsidies for Amtrack. (Few make better use of the railroad then Senator Joe Biden.) He would encourage banks to forgive interest on outstanding loans to Third World countries and to renegotiate principal payments. As for Social Security, Joe Biden takes a low non-committal profile, in contrast to the fiery stand of ex-Governor Babbitt. Senator Biden rules out any means test for benefits and endorses the status quo of taxing half the benefits of single retirees with incomes over $25,000 and couples whose income exceeds $32,000. True to form, he couches his opinion in moralistic rhetoric, "the best measure of the humaneness of a society is the way in which a society treats its elderly." I'm not kidding. But that's nothing compared to the way he carries on about children. "It is the plight of our children that is the moral test of our time." He can't seem to make up his mind!

But writer Laurence Barrett matches Joe Biden when it comes to imagery. Mr. Barrett painted the following masterful portrait of Senator Biden in action in the June 22, 1987, issue of *Time* magazine:

> His handsome features taut, his fist balled in indignation, Biden was in danger of losing his audience by painting a vivid picture of ghetto hopelessness. So totally did he capture his listeners, however, that their approval punctuated the meticulous cadence of his clincher: "And these are not someone else's children. They are our children. (Applause begins.) America's children. (More applause.) Blood of our blood. (A louder ripple.) Heart of our soul."

Senator Biden would like to see that every child born into a family at the poverty level receives health care up to age 12. It could turn into one more powerful incentive to remain poor—and under 12!

The Senator claims that only 19 percent of American children live in a two-parent family with a non-working mother and that programs and policies must adjust to that change. He and his colleagues never ask the citizens whether they want to reinforce the changes that have thus far taken place or stop or even reverse them—the silent citizens, not the most vocal. Perhaps there should be some attempt by our self-proclaimed leaders to encourage discussion among all the people as to goals and priorities. We should ask if men, women and children are benefitting from the changes that have occurred in the American family over the past twenty years. If the answer is negative then perhaps we should think twice before setting up programs to ease a path which leads to more people in need of psychiatric help, drug and discipline problems, truancy, illiteracy and unhappiness. Politicians love to cry that America's greatest resources are her human resources. How then could we be thinking of ways to turn the care of children over to day-care centers? Ask Leo Buscaglia, Mario Cuomo, Dick Gephardt and, yes, Joseph Biden—all who profess to come from poor non-college-educated families—if they were loved, nurtured and encouraged by having attentive parents rather than material riches. Which do you think the children of tomorrow would prefer if we were to give them a choice?

Joe Biden proved that he is a flexible speaker with his address to the American Bar Association's annual meeting which was held in San Francisco during August 1987. Imagery and theatrics were out and logic and reasoned persuasion was in. His topic was "The Constitution, the Senate and the Courts"—loosely translated as "Why The Senate Is Justified In Rejecting Robert Bork's Nomination To the Supreme Court."

He began by asking two questions: (1) Should the Senate consider the constitutional views as well as the professional fitness of a nominee to the Supreme Court? and (2) How should a Senator go about forming a judgment in order to carry out his responsibility? He told his audience, consisting mainly of lawyers and judges, that delegates to the Constitutional Convention intended to give the Senate exclusive control over Supreme Court appointments; that only in the closing days did the advise and consent compromise occur (Article II Section 2 of the Constitution). He reported that since 1789, twenty-six Supreme Court nominees have been rejected, withdrawn or never acted upon—in all but one case political or philosophical reasons played a part. Senator Biden referred to *stare decisis* (the practice of adhering to precedent and not to disturb settled points) claiming that as a Court of Appeals Judge, Robert Bork has been bound by *stare decisis*. However, the Senator pointed out, the Supreme Court is not so bound—they say what the law is! "As a Justice," Senator Biden continued, "Bork would have an opportunity to change laws." If Robert Bork had been on the Supreme Court years ago America would be very different today, according to Joseph Biden. The issue, the Senator claimed, is not whether the Court *should* change direction—it is about to change—the issue is can the Senate decide on facts beyond the intellectual and moral qualifications of a nominee. The

Senator went on to explain that Andrew Jackson had attempted to tilt the Court in the 1830s and succeeded. FDR tried in 1937 and failed. He compared FDR and Ronald Reagan as presidents who intended to shift the balance of the court. Both the Senate and the House repeatedly rejected Mr. Reagan's programs, he said, while FDR's social programs had the support of both Houses. Then showing precedent for what he hopes will be the Judiciary Committee's action in 1987, Senator Biden interjected a bit of drama. In May 1937, he said, the outcome was uncertain in the Senate. The Judiciary Committee was controlled by all New Dealers, but somehow they summoned the courage to condemn their hero's (FDR) court-packing plan. The Executive's attempt to dominate the Judiciary was defeated. (No one applauded but cheers seemed appropriate.) Exhibiting his mastery as a speaker, Joe Biden lightened the atmosphere at this point by injecting a little well-received humor. In FDR's case the balance of the court (voting) shifted on its own. "A switch in time saves nine," he chanted, referring of course to the retention of nine Justices rather than fifteen as FDR had proposed.

The Senator ended his address to the Bar Association:

> In case after case (the Senate) has rejected qualified nominees because it perceived those views to clash with the interest of the country. In the future . . . we'll have to make a judgment whether the case today—50 years after Roosevelt failed—150 years after Jackson succeeded (we) are once again confronted with (a) popular president's determined attempt to bend the Supreme Court to his political ends. No one should dipute his right to try to do that . . . but also no one should dispute the Senate's duty to respond . . . Let no one deny our right and our duty as Senators, to consider questions of substance in casting our votes—for the Founders themselves intended no less.

The distinguishing feature of Joe Biden's candidacy is his ability to move people. He sees the president of the United States as a leader not only of government but of society—as a crusader or missionary whose duty it is to motivate and change people's attitudes and lives. That is where Senator Biden leaves me cold—me and possibly a good number of independent, strong-minded Americans who are sick of being told what to do and what is best for them and their neighbors.

In a speech in Philadelphia on May 13, Joe Biden said a president

> must be able to mobilize America behind new patterns of work and behavior. He said he'd try to persuade business leaders to emulate the example of successful companies such as Ford and Federal Express, to promote day care, to convince schoolchildren to do their homework and skip watching TV.[8]

As far as I'm concerned that is not government's role and assuredly not the role of a president. Senator Biden professes to believe the people are disillusioned with government and yet he offers them more!

If political sages are correct, Joe Biden's downfall may be his reputation for inattention to detail. White House watchers point to the reactions voters have exhibited in the past. They turned from an old popular father figure with a loose rein (Eisenhower) to a young man full of grandiose plans (JFK), from a perceived scoundrel (Nixon) to a perceived missionary (Carter). These soothsayers predict the turn may now be from an old man with little grasp of detail (RR) to a young man who is detail oriented (alas, more like Gore than Biden).

On the other hand, the American Association of Political Consultants (who is more savvy in these matters?) in December 1986 voted Joe Biden as the front-runner for the 1988 Democratic presidential nomination.

Mike Dukakis

Michael Dukakis was born in Brookline, Massachusetts, in 1933, the second son of Panos and Euterpe Dukakis, both emigrants from Greece. Panos Dukakis had started life in America as a frightened 15-year-old with little command of the English language. Eight years later he was enrolled at Harvard Medical School. Euterpe Dukakis was the first Greek girl in Haverhill, Massachusetts, to go beyond high school; she became a teacher. Michael Dukakis is very proud of both parents.

After an illustrious high school career which included a stint as student body president, class brain and sports hero, he entered Swarthmore College, spent some time in peacetime Korea and then entered Harvard Law School. Like Joe Biden, Mike Dukakis' ambition bloomed and was expressed early. During his Swarthmore years he voiced his desire to become Governor of Massachusetts. Recognizing such a grand ambition early set him on the political track right out of law school. As a young lawyer he waged a reform campaign at the Brookline City Hall which soon spread to other parts of the state. He was elected to the Massachusetts legislature in 1962. In 1963, with considerable resistance from his parents, he married a Jewish divorcee with a five-year-old son, John. No one who has seen the two together can doubt that Kitty and Mike Dukakis is a good match. The two complement one another; she outgoing and impulsive and he more reserved and analytical by nature. In addition to John, the couple have two daughters, Andrea (born in 1966) and Kara (1969).

Unlike Joseph Biden, Michael Dukakis has experienced political defeat. He, along with his good friend and fellow governor Bill Clinton of Arkansas, who won, lost and then came back again, is a member of the "Phoenix Club"—those who have risen from the ashes of defeat. Mike Dukakis was in the state legislature for eight years, was defeated in a race for lieutenant governor and sat the next few years out as moderator of *The Advocates*, a national public affairs television program. In 1974 he was elected Governor of Massachusetts, but the elation proved to be short-lived. In 1975, when Massachusetts was laboring under a half billion dollar deficit and unemployment was just under 12 percent, Governor Dukakis reneged on his campaign pledge not to raise taxes and imposed the largest tax increase in Massachusetts history. (Now you know where the term "Taxachusetts" originated.) As fate would have it, 1978 was the year of the tax revolt, the year Proposition 13 was passed here in California. Not surprisingly then, Michael Dukakis was punished for his tax transgressions and soundly defeated in his bid for a second term as Massachusetts' governor. The political set-back was made all the more painful because of the debilitating effect it had on his father, Panos Dukakis. High expectations and unyielding standards were ruling factors in the older man's life and defeat was not easy to accept. Unhappily, Panos Dukakis died in 1979 with the taste of his son's political defeat not yet muted by the glorious victories that were to come.

Mike Dukakis took a couple years off and joined the faculty of the Kennedy School of Government at Harvard, where he had ample time to reflect on his mistakes and ended up perhaps learning more than he taught.

He returned to Massachusetts politics again in 1982 and by defeating Ed King, who had been plagued by a series of scandals during his term in the capitol, gained another try at the governorship. The success of this second term was evidenced by the landslide victory he enjoyed when he clinched his third term in 1986 with 69 percent of the vote!

Governor Dukakis' hallmark seems to be his penchant for plans and progrms. He's very much an activist governor who would like to be an activist president. Says Walter Shapiro writing for *Time* magazine, "Dukakis' strongest suit may simply be his record as an administrator who inspires creativity, closely monitors performance and eventually learns from his mistakes."[9] He certainly doesn't believe in laissez-faire and in fact his record as Governor of Massachusetts evidences his preference for a planned economy. Much in the cocky manner of a philosopher-king, Michael Dukakis did what *he* knew was the right and necessary thing to do in Framingham, Massachusetts, in 1985. General Motors gave the town an ultimatum—sell it the land adjoining its plant so it could expand, or face the closure of the existing plant and the loss of 4,000 jobs. Now what town wouldn't jump at the chance to sell a piece of vacant land in exchange for more jobs and an additional $250 million investment in its community (GM's proposal)? You guessed it—Framingham, Massachusetts. But Governor Dukakis didn't miss a beat and in his great wisdom he rode in like a knight on a white charger and saved the town from itself. How? He called upon the state's right of eminent domain, purchased the land and then sold it to General Motors. What a good feeling to play philosopher-king!

Praise from Robert Reich, a professor at Harvard University's John F. Kennedy School of Government, reassures me that I was correct in my dislike of Michael Dukakis' high-handed ways, which Professor Reich prefers to call "bold experimentation." Says the professor: "He (Governor Dukakis) understood the critical role that government could play in mobilizing resources and accelerating industrial development." Government's role may be critical, but critical in the negative sense of destroying personal freedom and fostering a nation of dependents.

In a recent study of Massachusetts' economic policy, which was conducted by Ronald Ferguson and Helen Ladd of the Kennedy School of Government at Harvard, Mr. Dukakis was lauded for his role as a catalyst in promoting development by bringing together business, academe, labor and government. A more apt description might be that of a broker. The governor has a sure-fire winning description for the process he imitates: "investing public resources in combination with private initiative and private capital."[10]

Michael Dukakis is running a quasi-socialist government in Massachusetts. To some that is good news because, after all, he has proved that socialism works! But let's recognize that not all Americans are pragmatists—some are idealists. A large segment of Americans would rather be free to make mistakes than be protected from their own folly by those who would play king. Besides there are many that claim the governor's policies are responsible for only a small part of the state's recovery and, if anything, laissez-faire capitalism would have speeded the process along and resulted in a greater boom in Massachusetts. (I know, you've heard that before!) These critics say Massachusetts could have had its cake and eaten it, too—freedom *and* economic recovery.

What *are* the facts? No one can deny (and most would not care to do so) that the Dukakis policy involves subsidies—direct and indirect—by quasi-government agencies created by the philosopher-king. Massachusetts has an Industrial-Science Agency that has made well over $3 billion in loans. Its "Centers of Excellence" indicate areas to be set aside for specific high-tech industries and offer grants to research projects jointly proposed by business and academe. The Massachusetts Capital Resource Co. and the Massachusetts Industrial Finance Agency lend money to businesses willing to invest in depressed areas. Massachusetts has in fact a state UDAG (Urban Development Action Grant) system. The governor believes in order to entice business or individuals to do what he wants (ah, there's the key—what the philosopher-king wants, not what *they* want!) incentives must be provided in the form of good infrastructure, educational facilities and favorable loans. After all, he believes, people cannot be asked to take risks.

Risks! Risk was his mother and father's middle name. Risk is what American freedom is all about! The arrogance of the son of a successful self-made man in espousing socialist policy is that the Dukakis or Gephardt or Cuomo ancestors may have succeeded but the rest of us must keep faith with the myth that they were super folks—that these men were not sired by ordinary mortals like you or me. The ordinary American needs to be enticed, coddled and protected from risk. What insolence!

Because much of the money has been raised through industrial revenue bonds,[11] boosters of the tactics claim the state has paid little and gained much. Perhaps you, too, recall a caution to beware gaining great riches at the expense of one's soul. I wouldn't want to get that dramatic, but it does seem a bit untoward for a capitalist nation to embrace socialist programs because they work. On the other hand there may well be more real socialists in the United States today than there are real capitalists. It is most certainly true that many people are tired of labels and don't particularly care to know what fits or doesn't fit, nor even care to examine their own positions. Ignorance is bliss and precludes the hard choices. The temptation is to simply drift into intellectual nirvana.

So let's look at the positive aspects of the Dukakis programs since the success of programs is assuredly the platform on which Michael Dukakis is seeking the Democratic presidential nomination.

After the gigantic tax hike in 1973 and the ensuing revolt which drove Mike Dukakis from office, the citizens of Massachusetts in 1980, under Governor King's leadership, passed Proposition 2½. One of Governor Dukakis' own advisers, Professor Ralph Whitehead, Jr. of the University of Massachusetts, admitted to journalist Charles Kenney of the Boston Globe that, "Without Proposition 2½ ... we would be on our way to becoming a banana republic." The remark, printed in the *Globe*, was widely quoted.

The high taxes of Governor Dukakis' first term discouraged all business investment within the state. (How ludicrous that government continues to get away with taking credit for solving problems it first creates!) There was a vast exodus of investment dollars to neighboring New Hampshire. (Lassez-faire and free market worked in this instance in New Hampshire's favor!) Proposition 2½ trimmed the Massachusetts tax burden from 11 percent above the national average to approximately 10 percent below. Proposition 2½ reduced Massachusetts' property taxes, which had been the highest in the nation, so that instead of property values increasing at 6 percent annually, as they had before Proposition 2½, they increased at the rate of almost 20 percent a year between 1981 and 1986. This meant that Massachusetts enjoyed more than a $90 billion increase in property wealth—over and above inflation! In 1985 Massachusetts could boast the hottest real estate market in the nation with construction jobs up over 56 percent between 1980-86 (as compared to 13.8 percent for the rest of the nation, according to the U.S. Bureau of Labor Statistics).

The excise tax on automobiles was cut from $57-per-$1,000 valuation to $25-per-$1,000 valuation and auto sales skyrocketed. Revenue from auto sales tax exploded from $102 million in FY1980 to $319 million in FY1986.

Thanks to Governor Dukakis and his industrial policies? NO. Thanks to Proposition 2½ passed under former Governor Edward King's stewardship.

Between 1981-86 Pentagon funds for research and development increased from $15.3 billion to $27.1 billion and Massachusetts' share grew from 4.7 percent to 5.9 percent or from $700 million to over $1.6 billion. Defense procurement spending increased by $2.4 billion making a total increase of $3.3 billion in Massachusetts' share of the nation's defense expenditures between 1981-86. In 1986 the state was awarded $7.7 billion in defense contracts.[12]

Thanks to Governor Dukakis and his industrial policies? No. Thanks to the much criticized defense spending policies of the Reagan administration.[13]

Manufacturing jobs, including jobs in high-tech industries, decreased by 4.3 percent between 1980-86. (The national average was a decrease of 5.6 percent.)

Thanks to Governor Dukakis and his industrial policies? Now what do you think?

An overhaul of the tax collection system and the offer of amnesty to delinquent taxpayers has been credited with injecting a sense of fairness and integrity into the process as well as generating enough revenue to allow Massachusetts to boast about a $584 million surplus in 1986.

Thnks to Governor Dukakis and his industrial policies? Thanks to Governor Dukakis and his *tax* policies!

Unemployment in Massachusetts was 2.5 percent in the summer of 1987 and the personal income of its citizens was the fourth highest in the nation.

Thanks to the industrial policies of Governor Dukakis? At least partially, but cause and effect is debatable. The high cost of housing in the state means new workers cannot easily afford to live in Massachusetts, and that helps keep the unemployment rate down. That and the 120 colleges and universities with their periodic releases of well-trained and creative young men and women into Massachusetts' economy. It has been estimated that approximately half the 2,000 Ph.D.'s produced each year stay. But if you ask Mike Dukakis how it was accomplished he would say,

> We worked at it. We invested public resources; we got the private sector in; we involved citizens, mayors, business people.[14]

And from that point the governor would no doubt launch a pitch for a regional development fund—an idea he would implement if elected President of the United States and a central part of his vision for the nation. "This country ought to be a one nation economy" he told his audience at the Southern Legislative Conference (SLC) held in Little Rock, Arkansas, in August 1987. He spoke of the great need for the nation to invest in education and training (who hasn't mentioned it?) pointing out that the average worker changes jobs five times during his or her lifetime. His proposed National Strategic Investment Fund would use federal funds to provide support for public private partnerships in parts of the country that are hurting. He admitted that such a plan would take an activist president to implement and, I might add, an elitist president. For who is to choose who should get what? We must have super-heroes! Mr. Dukakis calls them the new coalition. (The Reverend Jackson has been working on his own version of the ideal coalition, the Rainbow Coalition, for a long time.) The new coalition will be composed of mayors, managers, members of school boards, legislators and religious and civic leaders, all chosen for some reason by someone to meet and decide things for the rest of us—oh, yes—and to use our money. What an elitist ego trip! But that is the kind of "leadership" Mr. Dukakis intends to bring to Washington if elected. He'll be the guy who gets to do the choosing—what fun—what power! After all, he told the SLC audience, his dream is to establish a group council and advisory group at the national level.

He has tried to sell the idea to farmers in Iowa. "Iowa has great strengths. It's all here. But you need somebody . . . who understands how you take those pieces and build a partnership and make them work and builds a very strong and bright and promising economic future."[15] Iowans have heard more than their share of fine-sounding words in the past months, but Michael Dukakis has so far been successful in using the economic turn-around in Massachusetts as credentials for being a doer, not *just* a fine talker. But there is always the sneaking suspicion that maybe Governor Dukakis is merely capitalizing on his incredible luck of being in the right place at the right time. Even if one completely ignores cause and effect he is bound to look more competent than his fellows. Whether and how much Governor Dukakis is indeed responsible for the turn-around in Massachusetts may never be known, so it may be prudent to move away from his past record for a moment and concentrate on his stand on other issues.

Social Security

Michael Dukakis, along with thirteen other candidates for the presidential nomination, was asked by the Associated Press whether he would keep Social Security benefits and COLAs exempt from budget cuts. His reply was released by the Associated Press on June 14, 1987. He said, "I believe that the United States government has an obligation to help recipients of Social Security." Unfortunately, Social Security is not a contract between the payer-recipients and the federal government, or so the Supreme Court has repeatedly ruled. When Social Security was instituted in 1935 a hesitant population was promised a money-back guarantee. In 1939, when the refunds became too expensive, the government conveniently changed its mind. Then in 1945 the Supreme Court stated that benefits were to be given or withheld at the discretion of Congress—but no one seemed to notice. The point was made even clearer by Justice John Marshall Harlan who wrote the majority opinion in the 1956 Nestor case. There he boldly declared that Social Security rights were not property rights because that would deprive the system of the flexibility it needs to adjust to changing conditions. In his dissent, Justice Hugo Black pointed out that no private insurance company could get away with such shenanigans. He wrote:

> The court consoles those whose insurance is taken away today and

> others who may suffer the same fate in the future, by saying that a decision requiring the Social Security system to keep faith would "deprive" it of the flexibility and boldness in adjustment to ever-changing conditions which it demands. People who pay premiums for insurance usually think they are paying for insurance, not "flexibility and boldness."

Of course Social Security is not insurance in any true sense of the word, but the point here is that it is most definitely not a contractural right, either.

Welfare

But perhaps it is unfair to dwell so extensively on an issue which Mr. Dukakis is giving little weight in his campaign. Let's turn then to welfare reform, an issue on which the governor hangs his hat. He has won national attention for ET, Massachusetts' employment and training program that has reportedly helped over 30,000 welfare recipients off the welfare rolls and onto the taxpayer rolls. By some estimates ET has saved the state over $100 million. Each job placement reportedly saved the state almost $8,000 through reduced AFDC, Medicaid and food stamp outlays. ET provides not only job training but also one year's free child care, a back-to-work clothing allowance, a travel allowance and four months of free Medicaid to all participants. Sounds great, so why does Warren Brookes, in the January 19, 1987, edition of the *Wall Street Journal* cast his vote for New Hampshire's workfare program over ET? Mr. Brookes claimed FIP (Family Incentive Plan—New Hampshire's workfare) is less elaborate and more than six times cheaper than ET. Under FIP the New Hampshire caseload for AFDC fell 30 percent whereas the Massachusetts caseload fell 4.4 percent, according to Governor Dukakis, over the same period of time.[16] (Brookes claimed an increase.)[17]

New Hampshire's Governor Sununu attributes FIP's success to a booming economy with only a 2.2 percent unemployment rate (both Massachusetts and New Hampshire enjoy rates substantially below the national average) and caseworker incentives based on the number of AFDC recipients placed in jobs. New Hampshire also made an important commitment not to reduce staff as caseloads fell. Massachusetts may not have to cope with that problem. According to the U.S. Department of Health and Human Services over the slightly more than three years of ET's existence, new applications for welfare have increased 9 percent. Under federal regulations an increase in benefits expands the number of eligible families.[18]

Despite the increase in benefits afforded by ET, a welfare-rights advocate group called the COALITION FOR BASIC HUMAN NEEDS sued Masschusetts to force it to just about double its cash grants to welfare recipients. On January 5, 1987, Superior Court Judge Charles M. Grabau of Boston interpreted a 1913 Massachusetts statute ensuring adequate shelter to mean that the state must provide benefits sufficient to enable healthy circumstances for raising children. Admittedly vague, Judge Grabau has enlisted this broad interpretation of the statute to justify his ruling that monthly benefits to a family of three on Massachusetts' welfare roles be increased from $491 to $845. Massachusetts, represented by Judge Charles Grabau, is a state that would never think of legislating morality but it (he) is attempting to legislate compassion.

ET is all rights and no obligations. The only compulsion involved in ET is the registration. There is no requirement to work as in California (GAIN). Some experts believe that many of the 30,000 people ET is supposed to have helped were not really the underclass poor but rather those who simply took advantage of the help after a divorce, for example, and would have pulled themselves together and found a job without something like ET. That hard working poor should be taxed to let a proven able-bodied worker take a vacation and then get free babysitting services while looking for a job at his or her leisure is pure nonsense—no, it is outrageous! ET is sending the wrong message to society.

Trade

Just a word about Governor Dukakis' stand on trade. He approves some aspects of the Gephardt amendment but not enough to support it. He would provide protection for "endangered" American industries (here's more of those philosopher-king type judgment-calls) but would limit the protection to a specific time period. (More fun with rules and games.) He would make certain the protected industry takes certain steps to modernize and make itself more competitive. Governor Dukakis is the epitome of the old saw that "there's no such thing as a free lunch." Favors come with stipulations and business would soon become linked to government by chains consisting of past favors. All the governor's fine talk about permanent commitments—about a government guarantee encouraging private leaders to make loans—has one undeniable flaw. If it is a project that is desired by enough people they will prioritize and obtain it in an economic and forthright manner, but only if government first backs off. Government intervention skews business decisions in a most disastrous manner, leaving the mistakes for taxpayers to tackle and making wealthy men and women out of a favored few. (And you've heard that before too!)

Mandatory Health Insurance

As I write (summer of 1987) it is unclear whether Michael Dukakis will succeed in his attempt to communize health insurance in Massachusetts. ERISA (Employee Retirement Income Securities Act of 1974) prohibits states from requiring employers to offer health insurance benefits. Mr. Dukakis has Senator Edward Kennedy working on a waiver for Massachusetts that would allow the government to offer a bill requiring all companies (over three years old) to provide health insurance to employees and their dependents.

The candidate who is well known for his partnership proposals will have one more to add to his credit with the creation of the Massachusetts Health Partnership if and when the bill is passed.

Communist-type practices (the rights of the community over individual property rights) are well established in the Commonwealth. Under Massachusetts' comprehensive health care finance law, hospital charges have, for some years, been incresed 13 percent to pay the cost of care for the medically indigent. The new Health Partnership would place surcharges on hospital bills to fund health coverage for the unemployed and disabled. Not a bad idea—sure universal health insurance is costly but the coverage is *needed!* Principle? What about principle? The American principle based on capitalism says the surcharge must be voluntary—communism would see the efficacy in making the surcharge mandatory. Do we as a people want to change our principles? Could well be! Then let's be up front about it. From each according to his ability to each according to his need may yet become an amendment to our constitution. After all, the majority of those Americans in a recent poll identified it as part of our constitution in 1987—our bicentennial year, no less!

If Senator Kennedy fails to obtain the waiver for Massachusetts (after all, the Senator has larger fish to fry with his efforts to pass S1265)[19] an alternate plan calls for all employers in Massachusetts to contribute to a trust fund with those employers who already provide health benefits to employees receiving credit against their payments.

A Winner?

Governor Thompson of Illinois has been quoted as saying: "It's not in the cards for a sitting governor to run for President." "Indeed," says William Schneider, "every nonincumbent elected President since Roosevelt, with the exception of John F. Kennedy, was out of office at the time of his election."[20]

But it may be that Governor Dukakis is on an unbeatable winning streak. After all, members of the Southern Legislative Conference were told that in 1987 not only had Michael Dukakis been selected as the nation's most effective governor by his peers, but that *Playgirl* magazine had chosen him as one of the country's ten sexiest men!

Dick Gephardt

Richard Andrew Gephardt was born in St. Louis, Missouri, on December 31, 1941, the last day of the year. It would be understandable if he had a lapse of memory similar to Gary Hart's, as to the year, since only hours separated his birth from 1942. Only months separate his birthdate from Joe Biden's, so perhaps we'd forgive Mr. Gephardt if he tried to also pass himself off as a baby boomer. His birthdate definitely excuses him from service in WWII and explains his inability to present himself as a war hero or as a Vietnam veteran and true baby boomer as Al Gore can do. Nevertheless Richard Gephardt has a uniqueness all his own to commend him. What other candidate has been an Eagle Scout and has the wholesome "all-American-boy" look that Norman Rockwell made us believe requires red hair and freckles? What is more American than having a father who was a milkman and a mother who was a secretary? We can picture both in the "happy days" era in the midwest—and don't forget to add a brother.

Dick Gephardt received his B.S. degree from Northwestern in 1962 and his J.D. from the University of Michigan law school in 1965, the same year he married his lovely wife

Jane Byrnes. (You *knew* it was Jane, didn't you!) Between 1965-1971 he practiced law, fathered three children and served in the National Guard. In 1971 he won a seat on the St. Louis City Council and remained an Alderman until his election to the House of Representatives from Missouri's 3rd District in 1976.

Leadership

At a gathering in August 1987 in Baldwin, Iowa, his speech was full of what "we're going to do"—the "we" presumably Richard Gephardt and his cabinet if and when elected.

> We're going to perform and we're going to accomplish and we're going to renew hope and make people believers again. We're going to have policies that include all the people in the country. And when this country has spoken, and when this country has goals and when this country has leadership, it's going to be magnificent. We need leadership that inspires, leadership that motivates, leadership that looks long not short, leadership that unites us together in common goals and national purposes, leadership that is worthy of our values and worthy of our ethics and worthy of our beliefs. Leadership that leads us to a greater day than America has ever seen. It can be done.

During the debate involving, then, seven Democratic candidates for the party's presidential nomination which took place in Dubuque, Iowa, on August 22, 1987, Mr. Gephardt was again forceful in his advocacy of leadership. He told of an experience he had in New Hampshire where a high school student told him, "We don't believe in any of you anymore." Mr. Gephardt tried to attribute the cynicism of youth to the wrong values promulgated by the Reagan administration. "Indifference and selfishness" have flourished over the last few years and, he claimed, must be changed. He talked of the bankruptcy of Ronald Reagan's values—of the selfish attitude inherent in a "survival of the fittest" approach to the nation's social problems. Although he didn't say so, he obviously prefers the Robin Hood redistribution approach. He ridiculed Mr. Reagan's notion that "the government has no role in organizing and harmonizing for the people's benefit." He claimed that leadership is the answer—that we need to invest in people—manage people better, foster cooperation between government, business and labor. He said, "The free market doesn't work!"

Earlier in Baldwin, Iowa, he had expressed many of the same ideas: that we need a new budget, energy, trade and agriculture policy, but most importantly the people need to trust their leaders. "Too many Americans are cynical. In a democracy you're in trouble when citizens stop believing." He then recited a litany of those even remotely involved in scandal during Ronald Reagan's years in the White House and claimed that the "Iran-Contra affair means the crowd in Washington doesn't trust the people." Referring, of course, to the judgment of "the people" as represented by Congress and the vote to withhold arms to the Contras which "the crowd in Washington" found a way to circumvent. "The outfit in the White House," he went on, "knew better than the Congress."

And then in one of his famous turn-arounds, Mr. Gephardt asked elsewhere during the Dubuque debate,

> Why is this nation here? What do our basic documents mean? They mean that we trust the people, that we don't want a king, that we don't want a committee, that we want to diffuse the power, that we want the people to rule, that we want the people to set the policy, not the king.

There are two kinds of "people" in Mr. Gephardt's speeches. The ordinary people who have to be pushed around, motivated and managed, and the ruling people, meaning those who have been elected to Congress. When he says, "We need to ... manage people better ..." who is the "we" to whom Mr. Gephardt refers? Could it be the same elitist group Mr. Dukakis intends to pull together in his scheme for us ordinary working people, or is it the kingly (oops!) "we"? Is it the same "we" that is going to "perform ... accomplish ... renew hope and make (ordinary) people believers again"?

Chameleon Like?

This ability to change the meaning of words at will, or to about-face when there is a greater opportunity in doing so, has become almost a hallmark of Dick Gephardt.

Once Dick Gephardt fought labor on the minimum wage

issue, but now he's on the current bandwagon for an increase.

In 1979 Mr. Gephardt was allied with the American Medical Association in his advocacy of free competition among health care providers and institutions as the best means to keep health care costs contained. Now he has switched teams and lines up with Senator Edward Kennedy and various consumer groups as a co-sponsor of the Kennedy-Gephardt bill which calls for heavy government regulation. He would like to see Medicare and Medicaid merged (Medicaid is funded from the general revenue of federal and state governments) and long-term care for the elderly added as a benefit, apparently with no accompanying increase in Medicare Part B premiums. His bill also attempts to ensure that health care is provided for those who lose Medicaid by leaving the welfare roles and accepting low paying jobs. There is no doubt that changes need to be made in the system, but the Kennedy-Gephardt bill is a costly and inept solution to a very real problem and is an about-face for Mr. Gephardt.

Dick Gephardt sponsored a constitutional amendment to ban abortion, some say to please conservative voters when he was running for a city office; but somehow, now that he's running for the Democratic presidential nomination, he has seen a new light.

> I am not convinced that (a) it's (a constitutional amendment to ban abortion) not going to happen, and (b) that if it did, it would be disruptive and would not obviate the need we have in our society to deal with the underlying causes that drive people to need and want an abortion.[21]

An open mind may be praise-worthy but, nevertheless, Mr. Gephardt has done another about-face, this time on abortion.

At the Southern Legislative Conference in Little Rock, Arkansas, during the summer of 1987 he told the audience that we need to get our allies to help us with defense. We borrow money from Japan so we can protect the export of *their* oil. Mr. Gephardt incorporated this point into his answer to a question regarding the deficit posed at the Dubuque, Iowa, debate in August 1987: "It has taken us seven years to get into this mess and it will take us more than one or two to get out of it." His plan was hardly earth shaking—to impose an oil import fee, cut all spending, lower defense spending and, he advised, "the tax reform of 1986 will bring in more revenue than was originally thought."

During an interview telecast on C-SPAN on April 24, 1987, Mr. Gephardt told us that Ronald Reagan had cut taxes to 18 percent of GNP, raised defense spending and then made all the cuts in the 15 percent of the budget referred to as "all other." "This," he declared, "is everything you think of as the federal government. Veterans, Environmental Protection Agency, educational training, all the things designed to make the American people strong and high performance and for that reason many of these things need to be restored." To talk about reducing our deficit in one or two years while pledging to restore programs may involve some fancy about-facing.

Many of his views of yesterday regarding tax reform and less government are not highlighted in his campaign. Instead he would balance the federal budget by raising taxes from 18.5 percent to 22 percent of GNP. He leans toward higher rates for corporations and a steeper minimum tax for individuals. When asked during the August 22, 1987, Dubuque debate why he voted for Ronald Reagan's 1981 tax cut he replied, "I led the fight for the Democratic tax bill but didn't succeed. Reagan's bill was better than no tax cut at all . . . the recession (1982-83) was not as bad as it would have been with no tax cut at all." Another about-face? Perhaps not. Mr. Gephardt may have done the best he could with what was available.

Although in his clearer thinking days Mr. Gephardt favored cost-of-living freezes for Social Security recipients, he has found a renewed belief in COLA increases. The following is his answer to the Associated Press questions (see page 146) regarding Social Security and printed on June 14, 1987:

> Social Security should be taken out of the budget so that it doesn't become part of the budget battle each year. Social Security represents a contract with the American people—a pact. We must do everything that we can to ensure that present and future recipients are protected . . . I don't think Social Security should be subject to a means test.

His answer was somewhat similar to that of Mr. Dukakis who erroneously believed that Social Security represents a contract between the U.S. government and its citizens (see page 70). I was amazed that when asked by William Schneider for the *Atlantic Monthly*[22] about his proudest achievements,

Mr. Gephardt replied that, "He felt proud of his role in Congress in helping to stabilize the Social Security system"[23] and offered it as "one of the best examples of the effective use of government."[24] Although Mr. Gephardt may have done an about face on the means to achieve his goal, the goal—"stabilizing Social Security"—has not changed.

Education

Richard Gephardt has made education an issue in his campaign and never fails to mention the "60 million illiterate adults" and his goal to have by the year 2000 "the best educated people on the face of the earth!" He freely admits that such an ambitious goal will demand an immense increase in the federal government's budget for education. He told a New York audience that the federal government should be obligated to see that every American child has access to a first-rate education from kindergarten through college. The statement needs clarification. "Access" could mean schools that open their doors to all academically qualified or to everyone with no regard to qualifications of any sort or a myriad of other definitions. "Access" could mean that tuition, books or a portion of one or both be paid for out of general revenue or that loans or grants be available from or through the federal government or through private sources, guaranteed or not. "First-rate" is highly subjective and equally ambiguous. "Through college" however, needs no clarification beyond a detailed exposition of the estimated cost and where Mr. Gephardt intends to get the money for such largess! He wants to see longer school years, smaller class sizes, more advanced technologies (computers) and higher pay for teachers. As Morton Kondracke pointed out in his article for *The New Republic* which appeared on June 1, 1987, "There is not an item in the program that will displease the National Education Association—no merit pay, deregulation or teacher-certification procedures, voucher plans, or requirements for post-certification testing."[25]

Trade

Who in the United States today, if given an association test, would not immediately link Mr. Gephardt with trade?

(Premised, of course, upon the supposition that "who" knows who or what a Gephardt is!)

The Gephardt amendment has afforded Mr. Gephardt an immense amount of media coverage. An opportunist? Just because there's a Gephardt amendment for trade, a Kennedy-Gephardt health bill, a Harkin-Gephardt farm bill and there was a Bradley-Gephardt tax bill? The Congressman is obviously no slouch, but if you think his name just happens to "get around" withough strategic planning, then you underestimate Richard Gephardt. A man who could say in the summer of 1987 that he had already been campaigning for two and a half years, had been in 46 states, and had made 190 trips into the country in a twelve-month period doesn't just let things happen—he's a strategist extraordinaire!

The Gephardt amendment catapulted the 46-year-old Congressman into living rooms across America as he was interviewed on network television day after day and night after night during our trade difficulties with Japan in the summer of 1987. He was featured in newspapers and national magazines. David Shribman, a reporter for the *Wall Street Journal*, went so far as to claim,

> Mr. Gephardt, in fact, tailored his legislative tactics to fit his campaign strategy. He fought for his amendment on the house floor, where proceedings are televised, rather than in the Ways and Means Committee, which drafted the trade bill in a closed session and where he was unlikely to prevail. He orchestrated a series of press events in the days leading to the vote and, on Monday, lingered outside his own news conference because an aide had noticed that an NBC camera crew hadn't arrived.[26]

HR3 mirrors HR4800, a bill that passed the House in May 1986 but died when the Republican Senate in the 99th Congress failed to act. It would require punitive measures against Section 301 cases which relate to unfair trading practices by other countries. HR3 has entertained amendments mandating sanctions against the unfair actions of other countries that limit our access to world markets, changes in our laws to ease restraints on high-technology exports and giveaways to entice foreigners to buy farm produce and other American goods, provision for training programs for workers, funds for science education, mandates that the president work for a stabilization of currency exchange rates, provisions for economic relief to debt-ridden developing nations and provisions that require disclosure of foreign investment in U.S. businesses as well as a plan to create a new private-sector council on competitiveness.

Briefly, the Gephardt Amendment requires:

1) Our government to identify foreign countries who export at least 75 percent more to the U.S. than they import from the U.S.
2) Our U.S. Trade Representative, currently Mr. Yeutter, to determine those countries where the surplus can be traced to unfair trading practices (Sec. 301).
3) Our president to limit his time for negotiations in order to achieve an end to barriers or a method of retaliation.
4) Retaliation may be waived by the president for countries who have severe debt problems or whenever he judges such a waiver would be in the best interests of the United States. Congress, however, could overturn the waiver by a mere majority vote which the president could in turn veto, to be overridden this time by the usual two-thirds vote requirement.

The Gephardt amendment would force nations whose trade surplus with the United States can be traced to unfair trading practices to reduce that surplus by 10 percent a year. The mandatory percentage cuts have drawn the most criticism as they are seen by many as a usurpation of the president's discretionary power. Currently, Section 301 of the Trade Act of 1974 authorizes action by our country on a case-by-case, product-by-product basis. The Gephardt Amendment proposes a controversial "results oriented test" for determining how effective a foreign country's efforts at opening up markets to American goods really is. Such a test would penalize a government for the customs and habits of its people and encourage it to use coercion over its population. This is in direct contrast to America's traditional role in the world as a nation that enhances the expansion of freedom. Consumers in whatever country, should not be forced by their government to change their buying habits artificially. Competition and an open market should determine the purchases of all peoples. A results oriented test is a decidedly harmful, negative idea.

Another criticism of the amendment centers on its potential as a precedent. As Congressman Sam Gibbons of Florida has said, "We don't want to make surpluses bad, because we'll set ourselves in a trap." After all, American ingenuity, salesmanship, and an open market may make the

United States the country with a trading surplus in the not so distant future.

The House passed HR3 by more than a 2 to 1 margin on April 30, 1987. (Vote 190 to 137.) Mr. Gephardt's amendment was adopted the day before, on April 29, with appropriate drama. From a 209-209 tie, the fifteen-minute clock in the House quickly changed to register a final count of 218-214. Dick Gephardt enjoyed the victory, but the narrow margin almost ensures the amendment will not survive compromises which are bound to occur in joint committee with the Senate.

The Senate passed its version of the trade bill on July 21, 1987, by a 71 to 27 vote. The Senate considered 160 amendments including creation of a special inflation index for the elderly, a provision that meat sold in the United States be stamped with the country of origin, linkage of most-favored-nation status to human rights observances, and a requirement that both the budget submissions of Congress and the president include trade impact statements. Not all amendments were adopted. The Senate bill gives the president up to fifteen months to retaliate.

At this point it is not certain whether support for HR3 and the sponsorship of the Gephardt amendment is a political asset or liability, aside from the publicity it has generated. It may garner support from labor while conferring on its sponsor a reputation for pandering to special interests. Other groups have already pinned a great-big-button on Mr. Gephardt that reads PROTECTIONIST.

But Congressman Gephardt equates protectionism with competitiveness—you can't have the latter without the former. He says,

> If you aren't aggressive, enthusiastic and effective on trade-rule issues, you're in a poor position to advocate changes in behavior, investment and all the other things you will need to be effective and competitive.[27]

I'd like to see anyone argue with his position as expressed in the following statement:

> But we need the ability for American working people to be able to sell their products abroad as easily as other countries can sell their products here. Fairness. A two-way street.[28]

It's hard to argue with the truth, and unfortunately the Reagan administration is hard put to justify a policy of flexibility when it obviously hasn't worked!

Mr. Gephardt asked his audience at the Southern Legislative Conference (SLC) in Little Rock, Arkansas, (August 1987) if America could be the *best* economically and militarily at the same time. He claimed that was the challenge America faces. "We are trading $15-hour jobs for $5-hour jobs," he said, "and losing well-paying jobs to other countries." (Sound familiar?)

It's true that although total employment in the United States has grown by 10 percent since Ronald Reagan took office, we have lost approximately a million high paying manufacturing jobs. It sounds pretty good then when Mr. Gephardt advocates a tough trade policy in the national interest that will guarantee other countries treat us as we treat them.[29]

Today everyone knows about the unlevel playing field we are asked to play on.

> They put 40%-60% tarrifs on our goods in Taiwan and South Korea; we put a 4% to 6% tariff on their goods here. Taiwan doesn't let Korean or Japanese cars in. South Korean cars are not let in Japan. The Gephardt amendment says "open up and we'll compete—if you don't we're going to penalize your goods!"[30]

Mr. Gephardt reminded his audience that the world is not the same as it was in the thirties and that under Smoot-Hawley (that disastrous trade bill that many believed was wholly responsible for plunging the entire world into deep depression) there was a 60 percent increase in tariffs across the board. Although free trade is important to all countries, everybody believes in it and nobody practices it. There is no doubt the entire world's standard of living would rise under free trade.

A gentleman from Taiwan was in the SLC audience and asked that we recognize the progress that is being made. "Taiwan is attempting," he said, "to reduce tariffs on American goods to a high of 48 percent and an average of 35 percent." He said that 4,000 American cars were allowed into Taiwan but no one wanted to buy them because they were so big. (He forgot to mention how expensive they were with the addition of those tariffs!)

Most of us feel it's perfectly fine if folks around the world don't want to purchase our large cars, or tobacco or transistors or whatever, but we must get access or they don't get access! And not sham access with the imposition of tariffs or a myriad of safety inspections and prohibitive regulations.

One must give Mr. Gephardt credit for the evidence that many countries are now beginning, like Taiwan, to lessen their restrictions. Whether it will be enough and in time remains to be seen.

Agriculture

Dick Gephardt, the strategist, was well aware that his trade offensive might anger the farm belt so he covered his bases with the Harkin-Gephardt farm bill, which to obtain maximum voter appeal should be referred to as much as possible as "Save The Family Farm." Iowa's Senator Tom Harkin teamed up with Congressman Dick Gephardt to advocate mandatory crop reductions in order to raise the price of agricultural produce. Of course Mr. Gephardt is right when he says, "We're asking farmers to produce more when the world is in a glut." He's also right to realize the higher prices that would result from his bill would mean farewell to both domestic and foreign markets *unless* coupled with a new approach to trade.

It's hard to judge if a candidate is coming up with a reasonable solution to a problem unless one knows something factual about the problem. It is too easy to be led by emotion and totally disregard intellect. It is easier, too, for the candidates to depend on emotional appeal rather than buckle down and research and study the issues. But if we want to maintain a high standard of living in this country we can't let our hearts lead our minds at every turn in the road—hearts and minds must be joined. There is some hard work involved with success and to prove that I'm going to ask you to absorb some facts so that when Dick Gephardt tells you that farmers need price controls and supply management you will be able to intelligently agree or disagree.

I could take you back to 1948 when controls and supply management were used by President Truman, or to 1961 when President Kennedy did the same thing, but in the interest of time and because of the nature of this book I will only go back to 1972. It was in that year that President Nixon provided a price-income-support safety net—a floor below which farm prices would not drop. In 1972 Earl Butz, Nixon's Secretary of Agriculture, arranged for the Soviets to buy our farm surplus. Farmers expanded output after 1972. Why? Who encouraged it? Just keep those questions in mind. Wheat production soared from 1.4 billion bushels in 1970 to 2.4 billion in 1980. Corn production jumped from 4.1 billion bushels in 1972 to 6.6 billion bushels in 1982. By 1980 one-third of all farm land was committed to export production. Two out of every five tons of farm products traded in the world were produced in the United States of America. Foreign food consumption grew by 34 million tons a year. U.S. farmers added more acreage—from 293 million acres in 1970 to 352 million acres in 1980. Grain production skyrocketed!

Then fate, as it often does, took the hand away from the central planners. In 1972-73 El Niño, an unusually warm ocean current, ruined the anchovy harvest in Peru and there was an extreme shortage of high protein meal for poultry and livestock. The world turned to the U.S. but the Nixon administration had already committed her surplus feed grain to the Soviet Union. So the world turned to soybeans as a plentiful protein rich grain. In weeks soybeans went from $3 to almost $13 a bushel. President Nixon put a federal embargo on exports of soybeans and other feed grains. Who wasn't allowed to adjust quickly to worldwide change? The American farmer. Why? Who prevented it? You got it! It was an attempt by government to force the price of soybeans down in this country. It really hurt importers such as Japan who saw right away that it could no longer depend on the United States as a reliable source—the *United States*, as in government. The American farmer, if left alone, could have made a profit and adjusted to world markets. The whole world could adjust if planners would back off—and quickly and satisfactorily. Why don't demagogues understand! Anyway, can you blame the Japanese for turning to other suppliers? The Japanese began to invest heavily in Brazilian soybean farms. The Japanese government now has a joint farming venture with Brazil—a $300 million enterprise whose goal it is to produce 100 million tons annually. Other countries geared up also and stopped looking to the United States—

except for price supports. In the 1980s American policy has been to restrict production to keep prices up (sound familiar?) and the rest of the world merrily plants and plants and reaps the benefit of our policy. We are underwriting increased production throughout the world! It was one thing to provide a support and reduce risk for our own farmers, but according to agricultural economist Gordon Rauser at the University of California at Berkeley, U.S. agriculture policies determine commodity prices all over the world, injecting one more element of instability.

But the story is not over. As the 1980s progressed, world demand for food imports fell from 34 million tons per year to 19 million tons per year. Everyone was becoming self sufficient—something we as Americans had always thought we wanted. Remember all that talk of yesteryear about giving a man a hoe and he will provide for himself? Well, he did! Foreign grain production was increasing by 29 million tons a year by the mid-eighties. World wheat consumption in 1987 is estimated at a record 507 million tons but consumers will only import 85 million tons or 17 percent of the total. The dream has come true—the world has become pretty near self-sufficient, at least in the production of wheat. But that dream has become a nightmare for the government-manipulated American farmer. The U.S. share of world farm exports has fallen from 19.3 percent in 1981 to 14.8 percent in 1986. Feed grain dropped from 72 percent to 38 percent of the world market. Some observers blame the high dollar, and that has surely been part of it, but that is too simple. What we've got is a legendary example of bad social planning.

Politicians can't resist catering to the image of proud farmers working their land in order to feed a hungry America. Although farmers number under 3 percent of the nation's civilian labor force they evoke a great deal of empathy. No politician would dare risk coming across as "uncaring." Jesse Jackson is the best at making nonsense believable by appealing to emotion instead of intellect, but Richard Gephardt has his moments. "It's clear that our farm policies are failing to achieve the basic goal of preserving opportunity for a good life in rural America," he pontificated, even though the other 97 percent of the population is seeing to it that $25 billion a year goes into farm subsidies.

Mr. Gephardt is oh so correct when he tells us, "They're

farming this summer, not for corn but for green government checks.'' Agriculture Department officials estimate that $7-$8 billion worth of farm scrip will be in circulation in 1987.[31] The cutesy simplistic idea that all that needs to be done is "to put agriculture back in business so associated businesses can give farmers a *fair price* (?) for their products so they in turn will have money to spend in small business'' has been bantered about mercilessly on the Iowa circuit. The "how'' in this neat formula is the Harkin-Gephardt plan—greater supply management. You can see what central management has done to the farmer in the past. Do you want to let "them'' have another try at it?

Surely Mr. Gephardt is correct that if those who advocate an activist role for government are to be elected again in this nation, there is a need to restore the faith of the American people in our government and our leaders. It's wrong, he likes to say, when executives get increases and workers get laid off, and for every subjective "wrong'' there should be a government response, according to Mr. Gephardt's philosophy and Mr. Babbitt's and . . .

Rhetoric

More Gephardt favorites:

> We don't have and we need a national economy today because the heart of America's heartland is being torn out.

> We have failed values, not just failed economic policies.

> It is wrong to spend on Star Wars . . . It is wrong to kill children in Nicaragua . . . It is wrong to leave Iowa farmers out in the cold . . . (Iowans really like that one!)

> We have lost our moral compass.

> What self-centered men have torn down, other centered men can build up. ("Centered'' men?)

Mr. Gephardt often ends his presentations with the following:

> Give me your will.
> Give me your vision.

Give me your commitment.
Give me your belief.
Give me your heart.
Give me your mind and
together we will make America great and good and strong again.

A Hard Worker

When Richard Andrew Gephardt announced his candidacy on February 23, 1987, he declared that he would win the White House by being "the first to work each day and the last to quit each night." That is the Horatio Alger formula that many of us consumed with our mother's milk. There's no doubt that Dick Gephardt is keeping his part of the bargain. Will it work? To date James Garfield is the only president to have gone directly from the House of Representatives to the White House. What can I say? Assuredly Rcpublicans aren't as sore losers today as they were in 1881.[32]

Al Gore Jr.

Albert Gore Jr.'s roots may be in Carthage, Tennessee, but he was born on March 31, 1948, in Washington, D.C., where his father was serving in Congress (1939-1971). His claim to be "Southern-bred" may be disputed by the fact that he attended St. Albans, the prestigious prep school in Washington, D.C., and even married the lovely and outspoken Mary Elizabeth "Tipper" Aitcheson, a native of Washington, D.C. Al Gore studied government at Harvard, received his B.A. in 1969, and then entered the service and spent time in Vietnam as an army journalist. Upon his return in 1971 he worked as a journalist on a Nashville newspaper while attending Vanderbilt University, where he studied theology for two years followed by two years of law. Unlike Joe Biden and Michael Dukakis, who recognized their political ambitions while still undergraduates, Al Gore Jr. claims "that he wasn't interested in a political career until his newspaper work exposing corruption in local government made him realize that politics could be a positive force for change."[33] He left law school to run for the House of Representatives at age twenty-eight. (No fooling around with local politics for him!) He left the House to run for the Senate at age thirty-six. Now he would, at age thirty-nine, be happy to leave the Senate for the highest office in the land. To this point Al Gore, Jr. has succeeded in all his ambitions. Since 1977 he has managed to visit his home state every week and still maintains a 97 percent voting record. Tennesseans honored that commitment and in 1984 elected Al Gore, Jr. to the senate with the largest vote that state had ever accorded any person, including Al Gore, Sr.

"Youthfully mature, committed, experienced, attractive, vigorous and in tune" were the words used to introduce Albert Gore, Jr. to the Southern Legislative Conference (SLC) held in Little Rock, Arkansas, in August 1987.

Al Gore is as proud of his father as Michael Dukakis is of his. Proud that Al Gore Senior was one of only two Southern Senators to refuse to sign the notorious Southern Manifesto after Brown vs. Board of Education, the 1954 Supreme Court decision outlawing segregation in public schools. Proud not only of all the wins that went into thirty-two years of service in the U.S. Congress, but of Al Gore Senior's final defeat in 1970 which was due, at least in some measure, to his vocal and heart-felt opposition to the Vietnam War.

All politicians tell jokes—it lightens the atmosphere and warms up the audience—but Senator Gore Jr. is better at it than most, perhaps because he makes his jokes believable and personal. For example:

During one of his father's election campaigns an opponent had posted signs all over town proclaiming that "THE THINKING FELLER VOTES McKELLER." Al's mother, who practiced law in Arkansas, came up with "THINK SOME MORE AND VOTE FOR GORE"!

He tells another story about 140 people trying to get on a ballot and stresses the ingenuity of one hopeful who promised an income tax audit for dentists and divorce lawyers in the belief that he wasn't the only one to have experienced some pain in his lifetime.

Because the Iowa caucases in February 1988 are the first report cards to be issued to all the candidates, Mr. Gore has done his share of traveling to and addressing the citizens of that state. He's even picked up some new jokes: "It's beginning to look like the Publishers Clearing House Sweepstakes. Anybody can enter. Anybody can win." He has learned that a good bet is to acknowledge and poke fun at your own weaknesses before someone else beats you to it.

There was some truth to the "Seven Dwarfs" barb which pointed up the fact that many of the Democratic hopefuls were virtually unknown to a national constituency. When Senator Biden dropped out of the race, the label "mercifully" no longer fit, even though most of the six remaining Democratic candidates still had a problem with name recognition. Jesse Jackson is the only one, in fact, who can claim to have no problem in this area. Congressman Gephardt has been helped by associating his name with many of the bills before Congress and is well known to political enthusiasts. His national exposure has centered on his link with the nation's trade difficulties, which continue to receive national media coverage. Governor Dukakis of Massachusetts has received some national attention for his state's welfare program, "ET"—Employment & Training (Choices). But what can two rather uncontroversial junior senators and one ex-governor do to gain name recognition—besides staging a 397-mile bicycle ride?

Unfortunately, Mr. Gore's message is shop worn:

> America is increasingly divided between those getting wealthier and those getting poorer. Those with an excellent education and those that can't even read or write. Those with hope and those with despair. Those who say wait and those committed to make a difference.

The idea that runs so strongly through all the Democratic candidates' platforms that a new president must unify us—must heal the differences—is part of Al Gore Jr.'s presentations also. "We need a new sense of national purpose."

During the August 22, 1987, debate held in Dubuque, Iowa, on "The Economics of America" and involving all seven Democratic candidates for the presidential nomination, Mr. Gore failed to distinguish himself from the pack. He said things like, "The fiscal policy of Ronald Reagan has been misguided." "There has been a long decline in our productivity growth." "We must focus on shaping sharper minds, not lowering wages." "The world is inter-connected. We need an international outlook. We need economic growth on a global basis." He repeated essentially the same message before San Francisco's Commonwealth Club on October 26, 1987.

Mr. Gore stays away from controversy, although he's quick to attack fellow candidates. Seldom can anyone object to anything he says. "Instead of telling people what to do, we should listen and learn how to give them the tools to do what they want." What "they want" is the key—let everyone do what they want. I'm sure not disagreeing—are you? Of course his first job is to appeal to the Democrats. It's possible some Republicans could disagree depending on the interpretation of "give" (and the cost) and just what is meant by "tools" is uncertain. Could it mean a free education through college and a guaranteed job and house?

Mr. Gore claims that education is directly connected to our competitiveness—that we need the world's best education. Is that controversial? He claimed in his speech before the SLC (August 22, 1987) that there should be more federal support (dollars) for education and that the federal role had dropped from 10 percent to 6 percent of total expenditures on education. (According to the Reagan administration the federal government provides 7 percent of education's funds.) Al Gore, Jr. would like to see the system made more attractive in order to keep kids in school. I'll admit there's not universal agreement as to the two ways he suggests to reach the "world's best education," i.e. more federal dollars and making education "more attractive" which may or may not mean "more fun."

His observation that the Atlantic and Pacific coasts are doing well and mid-America is suffering is hardly earth-shaking. Nor is his prescription for a responsible fiscal policy and comment that each year the budget contains too much for arms. Slightly more controversial is his call to make more capital available to small businesses and his position that the Small Business Administration should be reshaped rather than eliminated.

Still speaking before the SLC, the Senator said that federalism has become a shell game where the Administration has said "we're not cutting programs, we're giving block grants to the states, so ask *them*, not the federal government for aid." But states' funds were cut, according to the Senator, and the states need more money for rural economic development, infrastructure, better health care, clean air and water and so forth. But, he declared, the states won't accept mandates without resources to meet those mandates. He discussed the need for a national energy policy and voiced his opinion that Louisiana, Texas and Oklahoma were heading for a crisis. He told his audience that Tennessee had a problem with its rivers in 1985 and linked that fact with FDR's creation of the TVA (Tennessee Valley Authority) implying that a similar response by the federal government is required now. He said the rivers are not a regional problem but are rather a national problem. It seemed like he wanted the entire country to come to the aid of the Southwest. Now *that* might stir some controversy!

On the subject of welfare Mr. Gore agreed with many other candidates that it is time to change the system so that a father has no incentive to leave the home and so that a family can keep health benefits if and when they leave welfare.

Senator Gore claims to be the only farmer in the race for the presidential nomination. His occupation has been listed as "journalist, home builder and politician" but never as "farmer." The fact that his family (the Senator has 4 children) lives on a corn and livestock ranch outside Carthage, Tennessee, which someone else works, doesn't qualify him as a bona fide farmer and he doesn't pretend that it does—his claim has always been humorous. But it doesn't take a bona fide farmer to see the problems or the solutions. The Senator's suggestion that we need *better* farm credit policies, however, tells us nothing. Everybody is for "better" everything, but what is "better"? Less costly? Geared to the "little guy"? More lenient? Here's controversy, but I don't know what Mr. Gore proposes beyond making the credit policies "better."

To the Southern legislators he said: "Agriculture is one of our strong suits in this country but we now have competition. China now exports wheat. Bangladesh is even an exporter. We need to negotiate international exporter agreements. We need commodity programs that are sensitive and that put a floor under the farmer."

A Mississippi catfish farmer stood up and declared, "We need market access, not subsidies!"

Al Gore Jr. is known to some of his colleagues as the Congressman who conducted hearings while in the House which focused on worthless insurance policies which were and are being sold to uninformed or misinformed senior citizens.

When asked by the Associated Press: "Will you keep

Social Security benefits and the annual cost-of-living increases exempt from budget cuts?'' he answered: ''I am adamantly opposed to any attempt to cut benefits to recipients and I strongly support the annual Social Security cost-of-living increases.'' Such an answer should make millions of people happy—a specialty of Mr. Gore's. To a second question: ''Do you favor any means test for Social Security benefits?'' he replied: ''I am strongly opposed to means-testing because the system is solvent and (it is) unfair to those who have contributed into the system.'' The answers of all candidates (Jesse Jackson chose not to respond) were issued by the Associated Press on June 14, 1987.

In the matter of taxes, Al Gore Jr. may offend a few people, but still in a gentlemanly manner. Some may be aware that he, along with Senators Biden and Simon, voted in the fall of 1986 to create a new 35 percent top rate above the 28 percent rate now prescribed by the 1986 tax reform bill. He opposes a value-added tax but believes a tax increase must be looked at as part of a comprehensive solution to reducing our federal deficit. During the Dubuque, Iowa, debate (August 22, 1987) Senator Gore attacked Governor Dukakis' figures. (The Governor had claimed that $110 billion could be saved by collecting delinquent federal taxes) and pledged that a tax hike would be undertaken during his presidency (if elected) only as a last resort.

Although Al Gore Jr. supports ''trade restrictions in cases of 'overwhelming unfairness' or where high penetration of foreign goods threatens to destroy a U.S. industry,''[34] he is nevertheless opposed to the Gephardt amendment. It is hard to support an opponent in a competitive race where the stakes are the presidential nomination. Senator Simon and the Reverend Jesse Jackson are the only candidates who have said that they would vote for the Gephardt amendment besides Congressman Gephardt himself.

The following statement made by Senator Gore, Jr. is unfair in its beginning and untrue in its ending. ''We've watched this administration double, and they'll end up tripling, the national debt in just two presidential terms, at the same time cutting the services that every American wants to see delivered in this country.''[35] The budget submitted by the President is a negotiating tool. No one ever expects Congress to accept it, but rather it is anticipated that Congress will dicker. It's nonsense to refer to "the president's deficit." If Congress wanted to chop the President's budget it would be chopped.

In 1982 President Reagn recommended a $695.5 billion budget. In 1982 Congress spent $745.7 billion.

In 1983 President Reagan recommended a $757.6 billion budget. In 1983 Congress spent $808.3 billion.

In 1984 President Reagan recommended an $848.5 billion budget. In 1984 Congress spent $851.8 billion.

In 1985 President Reagan recommended a $925.5 billion budget. In 1985 Congress spent $946 billion.

On March 23, 1987, Senator Gore Jr. announced that he would not be a candidate for the 1988 Democratic presidential nomination. On April 10, 1987, he announced he would consider running in response to an urging by Southern Democratic leaders who had each pledged to raise $250,000 for him (approximately $4.5 million). On June 29, 1987, he formally declared his candidacy both in Carthage, Tennessee, and in Manchester, New Hampshire.

If Charles Robb of Virginia, Sam Nunn of Georgia or Dale Bumpers of Arkansas had declared their candidacies, it seems safe to say Al Gore would not be running. Someone had to be the standard bearer for the South in 1988, and besides, there could be a repeat of the nation's 1960 craving for the "youngest" after experiencing eight years of the "oldest."

Jesse Jackson

Jesse Jackson was born in Greenville, North Carolina, on October 8, 1941, to Helen Burns, a high school student who two years later married Charles Henry Jackson, the man who was to become Jesse's stepfather. Jesse Jackson's genetic father, Noah Robinson, lived next door with a family of his own and, contrary to popular opinion, was proud of Jesse and acknowledged that he was his spittin' image! According to biographer Barbara Reynolds,[36] Jesse probably learned that Charles Jackson was not his real father and that Noah Robinson *was*, sometime between the ages of six and nine and was deeply affected by the information. Charles Jackson officially adopted Jesse when he was fifteen years old, and perhaps that made it possible for Mrs. Robinson to accept Jesse in her home. At any rate, Jesse Jackson ended up with two families.

This information only becomes important when seeking the common thread which binds all the candidates for the Democratic presidential nomination for 1988—excessive ambition and drive. Although in reality Jesse Jackson does not seem to have been rejected by the parties involved, *perceived* rejection is just as powerful a destroyer or, in Jesse Jackson's case, motivator.

Mr. Jackson graduated from Sterling High in Greenville in 1959 and entered the University of Illinois on an athletic scholarship. However, the racial realities of the time kept him from assuming the leadership position he so craved and so he switched to the predominately black Agriculture and Technical College (A&T) at Greensboro, North Carolina. There in 1962 he met and married Jacqueline Lavinia Davis, the mother of his five children. The civil rights movement had been in full force in Greensboro before Mr. Jackson's arrival, but by 1963 he had assumed a position of leadership. It was that year, after receiving his B.A. in sociology, that he decided to enter the Chicago Theological Seminary to become a preacher like the grandfather whose name he bears, the Reverend Jesse Robinson.

John Steinbeck once wrote, "Just because a thing never happened, doesn't mean it isn't true." Jesse Jackson would certainly subscribe to that view of things. In an effort to both gain acceptance and to motivate the truly oppressed he often leaves the truth, as most of us would call it, completely out of the conversation. In 1985 two biographers said the following:

> Jesse Jackson began by identifying himself as one of the dispossessed, a poor, underprivileged black from the rural South who understood all the hurt and deprivation felt by poor blacks everywhere. He identified himself as a "third-world" child, one who had lived in a "shack," who had stolen in order to eat, a ragamuffin grown wise and bold, who proposed to lead his people out of their degradation and into power and prosperity. Never mind that these stories of early poverty were untrue.[37]

According to biographer Barbara Reynolds, Jesse Jackson's "shack" was first "a spacious six-room cottage, trimmed with white asbestos siding, surrounded by well-kept shrubbery and a meticulously groomed lawn . . . by the time Jesse was in the sixth grade . . . they (the family) moved into a new housing development, called Fieldcrest, and then to an eight-room house on Anderson Street, where the Jacksons live today."[38] (1975)

On a Chicago television station (WBBM-TV) in 1973, Jesse Jackson, the preacher and man of God, said, "I used to run bootleg liquor, bought hot clothes. I had to steal to survive." These words at the time left Charles Jackson mystified. He told Ms. Reynolds, "We were never poor. We never wanted for anything. We've never been on welfare, because I was never without a job. We never begged anybody for a dime. And my family never went hungry a day in their lives.''[39]

A 1970 biography[40] which was written with the facts supplied by the Reverend Jackson himself, claimed that Jesse Jackson's mother was a maid and his father was a janitor—both, according to biographers, completely untrue.

Gary Hart was driven out of the race for the 1988 Democratic nomination because of lies—flaws in his character that we would not tolerate in a national leader—yet no one has had the courage to confront Mr. Jackson in the same manner.

Shortly after Joe Biden dropped out of the race for the 1988 presidential nomination, David Broder spoke of Doris Kearns Goodwin, Lyndon Baines Johnson's biographer, who, Mr. Broder told his readers, had recently reminded journalists how important it is to focus on the truthfulness of presidential candidates in their reflections of reality.

> The reason, she said, is that once behind the fence at 1600 Pennsylvania Avenue, there is inevitably a strong temmptation to reconstruct the world as you wish it to be. The same LBJ who invented a grandfather who died heroically at the Alamo, she pointed out, had no problem converting what was at best an ambiguous naval incident in the Gulf of Tonkin into the excuse for a massive escalation of the U.S. involvement in Vietnam. The fake grandfather seemed mere hyperbole, perhaps worth only a laugh. But the Gulf of Tonkin incident led to tragedy.[41]

According to biographers Landess and Quinn, Mr. Jackson, on April 21, 1984, claimed urban ties because it served his purpose. Before Southern audiences he had always claimed poor, rural origins. The stories that he made up and used for his own advantage and that alienated him from the old-guard black leaders following Martin Luther King's death reflect on his character. Character, or lack thereof, is something we must pay prime attention to in choosing our leaders. Who does not agree with the Reverend Ralph Abernathy who said, ''What is needed today is not *charisma* so much as character . . . (Moses) led his people out of Egypt, not because his words excited them, but because his goodness inspired them.''[42]

Tell me about the character of a man who would act in the following manner:

> Jesse was supposed to introduce Dr. King, but he took the opportu-

nity when the cameras were on him to deliver a lengthy, lengthy speech himself. You couldn't say he got carried away in his preaching because his remarks were all written down. When it was Dr. King's time to speak, he delivered only perfunctory remarks, 'cause he saw it had all been said for him.[43]

AN OPPORTUNIST?

Tell me about the character of a man who refers to the Democratic Leadership Council (DLC) as "Democrats for the Leisure Class"[44] and is himself

> ... treated like a monarch. A snap of the finger brings him a newspaper. A nod of the head brings a glass of lemonade. Oblivious of the hour, he rouses people with phone calls from six in the morning to long after midnight. Often he holds planes until the last minute before he arrives to take his first-class seat.[45]

A HYPOCRITE?

Tell me about the character of a man with a six figure income who continually denounces the wealthy in this country and himself was found to have given less than "one-half percent of his declared income" to charity. Charitable giving is normally one's private business unless one happens to be seeking the highest office in the land, as Jesse Jackson did in 1984 and was found not to be the lowest earner but the lowest contributor of all the candidates. What about a man who

> ... has grown prosperous and powerful on the business of being poor and has shared very little of his own wealth with those whom he most professes to pity.[46]

AN IMPOSTOR?

Tell me about the character of a man who while

> In high school ... worked at the Poinsett Hotel, across the street from a plaque enshrining the memory of segregationist John C. Calhoun, former Vice President and Congressman. Jesse relished the chance to show what he thought of Calhounism the only way he could, by spitting in the food he served whites.[47]

IMPETUOUS?

William Julius Wilson, a black sociologist at the University of Chicago, tells us about the importance of role models and the support of a community in providing values for the young. He claims that the success and mobility of blacks over the past twenty years has taken the props from under those left behind in the ghettos.

> Basic community institutions—schools, churches, stores, recreation centers—lost the support of the stable families that kept them viable . . . Crime and vandalism further hastened business flight, reducing employment and leaving little but the culture of failure, unemployment, hustling, drugs, and welfare.[48]

No one knows this lesson better than Jesse Jackson.

> Social morés were such that when Jesse was disruptive in class, he was disciplined at school, "whupped" at home, and the preacher . . . would publicly rebuke Jesse in church.[49]

The Reverend Jackson preaches self-help and personal improvement, knowing full well that *values* are the key to success. however, it would appear that he often forgets his own. If you want to believe that with dozens of biographers prying into their backgrounds, the other candidates, your own preacher, your neighbor and even yourself would come up just as "lacking," then that is your decision. However, I feel strongly that many of the problems that confront us today were caused by over-tolerance and low expectations of ourselves, our children and our leaders.

Jesse Jackson combines the strengths of the other candidates. He probably matches Senator Biden's oratorical skill yet manages to address specific issues.

> "The best measure of the humaneness of a society is the way in which a society treats its elderly."
>
> *Joe Biden*

> "We measure our character by how we treat children in the dawn of life,
> We measure our character by how we treat the poor in the pit of life,
> We measure our character by how we treat the old in the sunset of life."
>
> *Jesse Jackson*

Just as Senator Gore likes non-controversial issues, Jesse Jackson embraces controversy. Race, affirmative action, quotas, busing, South Africa, Nicaragua, Cuba—all are favorite topics.

We have seen how both Joe Biden and Mike Dukakis heard the call to greatness and set their sights on high political office while still in college, but Jesse Jackson has them both beat. According to a *high school* teacher,

> Jesse was always the candidate. Whatever office was available, Jesse would be there signing his name. He seemed to be saying, "whether you elect me or not, I'm going to run. I am the candidate!"[50]

When asked how he would bring down the federal deficit,[51] Mr. Jackson echoed Governor Dukakis' plan to concentrate on collecting delinquent taxes. He showed some originality and a willingness to talk about specifics when he explained his plan to get at a portion of the $2 trillion invested in pension funds by labor unions, business and government. He would like to see some of this money used to invest in infrastructure and to build affordable housing. He was enthusiastic about

> . . . using some of our own money to build bridges, make an energy efficient mass transportation system. Let Americans make the steel and lay the rails and drive the cars. It's called "better managing America's assets" for Americans.

He summed up by declaring that if businesses were paying their fair share of taxes, together with the collection of delinquent taxes and by putting America back to work using pension funds to tackle infrastructure projects (every 1 percent drop in unemployment saves $25 to $30 billion), we might have the deficit licked. If not, he would as a *last resort* (one of the more popular phrases on the circuit) raise taxes.

This particular spiel is very effective and never fails to impress an audience with what they suppose is lucid logic—a wonderfully simple and perfect solution to the deficit problem and a good many other irritations as well. But what no prudent pension fund manager (who, by the way, has a fiduciary duty) would do because of the risk involved and low return on the investment, our hero Jesse Jackson would not hesitate for a moment to do. But this is the Jackson trademark—surface solutions that sound good proposed by a demagogue with little grasp of the problem. "Full of sound and fury, signifying nothing." But, compared to his colleagues, as I said earlier, the Reverend Jackson has both a spellbinding delivery and offers specifics on every issue.

Education

> We must use our minds and resources. We must educate our children. It is immoral to cut back on education, to turn our children's sunlight into midnight. It's a mistake to tackle education from high-tech down rather than head-start up. It's a mistake to put more focus on private education than mass education. Democracy does not guarantee success but it does guarantee opportunity. To educate a child's mind is to give that child opportunity.
>
> To the issue of productivity—education is the key.
>
> To the issue of competitiveness—education is the key.
>
> To the issue of quality of life—education is the key.
>
> Education should not be reduced to an afterthought—it's our first line of defense. A full academic scholarship could cost less than $30,000—those same four years on a full penitentiary scholarship could cost more than $120,000. Education at its worst is better than jail at its best. We must educate our children!
>
> *Southern Legislative Conference (SLC)*
> *Little Rock, Arkansas, August 1987*

Beautiful—right? Now let's analyze what the great orator has really said.

First of all there is nothing moral or immoral about the issue. Secondly, absolutely no one is talking about cutting back on education. In our government almost inevitably any cutback is at most a cutback on the *growth*—on the ever increasing allocations. "Sunlight into midnight" is simply hot air. "From high-tech down rather than headstart up"—who's advocating such a thing? Nobody or entity that I ever heard of is focusing on private over public education (assuming "mass" means public). However, private education, as it is known now, could belong to the masses under a universal voucher system guaranteeing for every child the education of his or her parents' choice and making all the schools competitive and, therefore, eventually all excellent. How do you suppose Mr. Jackson would define "opportunity"? The three rhythmically perfect lines beginning "To the issue of . . ." make a charming litany and are an accurate observation that education makes a person more productive and competitive and enhances standards of living. The bit about providing a full scholarship or else . . . is just an example of blackmail, here couched as an appeal to economy rather than altruism.[52]

Agriculture

> We're the wealthiest nation in the history of the world and yet we've turned our backs on the hands that have fed us. That's a reflection on our character.
>
> *Baldwin, Iowa*
> *Summer 1987*

The cost of farm programs has increased six fold since Mr. Reagan took office, going from $4 billion in 1981 to $25.8 billion in FY1986. Is that turning our backs, Mr. Jackson?

Subsidies to farmers in various forms took 15 percent of the FY1986 budget. Is that turning our backs, Mr. Jackson?

The increase in farm support costs was between 500-600 percent in five years. Is that turning our backs, Mr. Jackson?

> Farmers and ranchers have fed America and the world. Farmers should expect mercy from us. Many farmers are in the cold without heat, without telephone, without medical care.
>
> *Before the Texas Legislature*
> *April 24, 1987*

Deficiency payments in FY1986 were double the payments in FY1985 and, consequently, participation in the program shot up to include 85 percent of all farmers. No wonder real per capita income in the nine grainbelt states has risen nearly 10 percent faster than in the nation as a whole. What about that, Mr. Jackson? In 1986 per capita income in Iowa was on a par with the rest of the nation, and yet that state consumed subsidies averaging nearly $18,000 per farm and worth close to $2 billion. One farmer received $9.9 million ". . . in the tax financed slaughter of his entire dairy herd in a program paying 12,000 dairy farms an average of nearly $105,000 each to get out of the business."[53] Under pressure from cattlemen, the federal government agreed to purchase the slaughtered dairy cows to prevent a glut in the meat market. A heartless administration, Mr. Jackson? Not on your life, but perhaps a mindless one. Our agriculture policy is a perfect example of the dangers inherent in leaving your business to the policy makers.

Farmers deserve fair prices for their production. Farm credit has taken acres from bankrupt farmers. We must give that land back. We must have an international congress on agriculture and food.

During debate in Dubuque, Iowa
August 22, 1987

The Farm Credit System lost $2.7 billion through mortgage and loan defaults in 1985—an historic record for a U.S. financial institution. But guess what, Mr. Jackson—Congress went back to the drawing boards and came up with the 1985 Farm Credit Corporation of America which it immediately authorized to tap into (steal) the $3.2 billion in surplus reserves held by healthy institutions, calling the theft "capital sharing." Examples are plentiful of farmers who have the federal government write off their loans but are then able to use fat federal payments to plant crops that, when harvested they will get paid to store. Farmers certainly aren't stupid, and although they can hardly help taking advantage of such stupid programs, they don't enjoy taking taxpayer money for being non-productive.

As for an international congress, President Reagan on June 5, 1987, appealed to other nations: "Let's jointly defuse this growing farms race by setting a goal of a subsidy-free world for the year 2000." Our government intends to bring before the 92-country General Agreement on Tariffs and Trade (GATT) a proposal for a phased reduction of all nations' farm-support programs—which, according to the World Bank, amount to a minimum of $110 billion a year worldwide—and suggest new trade rules to promote peaceful settlement of disputes.

What are you suggesting that isn't being done, Mr. Jackson?

I can't trust these multinational non-farming farmers who have no dirt under their fingernails. Land is real estate to them. I'm not asking for foreign aid—these are our farmers—they fed America—they fed the world.

A mother has five children and two pork chops. She won't run to a computer to prove that she has three excess children. She'll make gravy and cut the chops into five pieces because she's got common sense.

We can bail out the credit system.

We can bail out New York City (and we should have).

We can bail out Chrysler—and Continental Bank. We can have an

$18 billion cost overrun for the B-1 Bomber—if we can bail out Europe and Japan we can bail out the family farmer!

Address to the SLC
Little Rock, Arkansas, August 1987

As for "multi-national non-farming farmers," it's true that people who have analyzed the breakdown of the subsidy payments have found large amounts of taxpayer dollars going to foreign investors, executives with part-time farms and to the farmers with net worth's exceeding a million dollars who have the financial clout necessary to make it on their own. But bailouts and subsidies always, always benefit most those with clean fingernails. I discuss rice growers as an example in another book.[54] The "scam" goes something like this: the maximum government subsidy is $50,000 a year so the key is in knowing the exact number of acres to plant in order to qualify for that subsidy. The government presumes by having such a cut-off only smaller growers will benefit. (O, ye who underestimate the ingenuity of your fellowman!) All a large grower has to do is plant the right number of acres and then rent similar parcels to "new growers" (the ones with the clean fingernails), each for a handsome sum. Remember, each parcel is automatically worth $50,000 to each and every purchaser. There's no need for getting "dirt under their fingernails."

The Reverend was no doubt trained to use parables and his seminary should be proud of his mastery. In the SLC speech one can see the mother, children and chops and we feel good about her and her solution to her problem, but that feeling should not transfer to the Reverend's proposals regarding farm policy. Dividing pork chops may be *common sense* but expanding export credit and subsidy programs and paying farmers to idle up to 50 percent of all land set aside for certain crops is absolute *non-sense!* Farmers and others have learned how to "play" the federal government and can reap a record crop while receiving subsidies for idling land at the same time. On the other hand, "dividing pork chops" might bc the simplest and least expensive answer if done via direct money payments to farmers without all the hoopla. Let them plant or not and introduce the element of a free market with a gradual scaling back of "welfare" payments over time. Many believe such a plan would be cheaper than the present charade we are playing with agriculture. The 1985 Farm Bill spends billions of dollars undoing what other government programs have done and ends up giving the most dollars to those who need them the least. The acreage reduction program served as a signal to competitors to increase their own production. There is absolutely no doubt that subsidies are self-perpetuating as well as self-defeating.

Housing

> We must put every American in a house; it's our moral obligation—it's also cost efficient—it makes good common sense.
>
> *Before the Texas Legislature*
> *August 24, 1987*

Again, morality has nothing to do with government's role. Helping your neighbor stems from religious beliefs or a personal code of ethics. Socialism or communism attempt to legislate equality—morality, if you will—but a capitalist government rests upon opportunity and freedom, not redistribution (theft). Cost efficiency can only occur if one becomes *obligated* to do something more expensive as an alternative to putting every American in a house. (More blackmail.)

> It does not make good sense nor is it good morality to cut back on affordable housing for those who need them. Under the Reagan administration the HUD budget has gone from $32 billion to $10 billion in seven years. They're trying to privatize remaining public housing—3 to 5 million homeless people—others living double and triple up. PEOPLE DESERVE A HOUSE! We begin to provide homes for the homeless—we provide jobs for the jobless—turn welfare recipients, unemployment compensation beneficiaries into workers who generate revenue and pay taxes and reduce the deficit.
>
> *Before the SLC*
> *Little Rock, Arkansas, August 1987*

Let's discuss the housing budget. In 1981 the federal government's long term housing commitments amounted to almost $240 billion. Because of excessive costs and wasteful management, Congress, in 1982, brought a halt to all new federal construction programs. However, funds appropriated during the Carter years have produced units during the Reagan administration, as many as 76,000 in 1987 alone and 251,000 units in FY1981. The Reagan administration has opted for housing vouchers which cost taxpayers half as much as new construction, which incidentally ended up subsidizing developers far more than tenants. According to the Office of Management and Budget (OMB), tenants in government-subsidized construction projects receive thirty-four cents worth of benefits for every one dollar spent, whereas they receive eighty-four cents for every dollar spent in a voucher program. Dollars allocated to a problem rarely tell a complete and accurate story. Mr. Jackson may have wanted his audience to conclude that the present administration doesn't care about the problem. What do you think?

As for privatizing public housing, Mr. Jackson is absolutely correct. The Reagan administration is attempting to substitute loan subsidies for rent subsidies—home ownership for public housing. Rent for federally-subsidized housing is based on income, which means the more a person makes the more he pays. Not exactly an incentive for more work or a formula for getting ahead, is it? Low interest loans, however, often bring mortgage payments down to the level of rent and offer a family a real chance to get ahead. Home ownership not only enhances net worth but enhances self-worth as well.

Speaking of doubling and tripling up, check this HUD definition: "OVERCROWDING—more than one person to a room." Knowing the correct definition is the key to qualifying for most government programs. You can then make things fit. Bet you didn't know that "low-income household" means a household which receives less than 50 percent of the region's median income, or at most $21,000! To qualify, the fewer income-earners in the "house-hold" the better, and folks catch on to that quickly enough!

The Reverend's assertion that "people deserve a house" deserves a book in answer, but let me lightly skim the issue from a "right-to-housing" angle. The first "right-to-shelter" suit was filed in New York City in 1979 and many have been filed in various states since. The concept is an absurdity. There can be no right to shelter, only the right to acquire shelter, if not through purchase or rental as a result of one's own labor, then the shelter must be obtained through the charity of others, either willingly elicited or coerced—i.e., by government edict.

The first time I heard Jesse Jackson's "ABRA" (provide homes for homeless)-"CADABRA" (provide jobs for jobless) and "SHAZAM" (we've got taxpaying workers to reduce our deficit), I laughed my head off—but then I wanted to cry when I saw how unwitting audiences rose to their feet cheering. Forget the philosophy behind *government providing* homes and jobs—just look at the economics! Who pays for the homes and jobs? I guarantee that most of these new "workers" will be tax-exempt and that the cost will far exceed any taxes generated.

Energy

> Organize a PanAmerican energy and security alliance. Oil reserves of Canada, coal reserves of Pennsylvania and West Virginia can degasify and turn to methanol; corn reserves of the midwest from which we can make ethanol; oil fields which are not pumping in Louisiana, Oklahoma, Arkansas, Texas and Southern California combine with oil reserves in Mexico, Colombia and Venezuela. We can have a PanAmerican energy and security alliance in this hemisphere—make our oil more safe and more secure, get the oil wells pumping in Latin America—it will reduce their debt, reduce our deficit and put people back to work. That's the alternative to welfare and despair.
>
> *Before the SLC*
> *Little Rock, Arkansas, August 1987*

While we were once the world's leading oil producer, the United States now ranks behind the Soviet Union and Saudi Arabia. An alliance among oil producers in the western hemisphere as a protection against OPEC's potential stranglehold on us in the future is not such a bad idea. Even better would be government's backing-off (not subsidizing one over the other) and letting American ingenuity and the profit motive work out alternate energy sources. Increased subsidies for ethanol production is pandering to farmers. So far government subsidies and free corn have encouraged corporations to come up with 80-cent-per-gallon fuel for a mere $1.45 per gallon!

A call for "an oil import tax for revenue and energy independence" and to "get oil fields working again" went over big at a speech by Jesse Jackson to the Texas legislature on April 24, 1987. These men and women were particularly enthusiastic when he declared "the Northeast should help the Southwest . . . all bear and share burdens . . . just one America . . . world economy is interdependent."

Drugs

(Jesse Jackson spoke of the) agony of our children. 35 percent know someone dead because of drugs; 50 percent know someone in jail because of drugs; almost 100 percent know someone who takes drugs or know someone contemplating suicide.

Before the Texas Legislature
April 24, 1987

We can defend the borders of our allies in Korea, and we must. We can defend the borders of our allies in Europe, and we must. We must defend our *own* borders! To stop drugs we need drug sweepers for the Gulf of Mexico—to defend American borders. We know where drugs are grown, where they're coming from, who is dying from them. We've lost more lives by the dope than by the rope. They used to come at night disguised in sheets. Drug pushers come disguised as friends, as classmates, as teammates. They don't wear hoods—they *are* hoods and we must stop them!

Before the SLC
Little Rock, Arkansas, August 1987

The Reverend Jackson has spent more time than any other candidate speaking out against and drawing attention to the nation's nightmare affair with drugs. We should all be grateful for his oratorical skill in this area.

Trade

Many people believe Jesse Jackson makes sense and elicits the most audience response when it comes to the trade issue.

Thirty thousand of the best automakers in the world lost their jobs—that week thirty thousand new jobs opened in South Korea.

The #1 exporter from Taiwan is General Electric . . . also the #2 defense contractor . . . also owns NBC. (They run) "Buy American" ads while they close down plants here and take our jobs, repress labor and sell prices here at a high level. We need economic justice!

There is cheaper, not better labor elsewhere. (They) live in dormitories—can't organize—live under semi or marshal law—can't demonstrate. Labor relations and labor rights must be part of an (international) agreement. If they (foreign workers) get livable wages, it will reduce incentives for them to take our jobs. Livable wages means they can buy what we produce.

We cannot hurt somebody without hurting ourselves. We cannot help somebody without helping ourselves. It really does suggest that slave labor anywhere depresses organized labor anywhere. The Taiwanese, the South Koreans are not taking our jobs—the multinationals are taking our jobs *to* them—(the multinationals) export jobs, export capital, export our tax-base, destabilize our families. We must change direction—we must stop the process of merging corporations, purging workers, submerging our economy. The American worker can compete on an even playing field. Incentives must shift to the four Rs:

1) reinvest in America
2) retrain our workers
3) reindustrialize our nation
4) research for commitment

We're not working on competition, we're working on defense. (The) Japanese spend little on military. Who here owns a VCR? Raise your hands . . . Americans don't make them. Not because we're not intelligent enough to make them—they're not our priority.

Now, who here owns an MX missile? Raise your hands. (Laughter.) The point is we're making what the world is not requesting.

Before the SLC
Little Rock, Arkansas, August 1987

Some random comments: (1) "Economic justice" is subjective. (2) We have a hard enough time with "labor relations" and "labor rights" in this country. What country would submit to an outside international regulator? (GATT has little power.) Surely not the USA! (3) Who will provide "livable wages" to foreign workers? Only the market place can do that. If employers don't make a profit, they can't pay. (4) In a capitalist society (the United States is still one) the "4 Rs" can only be undertaken by private enterprise motivated by profits. The only place for the "4 Rs" in a political speech is as a strong appeal to socialism. If that's what you want, then recognize it for what it is and go ahead and work for it. People can change things. First, however, compare the history of socialism all over the world with the history of capitalism. Ask yourself why so many nations are turning from socialism to capitalism. If you're still willing to buck the trend, then join those who cheer and applaud speeches such as this one by Jesse Jackson.

Jesse Jackson's style is at its best when he uses simple imagery and asks for participation from his audience. Naturally everyone chuckled and felt warmly toward this "wise man" when he asked those who owned MX missiles to raise their hands. His wisdom extended to his observation that "we're making what the world is not requesting." Any fool capitalist knows the first rule for success is to make what people want! But this works only when people set their own priorities via their own pocketbooks and not their neighbor's. The system gets the wrong signals when government decides what people *should* want—what is *good* for them—and subsidizes one thing over another.

As for providing defense, that is one of the very few *obligations* of government (taxpayers).

In Baldwin, Iowa, during the summer of 1987, the Reverend Jackson, as usual, referred to foreign labor as "slave labor, undercutting organized labor" and facetiously complained that maybe the "American worker wants too many benefits—house, medical care, food, their children to go to college. They want too much."

When asked during the Democratic candidates' debate held in Dubuque, Iowa, on August 22, 1987, whether business or workers were the greedy ones when it came to the dispute over settling for a pay-cut or a plant-closing, he launched into a crowd-pleasing (unless the crowd is made up of CEOs) parable about executive greed:

> If all the fish in a pond are dead, look for the barracuda that killed all those fish. (He blamed GM for closing plants and suggested regulating corporations.) This government must *demand* that corporations retrain our workers—reinvest in America . . . don't over study the small dead fish, challenge the behavior of the international barracudas.

Another excerpt follows from his speech to the SLC:

> The UAW can't win with GM. The union is playing on a national playing field, the multinational is playing on an international playing field . . . FDR tackled monopolies in his day. We must tackle multinationals.

In case you are wondering what Jesse Jackson has in mind by "tackling multinationals," the answer is government. (Okay—so you're not surprised.) He advocates incentives and penalties to force corporations to behave the way he (and labor) would like them to behave—free enterprise and private property be damned in the process.

Jesse Jackson's tactic has always been to appeal to the discontented in our society. He told the 1984 Democratic Convention in San Francisco that:

> My constituency is the damned, the disinherited, the disrespected and the despised.

But he would never count himself among any of them—except publicly, of course.

He was eloquent when he addressed the Texas Legislature in April 1987. He spoke about

> ... locked out farmers, sold out workers and bought out middle managers ... not just the loss of jobs, but the loss of pride—not just the closing of a factory or the auctioning of a farm, but the end of a community—not just the loss of hope, but the growth of fear ... People without hope have lost faith in the American Dream—don't see a future for themselves—no chance of getting an education or a good job ...
>
> TEXAS—it's time to fight back.
> If we must fight—fight at the plant gate.
> If we must fight—fight at the farm auction for mercy.
> If we must fight—fight at the drilling site. (In Texas, remember.)
> If we must fight—fight at the drug exchange.

William Schneider, writing for the *Atlantic Monthly,*[55] reported that Jesse Jackson

> ... told me with pride that his Rainbow Coalition has been working with white unemployed shipbuilders, dispossessed farmers and several labor unions. Jackson has also been prominently associated with striking communications workers, laid-off oilfield workers and TWA flight attendants ... "His is an effort to take every political grievance that ever existed and make a political movement."[56]

Meat cutters asked for Jesse Jackson's help because black workers were crossing their picket lines. He said:

> Scabs ... take $10 an hour jobs for $8 an hour. There's a $6 an hour person waiting for your job! We must fight for livable wages everywhere. Having a job is *not* enough.
>
> In slavery we had full employment—everybody had a job but no security and no benefits and no qualitative future ...
>
> We must fight, but this time let's fight together.
> If we must fight,
> Fight at the farm auction which forecloses the farmer—
> Say "Take one, take all."
> If we must fight,
> Fight at the plant gate that closed on workers without notice.
> If we must fight,
> Fight at the shipyards where goods made by slave labor undercuts organized labor.
> If we must fight,
> Fight at the schoolyard where some child with a good mind could not gain admission because they could not get a scholarship or

get a loan or teachers couldn't get paid.

If we must fight,

Fight at the hospitals where somebody died because they didn't have a green or yellow card to go upstairs to an empty bed waiting for the rich to get sick.

Let's fight for the *right* fight! For jobs and peace and justice!

Before the SLC
Little Rock, Arkansas, August 1987

Jesse Jackson wants to see a reversal of power. He is a revolutionist. "We must look at every aspect of United States foreign and domestic policy that has favored the rich over the poor, the few over the many. As a nation we must change direction." During the debate[57] he claimed that "Gramm-Rudman supports the rich and locks the poor in the basement. It (G-R) levels the playing field as it exists." He clamors for a change. He would empower those who have little power now.

> This administration has tried to privatize public housing—tried to make a profit out of a public need. Nothing is sacred, including people's right to a house (?) . . . Cut housing, cut medicaid, cut education scholarships for their children, cut prenatal care, cut headstart education, cut job training; nothing is left but raisins that were once grapes. (?) The door of opportunity was closed in their faces.
>
> *In Baldwin, Iowa, August 1987*

No man should be given power over any other. When you have few (no matter that the few were voted into office) making decisions for many—directing programs, making rules and regulations for others to follow, distributing goodies and deciding how much to take from which "A Group" and how much to give to each "B Group"—then you are making men slaves to one another and encouraging corruption. Power corrupts no less when wielded by Madame Defarge than when wielded by Marie Antoinette.

"Deregulation is not right. Government has an obligation to regulate justice, fairness, order and peace," Mr. Jackson said at one point during the debate in Dubuque. Whose idea of justice and fairness? Yours? His? Mine? He has proposed taking dollars from Wall Street, patiently explaining to his audiences that if only 10 percent of the $2 trillion in pension funds could be available to use for low-income housing and meeting human needs, there would be a large change in society. "We are not asking money managers to contribute but to (let us—meaning all future pensioners) use our own money in our own behalf."[58]

The Preacher

Although Al Gore studied theology at Vanderbilt, Jesse Jackson is the only ordained preacher among the candidates for the Democratic presidential nomination in 1988. Some people think he uses his opportunity to speak at church services in an unethical manner. The allegiance a parishioner feels to a man-of-god is a special relationship, one in which the preacher has undue influence over the parishioner. Some mornings the Reverend speaks to two packed churches at once via video. Those who brush aside the fiduciary influence as nonsense nevertheless admit that the Reverend's years as an evangelist are serving him well on the campaign trail. The following is an account related in *Insight* magazine (July 27, 1987) which is a common occurrence in Iowa:

> "If you are eighteen or older, please hear this. You are 18 and older and you are not a registered voter, stand." And a few stand.
>
> "Eighteen or older," he continues, ever so softly and pleadingly. "Maybe your name has changed, your address changed, or you didn't think your vote was important. If you're 18 now or you'll be 18 by November of this year, stand!" And some more stand.
>
> "If your name changed, your address changed, you didn't vote last time, you're 18 or older and you're not a registered voter. Stand! And come down here right now!"
>
> And they do.

In 1984 Jesse Jackson received nearly 20 percent of the Democratic primary vote but only 10 percent of the delegates. Maybe we had better start taking the Reverend Jackson more seriously, because under the revised rules the same vote will earn him many more delegates in 1988 and, if anything, he intends to draw a far larger vote this time around.

Paul Simon

Just as Gary Hart, Joe Biden and others have tried to be identified with JFK in the public's mind, Paul Simon strives to achieve an identification with Harry Truman. He seems to have succeeded to a large degree, witness the *Boston Globe* (May 1987) headline "Simon Brings Truman-like Integrity to the Campaign" and the July 27, 1987, issue of *Insight* magazine, whose cover story on Paul Simon cried "A Harry Truman for Today." George Will titled a piece for *Newsweek* "Bow-Tie Politics" and told us that Truman was the last president to wear bow ties.[59].

Paul Simon is the oldest of the Democratic candidates for the 1988 presidential nomination and, if elected president, would be sixty years old when he took office. He was born on November 29, 1928, to Lutheran missionaries who had returned to the United States—specifically Eugene, Oregon—from China shortly before his birth. After high school Paul Simon attended the University of Oregon and then a small college in Nebraska, which he left at age nineteen to become owner-editor of a troubled newspaper in Troy, Illinois. He was too young for WWII but in 1951, at age twenty-two, Mr. Simon enlisted in the army and was assigned to the Counter

Intelligence Corps, where for almost two years he was a special agent along the Iron Curtain in Europe. He wasted no time figuring out what to do with his civilian life. Immediately upon discharge from the service in 1953, he began a successful campaign for the Illinois House of Representatives and was a member of that body until 1962, when he was elected to the Illinois State Senate. In 1960 he married Jeanne Hurly, his wife of twenty-seven years and mother of his two children. Like Harriet Babbitt, Elizabeth Dole and Elise DuPont, Jeanne Simon is an attorney and has also served in the Illinois legislature. In 1968 Paul Simon was elected to the office of Lieutenant Governor in Illinois along with a Republican governor. At the end of that four-year term, Mr. Simon ran for his party's nomination for governor and lost by a narrow margin. He then took his only respite from politics and taught history and government at Sangamon State University in Springfield, Illinois, betwen 1972-74. In 1974 Paul Simon was elected to the United States House of Representatives from Illinois' 24th District, where he served until 1984 when he was elected to the United States Senate. Over a period of thirty-three years, the junior senator from Illinois has been in twenty-two general elections and primary campaigns; the campaign for the Democratic presidential nomination will be his twenty-third. Along the way the indefatigable Mr. Simon bought and sold fourteen newspapers, wrote numerous articles, authored eleven books and taught at a state university for two years.

On February 25, 1987, Paul Simon declared that he would not run for the presidential nomination but would support Senator Dale Bumpers of Arkansas instead. However, when Senator Bumpers announced his decision not to run, Paul Simon saw a need for his kind of leadership and decided on April 9, 1987, that he would enter the race. Senator Simon formally declared his candidacy on May 18, 1987.

Paul Simon is not known for his spell-binding oratory but he projects a sincerity and honesty that makes him an effective speaker.

Employment

When he announced his candidacy in May, Senator Simon shared his vision of an $8 billion program to generate jobs, which would be funded by the federal government. Reporters asked if his jobs program would be similar to the old WPA (Workers Progress Administration) of the thirties and Senator Simon, without flinching, hedging or ho-hemming, simply answered, "Yes."

Actually, the Senator advocates not government programs per se, but government partnerships. He wants to encourage cooperative efforts between government, business and labor. (As Mr. Dukakis might well ask, "So what else is new?") Regarding the role of government, Mr. Simon has said:

> I stand unashamed in saying we have to use the tools of government . . . And if you let government be a dormant or semidormant partner in that relationship, this country simply is not going to move ahead as we ought to move ahead.

Lord Keynes also advocated a partnership between business and government. But as Ayn Rand pointed out, perhaps immoderately, in *The Fascist New Frontier:*

> There can be no partnership between armed bureaucrats and defenseless private citizens who have no choice but to obey. What chance would you have against a "partner" whose arbitrary word is law, who may give you a hearing (if your pressure group is big enough), but who will play favorites and bargain your interest away, who will always have the last word and the legal "right" to enforce it on you?

In 1982 the Office of Management and Budget (OMB) found that public works were a relatively high-cost way to create employment. It was estimated that only 12 percent of the jobs financed by the local public works programs went to the unemployed, and on average unskilled workers kept their jobs less than four weeks. Those with motivation and incentive would have found work on their own and the others were mostly workers brought in by out-of-town contractors. They were paid in conformity with the Davis-Bacon Act, which requires compensation to match the area's "prevailing" (read high union) wages. Such projects would simply put a lot of people to work for wages higher than those earned by two-thirds of the American workforce. Make-work programs raise the cost and reduce the supply of efficient production. Another case of the inefficient driving out the efficient. Federal public works expenditures merely replace state and local government expenditures, meaning there are no new jobs. In fact, other federal programs may be displaced with loss of government jobs as businesses are forced to economize. Although financing public works via deficit spending may have worked once (the ol' Keynesian solution), remember there is no longer the cushion we once had. The gargantuan budget deficit has used up the margin of safety we once enjoyed—we are more vulnerable to domestic as well as global uncertainties.

Mickey Kaus, a journalist for the *New Republic*, has proposed offering anyone who wanted it a government job, but at less than minimum wage so that there would be an incentive to move into the private sector. GAIN, California's workfare, will only give assistance checks to those either receiving job training, education or are in a workfare job. These government jobs are only provided if even after training a person is unable to find a job on his own. Failure to comply results in a gradual reduction in the relief check. Eventually, the relief package may get low enough so that it makes sense for a person to take a job. The problem is that now no person is required to take a job that pays less than the value of all the welfare recipient's benefits. (Massachusetts' ET "requires" no one to take a job—ET is voluntary.) When Medicaid, child care, transportation allowances and training is thrown in, the deal may be hard to beat for a person who wants to get off welfare.

The Job Training Partnership Act is a step in the right direction, but it would be even better with no government assistance, unquestionably so from a capitalist ideology and even so from a purely practical (non-ideological) point of view. For exammple, J.C. Penney, American Express, IBM and MCI all have pregnant dropout training programs. CBS News (May 27, 1987) featured a Norfolk, Virginia, businessman, Herman Valentine from Systems Management of America, who invested $100,000 in a program to train pregnant dropouts because it made good business sense.

Job training is another example of government rushing to fill a void that the free market would fill more efficiently and—best of all—freely, without coercion or incentives. But any pragmatist knows that is not going to happen—at least not any time soon. Employer incentives may be the best of a bad thing. Presently, employers who give jobs to the disadvantaged and the handicapped receive a tax credit equal to 40 percent of the first $6,000 of first-year wages. Minimum job durations are ninety days or one hundred twenty work hours for permanent workers, fourteen days or twenty work hours for summer youth. Some legislators would like to see this made a permanent program. Regarding growth in the service sector of the economy, Senator Simon has said:

> That represents a drop in the standard of living for most of the employees who have shifted away from manufacturing—pay is almost always less—and it reprsents a questionable policy for our nation ... To maintain a quality standard of living, and to improve it, we have to produce things that people consume. Our tax laws should encourage that.

From the preceding it would seem that Senator Simon should be in favor of taxing services as well as, or perhaps even instead of, goods, as Florida is doing now with it's new controversial tax.

According to the Bureau of Labor Statistics, between 1965-85 union wages outpaced cumulative inflation by 1.4 percent. (Not a heck of a lot.) Those in auto assembly lines were paid more, however, and thanks to union pressures $30,000 was not an unheard of wage for sweeping floors! It wasn't until 1984 that union pay hikes fell below the consumer price index for the first time. Growth in the labor force was a little over 2 percent during those years, and during the seventies alone approximately 20 million net new jobs were created. The projections of labor force growth from now to 1990 is 1.6 percent annually and is only 1 percent a year between 1990-95, with fewer teenagers included until 1992. Between 1972-78, real after tax income per capita was flat, but since then it has risen about 11.3 percent. However, it's true that many new jobs don't pay as well as the old. In 1983 the average employee in domestic industries made $16,000—in export industries he made $19,000. The new high-tech industries seem to pay either minimum wage for assembly line skills or high salaries for technical knowledge and training—no middle ground. Comparing American wages to other countries the Senator finds:

> The average worker in Japan now (summer of 1987) is making more

than the average worker in the United States. In 1950 the average Japanese made 5 percent of the average American's wage.

I don't know about Japanese wages in 1950, but from 1982 to 1985 Japanese workers were paid 50 percent less than American workers. However, by January 1987 the Japanese workers were paid only 21 percent less. In 1985 the wages and benefits of West German workers were 25 percent less than those of American workers but by 1987 those wages were 20 percent above the wages of Americans. The USA had become more competitive on labor costs than the Europeans, or to put it in the light it will be given by the Democratic candidates, wages of American workers are 20 percent lower than the wages of their European counterparts. All together between 1980-85, labor costs in this country rose 11.2 percent, about 5 percent under most other industrialized nations. In other words, wages rose 5 percent less here—but then look where they started.

Many European businesses have shied away from hiring in good times for fear of being stuck with too many workers when things slow down. (One reason for Europe's high unemployment rate.) German employers had to go through an expensive and complicated procedure in order to fire any employee who had been on the payroll for at least six months. Luckily a new law has put a stop to that nonsense and employers are allowed to hire workers on contracts of up to eighteen months and lay them off at the end of that period without a giant hassle. Activists in this country point to other industrialized nations as "way ahead of the USA in providing this and that," and yet those exemplary countries are beginning to copy us just as we are being urged to copy them. There seems to be no end to our self-destructive stupidity! Senator Simon says:

Let's move America forward. Forward into full employment.

Full employment has been defined as the level of unemployment that would exist when demand was adequate to keep the inflation rate stable. All unemployment at full employment would be voluntary in the sense that anyone who wanted a job would be able to find one by reducing his nominal wage enough to make employing him profitable to someone.

Partly to get away from the implication that full employment meant zero unemployment, economists adopted the term "natural rate of unemployment." The natural rate changes over time with changes in the age-sex composition of the labor force as well as for other reasons. In the forties and fifties employment was "full" if no more than 3-4 percent of the labor force was out of work. By the 1970s the acceptable level was 6-7 percent because the baby-boom generation was entering the labor market in droves, along with an influx of women.

Senator Simon reminds me of New York's governor, Mario Cuomo, who early in 1986 addressed the newspaper publishers in San Francisco:

> (The current prosperity) has been purchased at the expense of the well-being, the hopes and expectations of a large part of our nation, by the acceptance of such things as a level of unemployment that this nation would have considered a scandal only a decade ago.

George Will pointed out that at the time of Governor Cuomo's speech, unemployment was 7.1 percent and a decade ago it was 7.7 percent. Presently it is under 6.5 percent!

In the 1960s economist and Nobel laureate Milton Friedman claimed that at some point attempts to obtain further gains on the employment front simply result in an acceleration in wages and prices. In 1986 some economists thought an employment rate of 7.1 percent might just about be the inflationary flash point. The natural rate rises when skills offered by the pool of unemployed and new workers fail to match new openings, causing business to bid up wages. For instance, wage and fringe benfits rose by 7.2 percent in 1982, but the gain was only 4.3 percent in 1985 and was about a point lower in 1986.

Unemployment statistics regarding gains and losses are not reliable at any rate. Approximately four million people reach age eighteen every year in this country and many become statistical "have-nots" even though their minimum- or low-wage jobs are temporary and for "pin money." Many of the teenage girls who work at the local shopping mall are still living at home while attending local community colleges. They may be poverty statistics, but their low wages go to pay for school clothes and books.

In March 1987 the Senate Labor and Human Resource committee, the committee on which Senator Paul Simon serves, came up with legislation that would give financial bonuses: $3,700 for each former recipient of assistance who finds employment and remains employed for at least three years. The funds would come from the money saved by removing the former recipients from the welfare rolls and would not be paid until the savings were realized. During a former recipient's first year of employment, the state would receive 75 percent of the benefit that would have been paid to the person had he or she still received AFDC. That figure would drop to 50 percent during the second year and 25 percent in the third year of employment. After the three years, the average bonus per recipient would be almost $3,700. (Maybe a good time to quit and start the largess rolling all over again!) Also included in the target groups are the recipients of Social Security disability payments.

The plan may ensure federal budget neutrality, but what about the philosophy? The concern seems to be wholly practical with little thought to the ideals of the nation or whether it makes spiritual as well as economic sense. Does anybody care?

There are parents who *pay* their children for getting good grades or for cleaning their own rooms. Bonuses or incentives, they call it. What about instilling self-respect instead? Do it to please yourself, not so you can pick up a government check or for parental approval!

Those in authority, whether parent or legislator, tend to get what they expect. Keep the expectations low and you won't be disappointed. On the other hand, I am certain people respond to challenges and are capable of far more than they themselves realize.

That is the purpose of government—to provide opportunity and inspire citizens to do their best, not, as I read in one of my son's history textbooks recently, to redistribute the wealth of the nation.[60]

Social Security

Like the other candidates, Paul Simon was asked two questions by the Associated Press about his potential handling of Social Security. First, "Will you keep Social Security benefits and the annual cost-of-living increases exempt from budget cuts?" He answered:

> I would keep Social Security exempt from budget cuts and I would take Social Security as quickly as I could away from the rest of the budget . . . It is too tempting to use that as a means of balancing the budget.

I was intrigued by his answer.

M. Albert Linton, president of Provident Mutual Life Insurance Company of Philadelphia and advisor to the Committee on Economic Security in 1934, was concerned that excess funds, if allowed to accumulate, would prove too great a temptation for Congress to resist. To enhance their own popularity, elected officials would have only to liberalize benefits. Ironically, the same fears were expressed fifty years later by Stuart Sweet in an article discussing the effects of the 1983 Social Security Commission.

> And one doesn't have to be a cynic to see how tempting it will be for politicians to spend "surplus funds" that won't be needed for nearly sixty years. Who believes they will be able to resist handing out new benefits when a $20 trillion surplus will accumulate in OASDI funds if they forbear?[61]

Sweet claims, thanks to the 1983 reform, that the trust funds if anything are now *too well funded.* He estimated there would be an accumulation of between $20-73 trillion (worst to best scenarios) by the middle of the next century. He was adamant that we make certain such an enormous surplus never occurs.

An enormous surplus in the Social Security trust funds could effectively eliminate all interest expense from the federal budget—at least on paper. (Interest has cost as much as $200 billion in one year!) How's that for sleight-of-hand? Elementary really—interest paid and received by government entities shows up as intragovernmental transfers in the unified budget rather than as income or expense.

Even if surpluses were undisturbed, there remains the problem of investing such a huge amount of capital without crossing the traditional boundaries between the private and public markets. With just $3 trillion the government would have the ability to purchase all the stocks on the New York Stock Exchange!

Currently the trustees (Secretaries of Labor, the Treasury and Health and Human Services) are only permitted to invest in Treasury securities, such as T-notes, bills and bonds. 89.4 percent of the Social Security trust fund's total assets are invested in special issues which offer better yields than those available to private investors. Also making it easier for the trustees is the fact that they don't have to worry about capital gains or losses or the marketability of the Social Security investments. Our current trustees only have to work at placing a $27 billion surplus for a very short period. That does not pose much of a problem when the national debt is $2 trillion, but what will the trustees do when there is anywhere from $20-73 trillion to invest over fifty years? You don't suppose they'll think of raising the deficit, do you, in order to provide more treasury debt for those Social Security reserves?[62]

To the second question put by the Associated Press, "Do you favor any means test for Social Security benefits?" Senator Simon replied:

> I do not favor (a means test). Social Security should not become a welfare thing. Social Security is in a very real sense a retirement system that people pay into and I do not think there ought to be a means test to it.[63]

Education

> You talk about anticrime programs—the majority of people in the prisons of this country today are people who are functionally illiterate. The average grade level attained of those in our prisons today is fifth grade. If you want to talk about an anticrime program, let's move on education and not cut back as this administration wants to do.[64]

Senator Claiborne Pell suggested to William Bennett, Secretary of Education who was testifying before the Senate Labor and Resources Committee (Senator Paul Simon is a member) on January 14, 1987, that having to pay back college loans would limit the choice of jobs open to these college graduates. He pointed out that the lower-paying social service jobs would go begging. When Secretary Bennett recalled that he had owed the equivalent of $30,000 in today's dollars when he graduated from law school and was not deterred from choosing a career in the much lower paid educational field as opposed to law, Senator Pell would not concede but scoffingly complimented the Secretary, also pointing out that "not everyone has your drive and ambition."

In a similar vein, Senator Paul Simon told the Coalition for Higher Education Assistance Organizations about a medical school graduate in his district (Greenfield, Illinois) who was $80,000 in debt and although he would have liked to serve in an inner city area, he couldn't, according to Senator Simon, because he needed money to repay loans.

On January 19, 1987, Bruce Carnes from the Department of Education argued with Senator Simon that the new proposal for income contingent loans (ICLs) offered more access and flexibility than student aid in the past and was also fairer to the taxpayers.

The Reagan administration has pointed to the need-based student aid (Pell Grants, 1972) as being in part responsible for skyrocketing college costs which took off in the mid-1970s. In the past student aid has penalized savers (couldn't qualify) and provided no incentives for colleges to keep their costs down. Mark Tucher of the Carnegie Forum spoke of our backward incentives and offered the "learning disabled" label as one example. Schools receive more money for "learning disabled" kids and, therefore, there is a certain reluctance to improve these kids and lose the additional monies the handicapped bring via the federal government.

Furthermore, Mr. Carnes claimed the dropout rate for kids on loans was slower than for those on grants. Apparently it is easier to walk away from someone else's investment. In 1985 the Department of Education reported that former undergraduate and graduate students defaulted on $3 billion in low-interest loans to students through their schools. Most graduates were earning money and simply making economic decisions not to repay the low-interest loans.

Mr. Carnes, in an effort to show fairness, talked about borrowing from the taxi driver (the new symbolic average man) rather than making him provide as a gift, a college education which would almost assuredly net the recipient-student more than the donor-taxi-driver could hope to make in his working career. According to *American Demographics* magazine, households headed by college graduates had median incomes in 1985 which were 54 percent higher than incomes of those who had only graduated high shcool. Other studies have shown that the average college graduate makes $640,000 more than the average high school graduate over a lifetime.

Senator Simon and other critics are quick to point out that the taxi driver should subsidize the college student because his job and his future depend to a large extent on the college educated. The Reagan administration, as far as I can tell, agrees with this analysis, the only question being how much should the taxi driver be expected to pay? Don't forget he's being asked to chip in for child care so those with children can work, for farm subsidies so small farmers can keep their treasured way of life, for mass transit so people will have alternatives to his cab service, for parks, for highway, for schools he may never personally use—ALL FOR HIS OWN GOOD.

The ultimate show of concern for the taxi driver's wallet is expressed each and every day by the entire string of Democratic presidential candidates as they argue that college educations should be more fully financed because it costs on average $5,000 per year to send a person to college and to keep a person in prison costs closer to $20,000 per year. They may use a variety of figures, but their point is that the college educated are less likely to end up in prison. Voilà—a $15,000 per year saving by giving someone else's child a gift of a college education. With the number of conscientious officials and bureaucrats looking for ways to save him money "in the long run," our taxi driver won't have to worry about his own priorities—he won't have any income left for *them* anyway!

It's hard to believe members of Congress have any inclination whatsoever to curtail spending. I offer the following comments directed at Secretary of Education William Bennett at the January 14, 1987, committee meeting referred to earlier:

> There is no legal obligation put upon you (Mr. Bennett) to cut your budget.
>
> *Senator Lowell Weicker of Connecticut*

> Gramm-Rudman didn't dictate these priorities—only the bottom

line . . . Ted Bell (Bennett's predecessor as Secretary of Education) was in there fighting for every dollar from OMB (Office of Management and Budget)—I just don't hear that fight from the Secretary of Education today.

Senator Paul Simon of Illinois

Senator Simon went on to state that it is the function of the Department of Education to *demand* more funds.

My own angry notation: "My G-d, these Senators aren't trying to cut spending; they're trying to expand and scurry around, intent on ferreting every possible dollar!"

Over the past six years Congress has allocated $18.8 billion more than the Japanese have allocated to education; our system is simply inefficient and must be reformed. We can't go on viewing education as another target for the money slingers.

According to Secretary Bennett:

> We have increased education spending by 300 percent in real dollars in twenty-seven years and we have not increased the results in that proportion . . . The basic problem with American education is not that it is underfunded—it is underproductive and it is underaccountable. It is overregulated.[65]

Nevertheless a mind is under an individual's control and society, via government mandates and/or dollars, can neither dictate nor prevent its use. Many of America's greatest success stories began with a human being in abject poverty, often not knowing the English language (Panos Dukakis) and forced to support a myriad of relations. Man's indomitable spirit and determination can overcome anything and everything if it is only given the freedom to express itself; the freedom and the need. All the hand-holding in the form of grants and subsidies will never make up for the force of will.

The Disappearing Middle Class

> The ratio in income between the top 10 percent and the bottom 10 percent is about 14-to-1 in the United States. In West Germany it's about a 5-to-1 ratio. In Japan it's about a 4.5-to-1 ratio.
>
> Now what is wrong with having such a huge spread? Let me tell you, you have that huge spread and you have social dynamite. You don't know what's going to happen. And what *is* happening is we're gradually squeezing middle-income America, a few people moving up, a lot more moving down. And you can't have a lot of people

moving below that poverty line, moving down in income, without ultimately having major problems in our society.[66]

Wealth is a life cycle matter. The young accumulate debts, the middle-aged accumulate houses and cars and the older people have assets without mortgages and loans while accumulating medical expenses. This translates in numbers to a median net worth of $5,760 for those under age thirty-five, $73,660 for those age fifty-five to sixty-four and $55,180 for those over age seventy-five as they begin to sell off some assets in order to meet expenses and maintain their standard of living.

In May 1987 the Harvard Institute for Learning and Retirement had members of an illustrious panel voice their opinion concerning "The Disappearing Middle Class" (topic). Alan Reynolds of Polyconomics in Morristown, New Jersey, told the audience that a Federal Reserve study in March 1987 had found that 54 percent of the family heads earning over $150,000 per year had graduate school educations, compared to 10 percent of the population as a whole. Only 1 percent of the high-income families were headed by someone younger than age 35, compared to 31 percent of the entire population. In fact, 31 percent of all family heads didn't work at all, whereas in the high-income group 56 percent had two spouses working.

Mr. Reynolds concluded that the educated older families with two earners are likely to earn more than the uneducated younger families with one worker or less. "If this is shocking or unfair," he joked, "one might consider passing out a Harvard MBA to everyone in order to equalize things."

There has been a great deal of controversy surrounding the Joint Economic Committee's report on the concentration of wealth which was released in the summer of 1986. The study reportedly showed that the share of national family net worth held by the top 0.5 percent of the nation's wealthiest families had gone from 25.4 percent to 35.1 percent over a twenty-year period (1963-1983).

On August 21, 1986, the Joint Economic Committee press office admitted the Federal Reserve Board had made an error in its data. The corrected data showed that over the twenty years mentioned, the wealthiest 0.5 percent had increased their share of the wealth only 1.5 percent, which is an amount considered within normal statistical sampling error and, therefore, was statistically no change at all!

Taxes

It is likely that Paul Simon got his facts, directly or indirectly, from MIT Professor Lestor Thurow's assertion that income distribution is twice as unequal in the United States as it is in Japan.

> In West Germany, before taxes and transfers, 28 percent of the population has less than half the median income; in the U.S. the figure is 27 percent. After taxes and transfers, however, West Germany is left with only 6 percent of its population in that predicament, whereas the U.S. is left with 17 percent.[67]

Those enamored with the idea of using other countries as a role model consider this to be a valid argument for higher, more progressive taxation, whereas the facts show that the best way to "soak the rich" is by cutting their tax rates. In 1981 before the Reagan tax cuts, the wealthiest one percent of all taxpayers paid 18 percent of their incomes in taxes (on average); in 1985, after the tax cut and when they stopped hiding their income, they paid 22.1 percent.

This was not a unique situation. History shows that whenever marginal tax rates have been reduced, the results have been increased productivity, jobs, real disposable income and overall impressive economic growth. This was true of the Kennedy tax cut which took place in 1963 (and which Senator Simon has yet to mention), and going even further back it was true of the Coolidge-Mellon cuts of the 1920s.

In 1987 a book forecasting the "Great Depression of 1990" advocated, as a solution to our deficit problem, slapping a 5 percent surtax on Americans with incomes over $200,000 a year. As Peter Grace (as in "Grace Commission"), co-chairman of Citizens Against Waste, likes to point out to his audiences, putting a surcharge of 10 percent on all incomes over $60,000 will yield only $1.65 billion or 0.8 percent of the deficit. Even if 100 percent surcharge was put on incomes over $75,000, the government could only be run for 7.3 days with the resultant revenue. The truth that is seldom told is that less than 10 percent of all tax revenue is collected from those citizens with incomes over $35,000. To put it another way, over 90 percent of all tax revenue is collected from citizens with incomes under $35,000. Promises to tame the deficit on the backs of the rich are popular but ineffectual.

Although he is often mistaken, no one can doubt Mr. Simon is well-meaning. He is proud that he is the only candidate to have voted against the 1981 and the 1986 tax cuts, little realizing that this vote, if effective, would have done more harm than good to the economy and, therefore, to poor and middle-income Americans. He likes to quote Harry Truman who claimed that deficits help rich people. "Who pays the high interest rates?" he asked. "The poorest people." But he must also ask, "Who gets hurt the most when there are fewer jobs, less real disposable income, low productivity and a stagnant economy?" The answer would still be the poorest people.

Senator Paul Simon along with Senators Gore and Biden had wanted to see a 35 percent rate above the 28 percent rate in the 1986 reform. He does not advocate adding the higher rate now but would turn for additional revenue to an energy tax (oil import fee with rebates for the lowest taxpayers) and excise taxes on cigarettes and jewelry. He would also like to decrease the deduction for business meals from 80 percent to 50 percent and expand a telephone tax. Worst of all, in my opinion, he would decrease limits on contributions to retirement plans.[68] This is the same Paul Simon who at one time co-sponsored a measure that would have permitted taxpayers to stipulate that no part of their taxes be used for defense. More good feelings cloaked in bad policies.

In Iowa

> There are three things all candidates (Democrats) should agree on: (1) that too much is being spent on weapons; (2) that education should be a greater priority; and (3) a priority should be set on seniors' problems, there should be a vigorous family farm program and a jobs program. We (all seven Democratic candidates for the presidential nomination) should agree that on January 21, 1989, no matter who is elected President, to: (1) stop all nuclear testing (if the Soviets will agree); (2) attack adult illiteracy and provide funding

> for an intense pre-school education program; and (3) institute self-financed long-term (health) care for older Americans.
>
> *Debate in Dubuque, Iowa*
> *August 22, 1987*

Before another Iowa audience Paul Simon said:

> You in Iowa have more to say about who is going to be the next President than the people of Illinois, New York and California combined.

Unless you're from Iowa, that probably makes you mad. We'll take this up and discuss other injustices in the way we choose our political leaders in Section IV.

Section Three

Republican Presidential Hopefuls

George Bush

We've had educators, generals, haberdashers and peanut farmers as president of the United States, maybe it's about time we had a fisherman? Sure, I know George Bush has been billed as a New England aristocrat and a Texas wildcatter, and I must admit the fisherman label is rather farfetched and valid only if one is aware that, according to Standard and Poors, Zapata Corporation (George Bush co-founded the company) "engages in offshore drilling, marine services, dredging, petroleum exploration, coal mining, menhaden, anchovy and fisheries development." Menhaden is a compressed shad-like fish gathered for its oil and used as fertilizer rather than food—at least in this country. Okay—so I said "farfetched!"

In the fall of 1987 it appeared that four senators, three governors, two congressman, two preachers, one general and one vice president had thrown their hats in the ring. True, George Bush has the vice president category all to himself, but vice presidents have rarely won presidential elections. Although not an incumbent, Mr. Bush is the heir apparent; electable until proven otherwise. The burden to unseat Mr. Bush is on the other candidates. He needed no early entry in order to build name recognition, as did Dick Gephardt and Pete du Pont. In fact the longer Mr. Bush remains silent, the less chance of "foot-in-mouth" and other such diseases which could prove disastrous to one in George Bush's precarious situation.

George Bush was born in Milton, Massachusetts, on June 12, 1924. His father, Prescott Sheldon Bush, was a successful businessman, a New York banker and, like the fathers of both Al Gore and Pat Robertson, was also a United States Senator.[1] George Bush excelled in studies and sports throughout high school, and when he graduated from Phillips Academy in Andover in 1942 he immediately entered the navy as an Ensign and became the youngest navy aviator, attached to the carrier *San Jacinto* as a bomber pilot. He was shot down by the Japanese on September 2, 1944, and was rescued by a submarine near the Bonin Islands. Hard to imagine the George Bush that comes across in debates and is depicted often as a Mr. Milk Toast in the media, playing the part of 007! But there's more—

When the second world war ended in 1945 he married Barbara Pierce. Over their forty-three years of marriage they have shared many joys and tragedies. Joy over the birth of five children and tragedy over the death of a daughter to leukemia.

Most of his Andover classmates had gone on to college in 1942 and in 1945 it was George Bush's turn. He characteristically led his classmates in academics and athletics. During his years at Yale he found time to captain the baseball team while acquiring his degree in economics as a Phi Beta Kappa.

In 1948, with degree in hand, he took his family and headed for Texas in search of adventure. He started out as a drilling equipment salesman and soon founded Bush-Overbey Oil Development, Inc. in Midland, Texas. In 1953 he merged it into Zapata Petroleum Corporation, becoming in 1954 the first president of Zapata Off-Shore. When Zapata struck oil George Bush earned the right to call himself a self-made man—an entrepreneur! He had become wealthy not via inheritance, but by his own effort, intelligence and initiative. (Okay, sure, there was some luck, but remember that old definition of luck—"when preparation meets opportunity.")

With business success came the opportunity to pursue new challenges, and so in 1964 George Bush was encouraged to make an unsuccessful run for the U.S. Senate by Houston's Republican leaders. The failure only seemed to whet his appetite and he decided to meet the challenge offered by the political arena and sold his business interests in order to devote full time to politics. This decision paid off with a seat in the U.S. House of Representatives in 1966, a seat which he held for two terms. In 1970 he was again persuaded to try for the Senate, but it was not to be. In 1971 he began picking up a list of credentials which would serve him well in his quest for the 1980 presidential nomination. He was U.S. Ambassador to the United Nations 1971-1973, Chairman of the Republican National Committee 1973-1974, Chief Liaison Officer, People's Republic of China 1974-1975, Director of the CIA 1976-1977 and candidate for the Republican presidential nomination in 1980. Despite his strong criticism of Ronald Reagan, his most powerful opponent for the Republican nomination, he was asked to serve as Vice President on the winning 1980 Reagan-Bush ticket. There Mr. Bush seems to disappear from view—alas, the fate of vice presidents!

George Bush appears to be a rare combination of caution and bravado. His eagerness to rush into WWII when the majority of his prep school classmates opted for college and his severance from a secure New England existence were both audacious acts. On the other hand, those who knew him in the service described him as "... cautious. No unnecessary chances ..."[2] which is a description that would be appropriate today, over forty years later. A combination of courage and caution are highly prized characteristcs which should perhaps be required of any presidential candidate.

Education

Although Mr. Bush is most noted for his preeminence in foreign affairs, he has quite a lot to say when it comes to education.

In Alleman, Iowa, in April 1987 he told his audience that the United States spends more than any nation in the world on education—per student—but is not getting its money's worth. Like a business, we need to see a fair return on our investment, we need to see better results, more discipline, the inculcation of values and basic skills. Teachers and parents need to have high expectations. There should be more accountability and more homework. It was fortunate that the Vice President could point out to his audience that Iowa was number one in SAT scores. "It comes down to parents and caring," he said. He cited the following as his goals for the nation:

> By the year 2000 when kindergarteners are graduating from high school, every child should know how to read. (Now 13 percent of all 17-year-olds are functionally illiterate—even some college graduates.) Math and science (programs will be) better. I believe we can teach values—decency, kindness, duty, self-discipline, tolerance and respect for the law. Youngsters need to develop good character. We need drug-free schools ... Education will keep America first.

On April 15, 1987, he told the Middlesex Club of Boston:

> I have a goal in our fight against illiteracy. I want to cut America's illiteracy rate in half during the next four years, and I want to cut it in half again in the four years after that.
>
> We also have to put more emphasis on teaching our children foreign languages so they can step out into the world and compete in the global economy. We have to drill our young people in the basic skills—reading, writing and arithmetic.

In Forest City, Iowa, on May 9th he said:

> Education will be the way we outcompete the Japanese and the South Koreans and the West Germans ... Our educational system is antiquated—its technology and its calendar are those of the last century; its incentive and reward structures are outdated; its thinking is restrictive; and its costs keep rising without equal results.
>
> To give you a personal example of the thinking that holds us back: A few years after we moved to West Texas, I tried to volunteer to teach a couple of courses—I can't remember whether it was the high school or the new community college—but my Phi Beta Kappa in economics wasn't good enough for Ector County, Texas, because I didn't have the required education courses. I think I would've made a good teacher, but I wasn't allowed to contribute ... In the future, education must meet national expectations and national goals, as well as local ones. I also believe our educational system must become innovative and entrepreneurial if it is to carry the load it must carry in the years ahead.

At the Albion College Commencement in May 1987 in Michigan he told the graduating class:

> I believe that our educational system should teach ... the differences

between right and wrong. You often hear that you can't teach values. I don't buy it ... Yet for two decades, many schools have gone out of their way not to teach values. They have sought to remain value neutral. A *New York Times* article quoted educators who said they deliberately avoided telling students what is ethically right and wrong ...

Education and ethics go hand-in-hand. Like education, ethics are essential to a free society ... Our democratic institutions and our free enterprise system require a high degree of trust and confidence. If that trust and confidence are missing, regulation and legislation have to fill the void.

In the fall of 1987, Mr. Bush outlined a college savings bond program to ease the increasing burden of tuition costs on the average American family. The only trouble is the average family generally doesn't have $140/month to set aside for education.

Agriculture

Mr. Bush has had almost as much to say about farm policy as education and has quite naturally said it in Iowa. In Forest City in May he told his audience:

> There are unstoppable technological advances being made in laboratories right now. Corn that resists insects, wheat that withstands drought, strawberries that repel frost, cows that produce 40 percent more milk with the help of a special hormone—all those things are in the works or being tested right now. And they're going to make harvests larger which, as we all know, will make prices even lower. But technological advances will also reduce the cost of producing ethanol which will help reduce our grain surplus ...
>
> We must ... pursue rural development, diversification, retraining and education ... We can develop policies so that Iowans can remain in Iowa and close to the land, so that Iowa's children can be raised here, educated here, find good jobs here, keep the fabric of the family farm and the Iowa way of life ... We cannot allow a particular region of the country to suffer the way the farm belt has when the country as a whole has had fifty-three straight months of economic growth and prosperity.

However, Mr. Bush did not tell his Forest City audience what government policies would work the miracles he described. Also, unlike his challenger Pete du Pont, Mr. Bush failed to blame the administration's farm policies for the current problems. It didn't occur to him to mention that during the

Reagan-Bush administration the net worth of the average full-time farmer became ten times greater than that of the average U.S. household, in large part due to the eightfold increase in subsidies during that time.[3] It's not that the administration didn't know any better; they offered decent agricultural programs to the Congress in both 1981 and again in 1985 but were overwhelmed by the opposition. According to James Bovard, Mr. Bush has opted for the safe position in favoring a phase-out of agricultural subsidies *only* if our trading partners agree to do the same. "It allows Mr. Bush to support the free market rhetorically while posing little threat of actually cutting federal aid."[4]

Mr. Bush, along with his fellow Republican candidates for the presidential nomination, rejects the Harkin-Gephardt plan, which he sees as a way to reduce subsidies at the cost of raising good prices for the American consumer (and voter) There seems to be a certain amount of intellectual dishonesty in the stand as taken by Phi Beta Kappa economist Bush. Also, it is hard to understand his support of increased government subsidies for the conversion of corn into ethanol when it costs $1.45 to produce 80 cents worth of fuel. It has to be justified on environmental grounds. In Alleman, Iowa, in April 1987, he gave us a glimpse of the power inherent in legislators. It's easy to increase demand for ethanol—just increase the environmental standards of cities who will turn to ethanol in order to meet those legislated standards. Those weren't Mr. Bush's exact words, but that was the message.

Trade

As for trade, you can bet Mr. Bush is not for the Gephardt amendment, nor for the trade bill (HR3) making its way through Congress in 1987. During a commencement address to Waldorf College (Iowa) in May 1987, Mr. Bush pointed out that:

> Certainly there are unfair trade practices out there. And we must do all in our power to guarantee free and fair trade and to see that our trading partners play by the rules. But if every unfair trade practice in the world were lifted tomorrow it would reduce our $166 billion trade deficit by only 10 or 15 billion dollars . . .
>
> Protectionism . . . won't save jobs . . . won't cure our trade deficit. And protectionism . . . will invite retaliation . . . I believe we can

> compete successfully without protectionism. I believe Americans want to compete rather than hide ... Protectionism's backwardness is contrary to the American spirit ... I don't care if you're an auto company or a welfare mother or farmer, you're ruined once you come to rely on government protection for your economic well-being.

Competitiveness, Taxes & Deficit

In Boston on April 15, 1987, he talked about competitiveness, taxes and the deficit:

> To some people, competitiveness means massive new spending programs and government interference in the private sector ...
>
> We have a worker-adjustment proposal before Congress right now that will help thousands more displaced workers if necessary ... I want America to be known as the nation that's first in creating job opportunities, first in educating its young people, first in protecting the health of its citizens from drugs and disease and first for standing up for freedom around the world.

Mr. Bush managed to mention our drug problem, AIDS, health care and the Contras all in one sentence. Of course he gave no specifics on how to achieve his "wants." Mr. Dukakis, Mr. Babbitt, Mr. du Pont and Mr. Kemp can all spell out their proposals step by step; whereas, candidates such as Mr. Bush generally try to play it safe and often only give us their "wish lists"—their good intentions. Good intentions should not be enough for voters. They should demand to see how one intends to get from A to B—specifically.

Later on in his Boston speech Mr. Bush was more specific:

> A key to keeping America competitive is low taxes and the elimination of needless regulations that restrict investment and discourage risk-taking. I am chairman of the President's Task Force on Regulatory Relief. By ordering a re-examination of more than 150 regulatory programs, the Task Force has saved the private sector over 300 million man hours of paperwork and literally billions of dollars in government compliance costs ...
>
> We should not try to balance the budget by raising taxes. We should balance the budget by cutting unnecessary spending.

Of course we would all like some specifics on just where these spending cuts are to be made. He went on:

We are going to fight a tax increase every step of the way ...

Lincoln once said: "To (allow) each laborer (to keep) the whole product of his labor, or as nearly as possible, is a most worthy object of any good government."

Allowing working people to keep the product of their labor is not what some politicians have in mind. Our opponents would rather raise your taxes than reduce spending. They would rather take money out of your budget than cut the federal budget.

In Alleman, Iowa, in April 1987, Mr. Bush told his audience that the number one challenge facing the nation is to keep the economic expansion going. He admitted that in his adopted state of Texas, the unemployment rate in some areas was 14 percent. His priority would be to lower taxes (i.e., prevent raises) and lower regulation. He admitted a need to get federal spending under control but ruled out tax increases to balance the budget. "We need to cut the federal budget and leave the family budget alone."

Enlightened Capitalism

In his commencement address before the graduating class at Albion College in Michigan in May 1987, Mr. Bush defended Republican philosophy against the Democrats' charge of selfishness, greed and corruption:

Those of us in leadership positions in government, and in all walks of life, must make something very clear: Greed is not a legitimate force in this society.

Our nation believes in enlightened capitalism. We believe in bettering ourselves and pulling ourselves up. And we believe in free enterprise, not just because of the economic opportunities it provides, but because history shows that economic freedom is a condition for political freedom.

But just because we support free enterprise doesn't mean we can't be critical of its excesses. And as for those who go over the line into criminality, I say throw the book at them. I say treat white collar criminals as you would treat any other criminal. Lock 'em up. They have broken the law and they belong in jail.

Social Security

Not surprisingly, when Mr. Bush was asked "Will you keep Social Security benefits and the annual cost-of-living increases exempt from budget cuts?" and "Do you favor any means test for Social Security benefits?'' by the Associated Press, he replied with the standard administration line. The Associated Press reported on June 14, 1987 that ''The vice president said through an aide that he supports the Reagan administration's policy of keeping Social Security exempt from budget cuts and (being) in opposition to a means test. Bush, according to spokeswoman Gail Fisher, believes 'there is no reason to change Social Security for budgetary reasons. Anybody who contributes to the system should be entitled to their fair share of benefits.' ''

A superb example of hedging one's bets and a shameful display of intellectual dishonesty. There are plenty of reasons for changing Social Security but George Bush has only said budgetary demands is not a legitimate reason, in his opinion. That a person who contributes should be entitled to a ''fair share'' of benefits is hardly the issue. He failed to address the subsidies which amount to almost 80 percent in some cases. Can fewer and fewer workers be expected to SUBSIDIZE more and more retirees in the future? The system never has paid for itself and it is time that candidates other than Pete du Pont face the facts squarely.[5]

Contradictions

Congressman Richard Baker of Louisiana spoke on behalf of George Bush before the Southern Legislative Conference in Little Rock, Arkansas, in August 1987. He told the Conference that George Bush shared Ronald Reagan's long-cherished concept of federalism and that, if elected to the presidency, George Bush would no doubt allocate much of the responsibility for the welfare of citizens back to the states.

It will be interesting to see how Mr. Bush is able to reconcile the extra paperwork that will be involved in adhering to Ronald Reagan's proposed executive order requiring federal agencies to assess the impact of federal initiatives on families, with his role as chairman of the Task Force on Regulatory Relief. That Mr. Reagan might be at odds with his own programs and philosophy would not disturb anyone. The nation is used to that by now. However, reconciliation may pose a problem for candidate Bush.

Side-stepping issues and ignoring contradictions will not

gain favor with voters. The rare combination of courage and caution, instead of complementing, may end up negating one another to the detriment of George Bush. Perhaps character should be our first objective in choosing a president, but it becomes even more important when there is no visible disagreement among the candidates on the issues. The Democratic candidates are almost clones, but as a group they offer a clear cut choice between their party and the Republicans. The Republican candidates, however, offer differences among themselves and it will not be enough for George Bush to remain silent as to how he would proceed to end the nation's problems in the face of their specifics.

Finally, perhaps, Americans should consider if they are willing to pass the reins to another "economist"[6] (I use the term loosely) in view of the nation's soaring debt which, despite rhetoric and good intentions to the contrary, nevertheless took place under Ronald Reagan's watch. After all, for the truly committed there has always been the veto.

Robert Dole

In Bob Dole's own words, "There is nothing very complicated about Bob Dole."[7] He was born in Russell, Kansas, on July 22, 1923, one of four children to Doran and Bina Dole. Like many other candidates, Mr. Dole also has a claim to poverty. "My mother and father both worked for a living. My mother sold sewing machines and gave sewing lessons. My father ran a cream and egg station, and later a grain elevator."[8] Senator Dole likes to tell the story of the bicycle that took a whole year's work at Dawson's drug store and then had to be shared with two siblings. Bob Dole became an athlete, in part to qualify for a football and track scholarship, and the record he set in 1941 at the University of Kansas in the 440-yard dash held for thirty years. In 1943 he left his premedical studies at the University of Kansas to enlist in the army as a second lieutenant. He was trained by the 10th Mountain Corps in both California and Tennessee and was shipped to Italy in 1945, where in April of that year, while acting as a platoon leader in combat, he received devastating wounds. His entire right side was severely damaged and it was thought that he would never walk again. Robert Dole struggled in hospitals for thirty-nine months. When questioned about his war injuries he said:

> . . . it (the struggle) has made me a very strong person. And a very sensitive person when it comes to the handicapped and other vulnerable groups in America who haven't had it their way all the time.
>
> There is something about a recovery or a rehabilitation that I think makes you stronger. You get frustrated, you get mad sometimes, then you learn how to have a little patience. And you learn that other people have real problems. Yours may not be very much but other people have real problems.[9]

Robert Dole was discharged from the service with numerous medals and the rank of Captain in 1948. The GI Bill enabled him to complete his college education—first at the University of Arizona in Tucson and then at the Washburn Municipal University in Topeka, Kansas, where in 1952 he received his law degree. While still in law school he became a member of the state House of Representatives (1951-53) and went on to become Russell County's prosecuting attorney (1953-60). He likes to talk about his first congressional race, whose success he attributes to serving Dole pineapple juice in the first district in order to distinguish himself from his opponent Mr. Doyle. He was first elected to the United States House of Representatives in 1960 and served there until his election to the Senate in 1968. We witnessed his first defeat when he shared the ticket as Gerald Ford's running mate in the 1976 presidential election.

Medicare

The Senate's catastrophic health insurance legislation (S1127) was introduced on May 5, 1987, by Senator Lloyd Bentsen of Texas and supported by minority leader Senator Robert Dole. The key feature is an expansion of Medicare to cover unlimited hospital care expenses. The bill would cap a beneficiary's out-of-pocket expenses at $1,700, with that figure to be indexed to the CPI. The premium for Medicare Part B would increase by $4 per month plus a "supplemental premium" would be required, determined by the income of certain beneficiaries. The 1988 supplemental premium would be modest enough—only $12 per year for each $150 of tax liability beyond the first $150. For instance, if a beneficiary paid $750 in taxes, his supplemental premium would only amount to an additional $48 for the year. So who's going to object? That's what they're counting on and watch it RISE! (Social Security contributions were a maximum of $30 per year in 1949.) But we're talking as if the amount were the issue and it shouldn't be—the principle must be addressed.

This scheme may be a sound solution in a socialist country where those who work hard, are creative, sacrifice early gratifications, invest, are prudent and even sometimes lucky, are forced (not solicited for donations to charitable institutions to which the majority of highly "successful" people subscribe already), but are forced to pay more taxes to run the government—more taxes, dollar for dollar, than their neighbors. Then because they paid more in one instance, they are forced to pay more than their neighbors for mandated (no choice) health insurance. Why not? In a socialist society it makes sense—come on—you can recite it—Marx, Engels, Trotsky, Lenin and Co. would applaud. What wouldn't Madison Avenue give for such a slogan! "From each according to his ability to each according to his need." Is this what you want? Do you like this idea? Then for crying out loud be principled enough to come out and say so without all this hypocrisy. Too many Americans have been fooling themselves in the belief that "the slogan" is compatible with a free society based on capitalism. The two notions are incompatible.

The Reagan administration prefers a plan which could offer vouchers so that the beneficiaries could purchase catastrophic coverage from private insurers. As in all other areas the private sector will offer more and better options more economically.

Secretary of Health & Human Services Dr. Otis Bowen has advocated "steps to encourage personal savings for long-term care expenses and to stimulate the creation of private long-term care insurance policies."[10] Again I am appalled by our elected legislators: "... asking people to self-insure against the chance of needing long-term care thirty years down the road strikes me as absurd." (Senator John Heinz of Pennsylvania.)[11] He's right it's absurd, because the government has led its citizens into dependence and discouraged the self-reliant and prudent by taxing them above their more short-sighted fellows. Actually the President's plan, which did not translate to Capitol Hill, would have the Treasury Department study the feasibility of replacing Medicare altogether with private insurance. What an uproar that would have caused!

In his reply to the Associated Press questions regarding Social Security, Senator Dole said:

> Social Security is not a welfare program, and I do not support means testing of benefits. I do, however, support the provision adopted in the 1983 Social Security package to make a portion of the benefits taxable for high-income people.[12]

What kind of gobbledygook is this? Taxing benefits of high-incme people *is* a means test. Are we, the American public, supposed to hear but not listen—listen but not understand?

Bob Dole told William Schneider

> . . . that the "most exciting vote" he ever cast in the Senate was that 1985 vote to freeze cost-of-living adjustments for Social Security recipients. "In the U.S. Senate that morning," he told *The Washington Post*, "we demonstrated to the American people there was a majority willing to take on everyone in America for the sake of America, to put on the brakes and tell the American people that someone was willing to vote no . . . The deficit is not going to grow away or go away. We are going to have to address it head-on, without taxes, and we are going to have to do it the hard way."[13]

The package Bob Dole proposed on May 10, 1985, would have reduced the deficit by $135 billion over a three-year period without raising taxes.

The *Washington Post* on June 13, 1987, quoted Bob Dole:

> On May 10, 1985, in a Republican-controlled Senate at two o'clock in the morning, by a 50 to 49 vote, the Republican majority with the help of only one Democrat terminated fourteen federal programs, froze every cost-of-living adjustment in the books. We didn't cut any benefits . . . for once the Republicans in the Senate demonstrated to the American people, all those cynics out there, who are justifiably cynical about the Congress, that we were capable of making a difficult choice. It didn't last long, because the White House pulled the plug. But we made the tough choices. And I think it can be done.

A lot of citizens may feel as I do, that if I end up voting for Bob Dole for President it will be because he views the deficit as priority number one and has proven that he is tough enough to do something about it—a claim that can be made by no other candidate.

A Dichotomy

But there is, perhaps, an inevitable dichotomy here. Bob Dole the budget-cutter resides within Bob Dole the man of compassion.

> We've got to make some tough decisions. We're going to have to cut some spending in America. And it's not going to be easy ... And what I'm saying is this: If you don't want to make the hard choices, then I'm probably not the candidate.[14]

And then regarding AIDS:

> Whether it takes a hundred million dollars or a billion or two billion, we need to address it.[15]

On the one hand Robert Dole supports a Constitutional amendment to permit voluntary prayer in public schools, opposes federal funding of abortion (unless the mother's life is at risk) and has called for a Constitutional amendment to overturn Roe v. Wade. He opposes the use of quotas as reverse discrimination, backs right-to-work legislation, opposes tax increases and worked to confirm the nomination of Daniel Manion as a federal judge.

On the other hand he shepherded the renewal of the Voting Rights Act, backed the Martin Luther King, Jr. holiday, promoted the idea of a color-blind society and voted to support sanctions against South Africa. He is considered "accessible" by organized labor, fought against cuts in Medicare and Medicaid, joined with George McGovern to promote the food-stamp program and other anti-hunger programs and played a major role in getting a tax increase passed in 1982. Probably the latter has made him most unpopular with the conservative wing of the Republican party, who remember that the $98.3 billion tax hike of 1982 was followed by a $50 billion increase in 1984, which makes it hard for the Senator to be taken seriously when he claims he is against raising taxes. In 1985 he told the *New York Times*, "I'm perceived as a moderate Republican for all the work I've done on tax reform, voting rights, food stamps, all the stuff for veterans and the handicapped." In fact, Bob Dole thinks of himself as not ambiguous but rather as a "broad-based candidate"—naturally one that will appeal to the most voters.

He told William Schneider, "There is a role for government. There are vulnerable groups in this society for whom we have obligations as a government."[16] He echoed those feelings when he told his audience at the Southern Legislative Conference in Little Rock, Arkansas, in August 1987 that "I happen to believe the American people want a hands-on president." A president with power, which is one reason Bob Dole supports the notion of giving the line-item veto to the President. In fact he first proposed the line-item veto for the executive back in 1976 and has seen the argument for the proposal gain strength with every passing year and with the nation's ever-increasing debt.

Agriculture

Senator Dole was one of the chief architects of the 1985 Farm Bill and even though the price tag has exceeded $25 billion a year, he is against any radical overhaul of the program. Coming from Kansas may have something to do with his support for subsidies for ethanol production and the fact that one of the largest recipients of ethanol subsidies is in his district.[17] The Senator has worked to depress the effective price floor for U.S. crops in the hopes of boosting exports while at the same time he has fought to maintain the target prices for farmers. In fact, target prices were frozen at 1985 levels for the first two years of the bill. The idea is to protect farm income while lowering loan rates in order to make our farm products competitive on the world market. Mr. Dole somehow fails to recognize, as does Mr. du Pont, just how outrageous our agricultural policy has become over the past few years.

In just two years the honey support program cost taxpayers over $100 million with benefits going to 3,000 beekeepers, at most. You're right—an average of over $33,000 to each beekeeper. According to Peter Grace, "one producer in North Dakota collected a million and a half dollars from the program in just one year,"[18] which would, of course, cut into someone else's $33,000. Mr. Grace goes on to tell us that:

> In 1984 the federal government purchased 72 percent (119 million pounds) of all the domestically-produced honey at 66 cents a pound—fully a third more than the wholesale value of honey sold commercially in the U.S. that year.

Just the cost of administering the program (e.g., freight and storage costs) totaled $23.7 million in 1984—equal to the combined taxes paid by 10,172 median-income families in that year."[19]

The target prices Mr. Dole supports have been running 60 percent above the market price for honey (by government contract with the beekeepers) and since beekeepers are unable to sell at this inflated target price, guess what happens to the honey? You're right again—just as in other commodity support programs Uncle Sam buys the honey by forgiving the loans made earlier to the beekeepers. The government owned 5 million pounds of honey in 1980. You'll never guess how much your tax dollars purchased in this outrageous manner in just four years but I want you to try. To see if you are correct, turn to the footnotes to read the actual amount of honey in government warehouses in 1984.[20]

Mr. Dole is against the Reagan administration's proposal to impose a $50,000-per-farmer annual limit on farm subsidies although he "favors creation of a federal Rural Fund for Development, under which the Commodity Credit Corporation would back at least $1 billion in loan guarantees to encourage private investment in small rural businesses."[21] (Refer to the discussion on pp. 85-88.) David Rapp had an interesting article in the April 4, 1987, issue of *Congressional Quarterly*, "Farmer & Uncle Sam: An Old, Odd Couple" which had the following revealing quote: "... the notion that governments have a legitimate right to intervene is rarely challenged by society as a whole." Many a farmer in this country is most certainly wishing that he had challenged the government's right years ago.

Trade

Senator Dole supports the Reagan administration's proposal to stimulate competitiveness, S539, which he introduced to the Senate on February 19, 1987. He believes relaxing anti-trust, limiting product liability and further deregulation in certain areas would result in America's greater competitive ability.

On the other hand the Senator opposes Congressman Gephardt's amendment to the House trade bill (HR3). In that regard he told the *Washington Post* (June 13, 1987) that

> If some other country is making something that is competitive, they ought to be able to get it into this country . . . If we're not competitive, we shouldn't blame someone else.
>
> But if we are competitive, then we ought to have the right to get into those markets.

Senator Dole favors a four-point program for promoting competitiveness: (1) strong action against nations that erect market barriers to our products; (2) stronger statutes to ensure relief to industries injured by unfair trade practices; (3) addressing the broader economic issues that contribute to trade imbalances; and (4) improvements in research, education, labor-management cooperation and regulatory reform.

Robert Dole supports the Bentsen-Danforth trade bill, S490, which enlarges assistance to "displaced" American workers and toughens retaliatory measures to be taken against nations who engage in unfair trading practices. Under S490 the presdient would be required to take action if such action was recommended by the International Trade Commission. $4,000 per worker would be provided for retraining, and the retraining opportunities and other benefits would be extended to include not only those directly harmed by imports but those indirectly injured as well. Special weekly allowances for displaced workers would be extended from 54 to 78 weeks. These so-called entitlementss would be paid with the fees (.1 percent to 1 percent) to be levied on duty-free items. S490 would require the U.S. Trade Representative to investigate allegations that other countries are violating their trade agreements with the United States. One can hardly tell the Republican trade proposals from those of Democratic cpponents on the campaign trail.

Taxes

A choice is more readily apparent when it comes to taxes. The Democrats as a whole believe the tax code would be fairer if tax rates were raised on the most wealthy citizens. Senator Dole, however, has introduced into the 100th Congress a resolution to preserve the lower income tax rates the 1986 tax reform mandated for all citizens. He has come out as "staunchly opposed" to reducing the deficit by raising individual tax rates. He is against excise taxes because they are regressive and additionally take away state revenue. He would support an oil import fee, although more as a conservation measure than a "revenue enhancement." He is definitely alarmed by the fact that 41 to 42 percent of our oil is now imported. He has been saying over and over that this nation must explore alternative energy sources. With oil at $21-$22 a barrel there may not be a need for subsidies, but nevertheless Senator Dole has led efforts to ensure necessary incentives to stimulate domestic oil and gas production.

UDAGs

In the name of fiscal responsibility Senator Bob Dole has gone on the record as referring to UDAGs (Urban Development Action Grants) as corporate welfare—subsidies which line the pockets of contractors at taxpayers' expense. Senator Dole opposed S825 which the Senate passed on March 31, 1987, and which authorizes $31.2 billion for housing and community development, calling it a "budget buster." There had been a provision to kill the UDAG program within S825 but it was removed by amendment, which did not improve the bill for Mr. Dole.

Education

The Senator has long been a supporter of tuition vouchers which he sees as a way to increase competition and expand the educational option of students. Senator Dole is the sponsor of the "Education Competitiveness and Improvement Act of 1987," which targets federal aid to the children who most need it and gives priority to funding programs of proven effectiveness. It would stimulate partnerships between public schools and the private sector in the hopes of devising programs that will result in a more competitive American labor force. Senator Dole has proposed several bills that would encourage private savings for higher education. One would function in the manner of an IRA, providing tax credits for contributions to education savings accounts and allowing any interest to accumulate in the account tax-free. Up to $1,000 could be deposited each year in the education account and a 15 percent tax credit would be applied to the contributor's tax return. Contributions could be made until a child reached age twenty-one or enrolled at a qualified college or post-high school training program, whichever came first. This would not be a subsidy because Mr. Dole intends to have the tax-credit paid back over a ten-year period once the child reaches age twenty-five (surely no longer a child) as one-tenth of the credit would be added each year to the subject's income between ages 25-35. (That's specific!)

The Senator's other bills are similar but would either not allow tax credits for the contributions, only tax-deferral, or if credit is allowed the earnings (interest) would be subject to tax currently. The final proposal is a variation of Mr. Bush's proposal using savings bonds for education.

Robert Who?

Almost all potential voters are familiar with George Bush, whereas few outside the beltway could identify Robert Dole before September 15, 1987, except, as he likes to joke, as Elizabeth Dole's husband.[22] And that, even though Robert Dole ran for national office in 1976. How soon we forget!

Pete du Pont

Pete du Pont declared his candidacy for the 1988 Republican presidential nomination way back on September 16, 1986. He knew getting the nomination would be a long-haul and a long-shot. For starters he had two blaring handicaps to overcome—wealth and a name like Pierre Samuel du Pont IV. Such handicaps, at least singly, have been overlooked in the Democratic party as witnessed by the popularity of such recent aristocrats as FDR and the Kennedys. However, if you will recall, Rockefeller couldn't make it to the "big-time" on the Republican ticket; not with the party trying constantly to deny its image as the party of the rich. In this game of "humble heritage" Pierre Samuel du Pont IV is a clear loser. Even going back to 1799 we find his immigrant ancestors were anything but poor—at least in France.

Pierre du Pont (it would help if *everyone* would remember to call him just plain 'ol Pete)—Pete du Pont was born in Wilmington, Delaware, on January 22, 1935. Like his rival blue-blood turned wildcatter, George Bush, Pete du Pont attended Phillips Academy, only at Exeter. He went on to Princeton where he got his B.S.E. in engineering in 1956. In 1957 he married Elise Wood and joined the navy (1957-

1960)—no reflection on the marriage which has prospered over thirty years and produced three sons and a daughter. In 1960 Pete du Pont entered Harvard Law School, graduated with an J.D. in 1963 and went to work for the family firm. He eventually became a partner in the Wilmington law firm of Richards, Layton and Finger.

Mr. du Pont was elected to the Delaware General Assembly in 1968 (1968-70), the U.S. House of Representatives in 1971 (1971-76) and was Governor of Delaware for two terms (1977-85).

And to what particular talent do we credit Mr. du Pont's candidacy? One might well ask that question of Mr. Dukakis, because if bringing a state out of the depths of despair and into prosperity is any qualification, then Mr. du Pont yields to no one in his ability to do just that.

In 1977 when Pete du Pont took over as Governor of Delaware, that state had the worst economic performance of any state in the union. Between 1972-77 taxes had been raised twenty-two separate times and the budget was in deficit, despite the raises, in four out of five of those years. Unemployment was well above the national average because businesses were pulling out to escape the high taxes. The state had the lowest bond rating of any state in the nation. If you didn't get the message with all my earlier chatter about "long-hauls" and "long-shots"—the message that Pete du Pont likes a challenge—maybe the preceding description of the *state* of the state of Delaware when Pete du Pont took over will make it clear. Here's how Pete du Pont tackled that challenge:

First he eliminated all short-term borrowing and reduced state spending. He BALANCED THE BUDGET EIGHT YEARS IN A ROW!! (Who did you say you were going to vote for in 1988?) He was instrumental in amending the state constitution to limit spending and tax increases in the future and he signed into law two income tax reduction measures. A 30 percent decrease in income taxes meant a 20 percent increase in job opportunities. Lower taxes meant a return of some old employers and served to attract new industries. Cutting back on bureaucratic red tape and unneeded regulations didn't hurt either. Delaware continued to grow even during the early eighties when most of the nation was in recession. A new law enabling out-of-state banks to set up Delaware subsidiaries created 9,000 new jobs alone, as banks from New York, Pennsylvania, Maryland and even Texas rushed to open subsidiaries in Delaware. Delaware is now the nation's credit card headquarters. Pete du Pont didn't just talk "free market," he *created* a free market in Delaware.

In the du Pont v. Babbitt debate held at Drake University in May 1987, the differences between Mr. Dukakis' accomplishments and Pete du Pont's became clear. Mike Dukakis used $10 million to take 4.5 percent of welfare recipients off Massachusetts' rolls, whereas Pete du Pont removed 25 percent from Delaware's rolls by cutting taxes, deregulating business and empowering families to take advantage of opportunities. Okay—cutting taxes and empowering took place in Massachusetts also, only not to as great a degree and the de-regulation was more like *re*-regulation. Mr. du Pont prefers fewer mandates and because parental leaves are mandated he is against the parental leave bill before Congress, naïvely believing agreements should be freely entered into by both parties in a country where free enterprise is practiced.

Welfare

At the Drake University debate Pete du Pont said, "Welfare isn't a sign of caring, it's a prison for recipients. It takes from them a chance to care for themselves and their children. There are 800 million more (people) in poverty today than (there were) ten years ago." He would like to end the inefficient AFDC program and put all recipients of welfare to work, even at make-work jobs at sub-minimum wages. His reasons were explained in campaign literature:

> In the past ten years, our welfare system has given people over $300 billion without requiring them to work. Yet today, more of our citizens live in poverty than ten years ago. We should have learned by now that government spending doesn't cure poverty. Only opportunity can do that. Instead of a handout, we need to provide poor people with a job and everything that comes with it—a paycheck, a boss, responsibility for mistakes, rewards for initiative, and a chance to move up to a better job.
>
> Our first effort should be to help able-bodied people find jobs. If a person still can't find work after exhausting the counseling and retraining programs, he or she would have to go work for the government at 90 percent of minimum wage with day-care being part of the package.

Our policy in this country must be: "If you don't work—you don't get paid.

Jobs

At an appearance before the National Press Club on September 9, 1987, Mr. du Pont was asked to discuss his proposed job retraining program. He may have sounded a bit harsh to some when he said that in order to provide opportunities for the unskilled you have to just come out and say that starting six months from today there will be no more welfare checks. Approximately 20 percent will find work. To the remainder we say, "We'll put you to work, maintaining parks, sitting with the elderly, working in day-care situations and so forth."

When asked about his feeling for labor unions Pete du Pont answered that labor unions are important—they are the way people increase their opportunities. Apparently there wasn't time to get into the problems that his "workfare" scheme would run into with AFSCME (American Federation of State, County & Municipal Employees), one of the nation's largest unions.

Damn Right

Pete du Pont reportedly carries a three-by-five card in his breast pocket containing five "damn right" issues. To these issues listeners reportedly say, "You're damn right!" These issues are: (1) work for welfare, which we've discussed; (2) a private alternative to Social Security and a Medicare voucher; (3) a proposal to abolish farm subsidies over five years; (4) vouchers for education; and, (5) a proposal to tie driver's licenses to testing "drug-free" in schools.

Deficit

As a true supply-sider, Mr. du Pont believes government deficits will evaporate as primary attention is focused on expanding the economy and tackling the "damn right" issues. You've heard that growth alone will end the deficit from Jack Kemp, Phil Gramm and others. Pete du Pont was converted to the supply-side ranks by the miracle that was wrought in Delaware following supply-side prescriptions. As they say, "Seeing is believing."

He told a National Press Club gathering that the deficit is important but that keeping inflation down is more important, as is a high level of employment, a growing economy, job opportunities, low taxes, spending less and giving the president the line-item veto. He told the audience that Europe and Japan should be made to pay more for their own defense since $150 billion of our defense budget is earmarked for that purpose.

Pete du Pont really means it when he says, "The spending side of the equation is not as important as empowering people." On other occasions he has expressed genuine concern over the deficit.

> There are four things you can do about the deficit. We're doing the third worst one—that's ignore it. The worst thing is to inflate the economy, because that's a tax on everybody. The second worst thing you can do is increase taxes.

Social Security

Pete du Pont is one of the few leaders in America to tackle the problems inherent in the Social Security system head on. In a pay-as-you-go system, everything works nicely when there are more people paying than there are taking. That has been the case in the past, but ten or fifteen years into the next century and the tables will be reversed. (Remember the baby boomers!) In Mr. du Pont's own words:

> We need a Financial Security Program to run parallel to the Social Security System. It would maintain the Social Security program in exactly its present form and make it solvent. American working men and women would be given the option of using a variation on the individual retirement account (IRA) concept to provide some of the coverage they now get from Social Security. These new accounts would be called FSAs, or Financial Security Accounts.
>
> This program protects the Social Security benefit of today's recipients, tomorrow's recipients and any taxpayer who has a call on the Social Security system for generations tocome. It avoids the tax increases on the children of the baby boom, which this generation of leadership cannot conscionably impose on the school children of today. This idea increases benefits, it increases Americans' control over their savings, it geometrically increases the size of Americans' personal savings and it stimulates growth.

What bothers me about Mr. du Pont's plan is that workers who opt for the FSAs are still required to pay the payroll taxes as before. He thinks giving a tax credit (not for the entire amount paid in payroll taxes) and reducing future Social Security benefits proportionately will even things out. Who can afford to continue having automatic deductions taken from a paycheck and still find enough to put aside in a FSA? Only those who are supplementing or discounting their future Social Security benefits already. Such an idea takes discipline as well as money. The more affluent would benefit from the tax credit but those who pay little or no taxes are also the ones that will need more when they retire and are unable to invest in anything that promises a decent return now. Social Security offers a minus return on the investment of middle and high income earners and a top 2 percent return on the investment (contributions) of the lowest earners. The du Pont idea is better than doing nothing, I'll grant you. It will lessen Social Security's future liabilities, give some people better retirement benefits than they would have otherwise and the IRA-concept will create new capital for the growth of the country. (For a plan that goes all the way, rather than half-way and is fairer, see *Social Security: An Idea Whose Time Has Passed*.) Of course the main objection is the cost of letting people opt out of the system. Mr. du Pont estimates his plan would cost the federal government about $20 billion a year at the beginning, and that depends on just how many people would take advantage of FSAs. But remember the savings that will occur in the future when the real problems will otherwise arise. For each year a taxpayer chooses to opt out of Social Security, his ultimate benefits will be reduced by one-fortieth.

I couldn't forget to include Pete du Pont's answers to the Associated Press questions. Here they are as printed on June 14, 1987:

> The first step in my financial security program would be to pass legislation that puts the full faith and credit of the U.S government behind Social Security benefits for all Americans that have a claim on the system, much like the security provided for with government bonds. Further, my plan ensures benefits for this generation's retirees while allowing younger workers to set up IRA-type accounts and build their own nest egg . . . I oppose any means test. We should be treating people more alike . . . not finding ways to further segment the population.

Agriculture

Just as he tackled the Social Security system straight on, Pete du Pont is not skirting the farm problem. He says,

> Farm-crop subsidies clobber all Americans who share two common traits—the payment of taxes and the consumption of food. Altogether we are paying for this more than $30 billion a year in taxes and higher food costs; enough to feed everyone in Iowa, Nebraska, Kansas and Missouri, with enough left over for Connecticut and Delaware. We simply cannot continue to pursue anticompetitive and counterproductive agricultural policies that raise consumer costs without helping farmers ...
>
> Farmers should be free to make their own decisions as to what crops to grow, where and when to grow them, and what markets to sell them in, without having to worry about how the bureaucrats in Washington will react.[23]

He would phase out farm subsidies over a five-year period—gradually reducing payments 20 percent a year. For instance, if a farmer receives a $20,000 subsidy one year, it would drop to $16,000 the next, then $12,000, $8,000, $4,000 to zero.

> These transition payments are not income-support payments designed to guarantee some minimum standard of living. They are not welfare for farmers. They are an implicit admission that an intrusive federal government has helped to create the current mess and, therefore, has an obligation to help clean it up.[24]

Some farmers like Mr. du Pont's message. The president of the American Farm Bureau Federation, Dean Kleckner, supports him. He, and many other farmers, want to be able to depend on the market, not the government.

On September 9, 1987, Pete du Pont told the National Press Club that farm subsidies, instead of helping farmers, are actually holding them back. "Fourteen thousand Iowa farmers have gone under—who needs it?" he said. He wants to phase out export subsidies and instead open foreign markets to U.S. agriculture. If president, he vows he wouldn't sign a GATT agreement without first winning major concessions in this area.

If a name will help sell an idea, then Pete du Pont is on the right track calling his proposal for Social Security reform the Financial Security Account and his farm program the

Farm Opportunity Plan. Part of the plan is to give the states access to the equity in the commodity stockpiles over five years so that they can use that equity to fund new development and attract new industries to rural areas. So as not to topple prices the stockpiles would be sold off gradually. Again, in Mr. du Pont's own words:

> During the past five years, spending on price support programs has increased more rapidly than any other budget item—even defense—from $4 billion in 1981 to more than $25 billion this year. And the farmers aren't any better off—in fact, they're worse off.
>
> No wonder. Our own government policies and foreign subsidies have made it impossible for our farmers to prosper. Our programs are contradictory; we pay farmers to grow more, to grow nothing, to store their crops rather than sell them. Government support programs are a trap for the farmer and a fleecing of the taxpayer.
>
> I believe the government should be out of the agricultural marketplace in five years. We should stop playing politics with price-fixing schemes, and start making payments directly to farmers during this transition period. Our farmers are the most productive in the world, and it's high time we gave the American farmers the chance to be their own masters once again.

Education

Most politicians stop after telling you everything that's wrong with a system and that there is a need to change it—as if you were some kind of idiot and couldn't see that for yourself! Mr. du Pont tells you what and how to do something *about* the problems. From his campaign headquarters comes "Pete du Pont on Education":

> I would begin by providing current education assistance to the needy in the form of vouchers.
>
> If America is to be competitive, education and training must continue throughout our lives. We need to help those who must prepare for second and third careers—for new work in new industries.
>
> We need a national schooling and training bank. It would have simple rules. Everybody in our country would have the opportunity to receive schooling, training or retraining. Eighteen-year-olds could go to any college or to any vocational school where they are accepted. So could forty-year-olds. You could borrow as much money as you need, and the government would guarantee the loan. But you'd have to borrow it at market rates and pay it back yourself. The opportunity is there, but it's your responsibility because it's your future.

"People should be empowered to invest in themselves"[25] is the central theme in all Mr. du Pont's speeches and articles. He told C-SPAN in April 1987:

> I think we have to change our education system. After all, it's a system that was designed in the 1880s, after the Civil War, when things were very different in America. I think the problem with education is, it's a monopoly. The government tells you where you're going to go to school; who's going to teach you; what he's going to be paid; what courses you're going to take; what books you're going to read; what you're going to learn. I think we have to bring competition into education, and the best way to do that is to let you, the parents, choose which public school your child's going to go to. Think of the competition that will place in front of the school system. They've got to compete for your business. That would make American education strive for excellence instead of just worrying about a uniform program for everybody.[26]

All seven candidates for the Democratic presidential nomination and only two Republican candidates showed up for the debate on education which was held on September 11, 1987, at the University of North Carolina at Chapel Hill. I mentioned earlier that Jack Kemp was one of the two Republicans, and Pete du Pont was the other. When asked if the federal government should take more responsibility for the quality of education in America, Pete du Pont responded that the Constitution puts certain responsibilities on the federal government and others on the states. Responsibility for defending our nation, for maintaining a sound currency and for creating a climate of economic opportunity belongs to the president. Education is the responsibility of the governors. Mr. du Pont mentioned that as Governor of Delaware he saw to it that classes were started for disruptive children and volunteer classes were held for the basics—programs which improved the quality of Delaware's education without costing Delaware taxpayers a lot of money.

Mr. du Pont told the North Carolina audience that he supported merit pay in teaching. Under a competitive system the school where the most people wanted to go would become the most valuable and teachers there would be paid the most. In order for parents to make informed decisions when choosing schools teachers would face testing and evaluations periodically. (You know who *isn't* going to vote for Pete du Pont!)

Edward Fiske of the *New York Times* asked the candidates if they thought the country would have to make a "multi-billion dollar federal commitment to education." That is the question to which Mr. Kemp gave a flat "yes" answer. Mr. du Pont talked about a group of corporate leaders who in 1966 favored a voucher system and now, more than twenty years later, were saying feed the system more money. What we need, according to Mr. du Pont, is not more dollars but more choice. In his opinion the federal government does *not* need to spend more, though he conceded individual states might *want* to spend more and implied that that should be left up to citizens and their governors. When asked about the $12 billion in cuts which allegedly occurred since Ronald Reagan took office, Mr. du Pont admitted the cuts were too large. He told the audience that in the past the federal government has assumed as much as 9 percent of the nation's bill for education and that has been cut to 7 percent under the Reagan administration. He felt that college loans shouldn't have been cut. He garnered a round of applause when he asked interviewer Judy Woodruff of Public Television, "Why do you want to measure America's commitment to education only in dollars? Whatever happened to quality, whatever happened to choice, whatever happened to empowering people?"

Mr. Fiske wondered why vouchers have never been tried and thought that meant they were unworkable. Mr. du Pont was quick to point out that vouchers have been working for one hundred years in Vermont, where students are given their choice of public, parochial or private schools. Mr. Fiske countered that Vermont was a special case because it is a rural state. Mr. du Pont was undaunted and went on in favor of the voucher system: "I'm for empowering people to make their own choices and I think vouchers would help, particularly poor families, to do that." He told Mr. Fiske that 46 percent of Chicago's teachers send their children to private schools. Fears were expressed that if given complete freedom of choice everyone would flock to one particular school. Mr. du Pont offered in rebuttal the experience of Cambridge, Massachusetts, which offers complete choice and has not experienced that problem.

Mr. Fiske suggested there is evidence that early education will pay for itself, to which Mr. du Pont volunteered,

"A commitment at early ages is more valuable than later." He again brought up the Chicago school system where for the seventh time in nine years Chicago teachers were on strike, leaving 500,000 students in the "Windy City" without schooling.

Pete du Pont said the following in his closing remarks:

> America is a land of opportunity ... the role of the federal government ... is to give people the power to do the best things they can in their lives ... The President of the United States ought to be giving people all the power that he possibly can to make decisions in their own lives. That's the American tradition. We believe in people. We understand the faith in the individual. We understand that America is a diverse land, that everyone's priorities are a little bit different, that government's primary role is to empower the people to help themselves.

Drugs

There are those that say Pete du Pont's most controversial stand concerns drugs in America's classrooms. Here is what he has to say about that:

> The one place kids should be safe from drugs is in the classroom.
>
> The only way we'll ever guarantee drug-free classrooms is comprehensive drug testing of teenagers in our schools. If we can require vaccinations before kids go to school, we can require drug testing while they're in school.
>
> Of course, we must provide counseling and help for young people who need it. But we have to let them know there are penalties—and consequences—for drug use. We have to say, "If you use drugs you won't drive ... because you won't have a driver's license."
>
> For a long time we've gone after drug pushers. Now it's time to get tough with drug users, too.

As a mother of five sons, I find it hard to understand how such a sensible solution to drugs in the schools can be considered by anybody to be Mr. du Pont's most controversial stand. Ask any parent how he or she feels.

AIDS

If it's controversy you seek then the National Press Club is as good a place as any to look. There in September 1987, Pete du Pont was asked about AIDS.—an issue Mr. du Pont has managed to use to alienate even people with opposite points of view by maintaining it is not a civil rights issue but rather a serious medical problem. "Traditionally, when it came to diseases like tuberculosis and polio, we found out who had the disease in an attempt to prevent its spread." (That alienates those who oppose testing.) Early in 1987 he was booed at a religious convention when he said he believed AIDS was a medical rather than a moral problem and you can understand that alienation quite easily. In an attempt to please, at least the former group, he has sometimes added, "Of course we have to put up the money to find a cure and/or antidote."

Abortion

He manages to alienate, or at least not to please, both groups when it comes to abortion also. He favors reversal of Roe v. Wade but feels that then the issue should be left to the individual states. In other words he doesn't support the New Right in their call for a constitutional ban on abortion. The reason? It's simply not a constitutional question. Practical, straightforward and to the heart of the matter—that's Pete du Pont!

South Africa

He pleased the left and offended the right by supporting sanctions against South Africa. In his mind it is the duty of the United States to "signal the world that we don't accept white racist dictatorships any more than left-wing dictatorships."[27]

Give Him A Chance

Here's the bottom line. Mr. Bush needs 70 percent to be declared the winner in Iowa, where Pete du Pont only needs to beat somebody. In New Hampshire Joe McQuaid has been urging readers of the *Union Leader* to "TAKE A LOOK AT DU PONT!"—and that's a good sign.

Pete du Pont has become associated with "empowerment" and I think that, too, is a good sign. William Schneider quotes Pete du Pont:

> We used to have a Republican Party that was a party of accountants, and that's when we could only hold the majority in boardrooms and country clubs. The challenge post-Ronald Reagan is to extend this idea of empowering people to make decisions in their own lives, to extend it into areas that aren't directly economic, into what I call the opportunity issues . . . when you empower people, good things begin to happen.[28]

I find myself hoping good things happen for Mr. du Pont in 1988.

Alexander Haig

Alexander M. Haig, Jr., is the third oldest candidate to try for the 1988 presidential nomination. He was born in Philadelphia, Pennsylvania, on December 2, 1924. Although less than six months younger than George Bush (who at age 18, you will remember, rushed to enter WWII), General Haig was not in World War II.[29] He attended Notre Dame and then switched to West Point, where he received his B.S. in 1947. That year he married Patricia Fox, his wife of thirty-seven years and mother of his three children, and was commissioned as a 2nd Lieutenant. Alexander Haig graduated from the Naval War College in 1960, the Army War College in 1966 and served as military assistant to the Secretary of the Army in 1964, Assistant to the President and Chief of White House Staff in 1973-1974, Commander-in-Chief NATO in 1974-78 and emerged from the army in 1979 with the rank of General. The general was Ronald Reagan's Secretary of State 1981-82.[30] He has also served as President and Chief Executive Officer at United Technologies, a firm which according to Standard and Poors specializes in:

> Air craft, industrial, marine engines; rocket motors; airborne sys-

tems, automotive and space equipment; commercial and military helicopters; elevators and escalators; energy conductors, controls and devices; military electronic systems, air conditioning and energy process equipment, wire and cable products.

General Haig is taken less seriously than most of the other candidates for the 1988 presidential nomination because, although he has a small loyal following, he also has a negative image with a good number of Americans. Name recognition may do the general more harm than good, if, as William Schneider claims:

> Three out of four voters who had heard of him at the time of his announcement (for the presidential nomination) said they didn't like him. That is most likely a residue of the day Reagan was shot when Haig presumptuously announced, "I am in control here."[31]

The General's campaign literature suggests that "Al Haig possesses a clear vision of where our country should be moving as we head into the next century." He is credited with having "both fiscal realism and compassion." (Shades of Robert Dole's dichotomy. See page 153.) He sometimes sounds as optimistic as Jack Kemp: "We have the talent, we have the resources and with the renaissance of the American spirit we have the will." On other occasions he reminds one of Mr. Dukakis and the other Democratic candidates, as he calls for "a partnership with private enterprise in addressing the problems of urban and rural America."

Social Security

On June 14, 1987, the Associated Press printed the General's answers to the questions they asked every prospective presidential candidate concerning Social Security.

> I believe in the preservation of the Social Security system, which has been a bedrock of economic stability and dignity for the elderly. Indeed, Social Security is also at the very center of the social compact that exists between our government and its citizens. We need to do everything to ensure the sustainability of the system, so that future generations will not have to bear undue burdens. Our elderly and those who will soon enter the retirement years have been caused needless aggravation over the politicizing of Social Security as an issue."

It would be interesting to know just what the General would do "to ensure the sustainability of the system, so that future generations will not have to bear undue burdens," because as the system is structured now the only way to sustain its economic viability in the future *is* by putting undue burdens on future generations. Only Pete du Pont and Pat Robertson have tackled this problem and come up with a viable solution. The other candidates, including General Haig, seem to be intent on making the elderly feel secure and content, ignoring their intelligence, sense of responsibility and the love that they have for their country and future generations. These candidates continually speak out of ignorance of the facts or with their own short-term good in mind rather than the long-term good of the nation.

The following are General Haig's stand on several issues as presented by his campaign headquarters:

AIDS

AIDS is more than a medical problem; it is a moral challenge. We've got to deal with both aspects of it if we are to prevent disaster. As scientists search for a cure, we must act to prevent the disease from spreading. I favor testing for a marriage license—we have long had such tests to detect venereal and other diseases. We ought to test immigrants for AIDS—we test them already for other communicable diseases. And in our prisons, the prison population as well as society should be protected by separating AIDS victims—just as we would do with any threatening disease.

The moral challenge is for us to educate Americans, especially our youth, in the behavior that prevents AIDS. It would be a grotesque abdication of our responsibility to our children if we instructed them simply in how to use condoms. True sex education informs the youth of the nation that abstinence before marriage and monogamy after it are the safest and the best ways not only to avoid AIDS but to live a better life.

Education

I detect a consensus in America to reestablish the basics in our schools, to teach students to think, to reason and to become fluent in the languages of our times—whether it be the foreign cultures of our global community or the mathematical skills of the computer age. Private schools, essential to America's diversity, must be enlisted in this effort as well as public schools. America needs a five-point blueprint for excellence in education:

1) Virtues, not just "values"—our children need a solid foundation in democracy and why it works.
2) Realistic standards for teachers—merit plans will attract a few good teachers but we need to uplift standards for all teachers—and we cannot attract and retain good teachers unless we pay them more and hold them in higher respect.
3) Higher standards for students—improving elementary and secondary skills are the key to a better performance overall and those skills must be exercised.
4) High standards for parents—schools cannot compensate for lack of parental involvement or a home that stresses the importance of doing well in school.
5) Quality higher education available for the qualified—colleges and universities, too, need to tighten their standards. In addition, we need a form of cost-containment for excessive tuition increases and a better way of financing higher education. We should separate the issue of *collecting* delinquent loans from the issue of *investing* in higher education by making monies available. Alternative financing plans need to meet the criteria of responsibility to both the student and the taxpayers. We ought to investigate the possibility of a revolving fund that might eventually be made self-financing. I also favor tuition tax credits for parents who choose to use private rather than public schooling.

Defense Spending vs. Domestic Spending

Some people forget that during the Kennedy Administration, we were debating whether 49 percent of the federal budget for defense expenditures was too much for the nation to afford. Today, that figure is around 26 percent . . .

The defense budget ought not to be made the whipping boy for excessive spending in the domestic sector. Like those in other branches of government, defense planners should demonstrate restraint as we begin to attack this deficit. I would much rather have preferred a gentle glidepath of defense increases rather than to "front load" spending and have to settle for dangerously small increases later on . . .

1) No one section of the budget should bear the principal burden of reductions, especially defense;
2) Every area of expenditure must be scrutinized before revenue increases are put on the table; and
3) Reform of the budget process, especially giving the president the line item veto, is far to be preferred to legislating economic morality, such as constitutional amendments to balance the budget.

The American people will not understand why the $25-$30 billion reductions necessary to get on the glidepath cannot be found in a billion dollar budget.

Welfare Reform

As a humane society rooted in the Judeo-Christian tradition, we support a "safety net" for the weaker members of society. But a net is not enough. We need programs that encourage dependents, especially young mothers and their children, to escape from the welfare net through handholds on the ladder to success: to finish high school; to get a job; to establish a stable family.

Workfare programs, run by state and local governments, have shown some success in reducing the long-term dependency rate. But before we turn this aspect of welfare reform into possible self-defeating large-scale expenditures, repeating the errors of the War On Poverty, we need a more comprehensive approach. That includes improvements to inner-city schools in poor neighborhoods. It also requires a mobilization of private and public agencies, especially our churches, to add the missing moral dimension to our growing young populatiin of dependents.

Trade

To rectify the trade gap, we've got to free up more of our own funds for investment and that means a reduced federal budget deficit, which will help to bring lower interest rates and a more stable dollar. Government at all levels has to examine its tax and regulatory policy to improve our ability to compete in an increasingly "globalized economy"—including revised antitrust laws and the restoration of tax credit incentives for new investment. In our dealings with other nations, we must lead the march once again toward more free and fair trade in agriculture services and finance—using the annual economic summits to guide the process and to speed it up.

Finally, whatever government does will not be enough unless American management and labor make the changes mandated by the new technologies of computer-aided production—changes which are key not only to new products but the survival of traditional industries. A level playing field isn't much use unless we're prepared to play on it.

Charisma or Issues

Most of the candidates have worked more on their charisma and less on the issues. General Haig has chosen the opposite course.

The Haig candidacy is analogous to the country's lament over the deplorable movies and TV it is offered, but when documentaries and shows with substance are presented the public ignores them. Maybe we'd rather be won over by a charming personality than listen to a discussion of the issues, and if so maybe we deserve what we get!

Jack Kemp

Foreigners are always amazed that everyone in America has the potential of one day becoming President of the United States—yes, even a football player. Jokes were made (and are still being made) in some quarters about the qualifications of an actor for the real life role of president. But in hindsight, acting, or to give it more substance we might refer to it as "communication," has served the office in good stead on more than one occasion. Similarly, the talents required of a good quarterback are also those we seek in our highest office holder. Both must excel at calling the plays and attaining goals through team work. Of course, it will take more than this ability to win Jack Kemp the presidency or even the nomination in 1988.

Jack Kemp was born in Los Angeles on July 13, 1935. He attended Occidental College in southern California where he received his B.A. in 1957, the year he also married Joanne Main. Needless to say, the young Jack Kemp excelled in athletics, in fact he was good enough to make football his career for thirteen years. He led both National and American League teams to victory and collected numerous awards over the course of his career. The Kemps have two daughters, a teenage son and an older son who is a quarterback with the Seattle Sea Hawks. Jack Kemp's career took him to the Buffalo Bills, where he was first elected to the United States House of Representatives from Buffalo, New York, in 1970.

Mr. Kemp can match Mr. Gephardt's energetic work schedule as few can. Between 1985 and 1986 he delivered 512 speeches and was constantly on the go. But like Senator Al Gore, he is a stickler for details and sometimes talks above and beyond his audience. He is often criticized for his inability to give a short direct answer to any question, using fifty words when five would do. William Schneider gives what he calls a "classic Kemp sentence" in the July 1987 issue of *The Atlantic Monthly:*

> It is absolutely essential to our hopes for peace, stability, democracy and better foreign policy to have a world that is growing and expanding with a tide that is rising, upon which all boats can rise, as opposed to this zero-sum, fiercely divisive Darwinian struggle in which nations are locked into mercantilistic practices and protectionist policies that drive people apart, as opposed to bringing people together in a liberal democratic fashion as I think America was founded upon two hundred years ago.[32]

Of course it is only fair to add that the sentence was spoken, not written.

Mr. Kemp's words are full of optimism and expectations of great things for the future but his manner always appears a bit desperate, as if to deny his words. He often appears to be too intense for his message. He writes and speaks in the Biden-Jackson style as evidenced by this piece from the *Policy Review*, Spring 1986:

> Clearly the work is just beginning to give a new burst of freedom to our country, to get spending and government under control, to renew the values of individual dignity, self-reliance and the sanctity of human life, and to create a true American renaissance of spiritual, political and economic dimensions.
>
> A revitalized America will help secure the blessings of liberty and a free economic order to all people both in the USA and abroad. It will not usurp the responsibilities and energies of the individual, family or society, but help foster the happiness, prosperity and true welfare of our people by devising prudent, intelligent laws and by promoting equal opportunity for all to reach their God-given potential.

The above was written!

Abortion

The Right To Life Convention, consisting of three hundred-plus people, chose Congressman Kemp by a margin of 37 percent to 31 percent over fellow pro-life candidate Pat Robertson. The Congressman told his audience at the Des Moines convention in September 1987 that, "I will appoint pro-life ... judges to all courts if I am elected president in 1988." He talked about the one and a half million lives claimed by abortion in 1987 and told his audience that it was time to care for a child not only before but after its birth by allowing deductions in the tax code for the costs of adoption as well as abortions. His campaign headquarters released the following:

> Jack Kemp believes that the Supreme Court's decision to legalize abortion in Roe v. Wade was a travesty of justice that must be reversed. He has worked in Congress to restore the right to life of the unborn to its rightful place as a pillar of the Constitution. He is a prime sponsor of President Reagan's pro-life initiative to terminate all federal involvement with abortion and affirm the humanity of the unborn child, which was introduced by Congressman Henry Hyde and Senator Gordon Humphrey. He has helped lead the fight to end federal funding of abortion for organizations—foreign or domestic—that promote abortion as a method of family planning. His voting record has been 100 percent pro-life since coming to Congress in 1970.

Tolerance

In March 1987, Congressman Kemp called for constitutional protections for the unborn and for a mandatory AIDS testing program for couples applying for marriage licenses. In an attempt to strengthen the family, Mr. Kemp has worked for legislation to combat child pornography and drug abuse. He has proposed legislation that would mandate life imprisonment for dealers who sell drugs to children.

Jack Kemp uses children just as Bruce Babbitt does—to elicit emotion and win agreement from his audience. Who can disagree that our children are important, that they are the future of this nation? Jack Kemp actively tries to prevent the Republican Party from being perceived as Puritanical, illiberal or intolerant and is one of the few Republicans that can get along with the Congressional Black Caucas, no doubt because of his vote to institute sanctions against South Africa and votes on other occasions to extend aid to that continent. Anti-establishment appeal is notoriously lacking among most of the Republican candidates, although Pete du Pont supports sanctions against South Africa also.

Monetary Policy

Those not alienated by his stand on AIDS testing and abortion may well be by his extremist views when it comes to monetary policy. Political wisdom is that no one can be elected president who has not first won New Hampshire's preferential primary. C-SPAN interviewed Joe McQuaid of the New Hampshire *Union Leader* in September 1987 and was told that many of the paper's readers were put off by Kemp's continual emphasis on the gold standard. His own political advisers have urged the Congressman to play down the "gold issue," but Jack Kemp feels strongly about this. He has worked tirelessly in the House for reform of the nation's monetary policy, advocating a stable exchange rate and a dollar backed by gold, contending the reform would work to keep inflation in check and promote growth.

Deficit

Mr. Kemp uses his conservative philosophy aggressively rather than defensively. He was one of the few Republicans to vote against Gramm-Rudman, with its automatic cutting mechanism. Like Phil Gramm of Texas, he seems to think that growth and opportunity will solve all our problems with no reason to balance needs or cut programs. Appealing perhaps, but not believable as far as most voters are concerned. He is certain we can grow our way out of any deficit. "The deficit is not due to the tax cut (of 1981)," he has said. "There is plenty of room for a deficit in this economy."[33] If there are going to be cuts, however, Jack Kemp has expressed opinions on what he would like to see cut:

> The Export-Import Bank direct loan program ($1.4 billion) should be eliminated because it funnels export subsidies to a handful of the nation's largest corporations. The SBA's direct loan and loan guarantee program ($1.9 billion) benefits a tiny fraction of the small

business community, and its elimination has been sought by many small business associations.[34]

Jack Kemp espouses tax reductions and enterprise zones as indispensible parts of any plan to create new jobs and bring the economy to full production capability. He accuses the Democrats of wanting to balance revenues up to current expenditures which, he says, will lead to greater and greater spending. He advocates balancing expenditures down to current revenue so that citizens will be able to keep more of their own money. Besides, he points to the fact that despite the recent tax cuts we have more revenue to work with than ever before in history. It's just that spending has gotten out of hand—mostly automatic spending with so many transfer programs being tied to the CPI. He warns that higher taxes would only lead to more unemployment, less growth and even less revenue. Jack Kemp feels certain that the deficit problem has been blown out of proportion and that, if handled calmly and patiently, it can be brought under control painlessly. He sees the key in keeping inflation and interest rates low so that, even with an economy that is growing slowly, the budget will be gradually balanced. Oh yes, he would like to see the recommendations made by the Grace Commission implemented also.

Trade

The Kemp-Gramm bill has not had the media coverage accorded HR3 and the Gephardt amendment, but it is proposed trade legislation. It would set up reciprocal free trade agreements to open new markets for American goods. No tariffs and no protection for privileged industries, just reciprocal free markets. Desirable, but not workable, has been the general verdict. Mr. Kemp would like to expand the new GATT (General Agreement on Tariffs & Trade) round of negotiations to include agriculture and services.

Taxes

Jack Kemp, a loyal supply-sider, would like to see an essentially flat tax. His industrial strategy for the nation would include further lowering of taxes on business in order to stimulate capital formation and more enterprise zones in the inner city. If he had his way he would do away with the capital-gains tax entirely.

Jack Kemp's campaign manager, Edward Rollins, spoke on Mr. Kemp's behalf before the Southern Legislative Conference (SLC) in Little Rock, Arkansas, in August 1987. He told the audience that Mr. Kemp thought the individual could do a better job with his own money than Congress could. (Sounds like a popular idea, doesn't it?) He pointed out that most Americans are currently paying about 50 percent of their income to the government in one form or another. Roughly 28 percent in income taxes, 6 to 11 percent in state taxes and then various amounts in excise, sales and property taxes along with user fees.

Mr. Rollins said that the Congressman views the state as a partner with the federal government but that the closer to home power is kept, the better. Jack Kemp told Mr. Schneider, in the *Atlantic* interview, roughly the same thing. "I am not anti-government. I would not run a campaign against government," he reportedly said.

> He explained that whereas government has an obligation to promote opportunity—mostly by lowering taxes and getting out of people's way—"security is another aspect." He said, "People want opportunity so they can earn security." Kemp sees himself as a "use-government-where-you-can conservative" rather than a "fight-government-at-all-costs conservative."

Mr. Rollins told the SLC audience that "Kemp is a very open-minded pragmatic man." He said Mr. Kemp saw safety as an obligation of government and agreed that adequate facilities and traffic controls were needed for the country to run smoothly. When speaking of deregulation he admitted that the Congressman would stipulate a need for better enforcement of safety laws and that perhaps the loss of service in certain rural areas was not a good by-product of deregulation and might need to be attended to in the future.

Education

On September 11, 1987, Mr. Kemp debated Pete du Pont at the University of North Carolina at Chapel Hill. The subject was "Education '88." Mr. Kemp defended the administration's expenditures on education by pointing out that more was spent on education (6.6 percent of GNP or $308 billion) than is spent on defense (6.5 percent of GNP or $288 billion), despite popular opinion to the contrary. He reiterated his stand against austerity and in favor of growth to provide the revenue to do all the things he thinks a government should legitimately do. He favors expanding the IRA concept to education. He attacked Mr. du Pont's support for education vouchers, claiming that all mandated vouchers would interfere with public schools and vouchers from the federal government would interfere with private education as we know it. He believes if parents are allowed to send their children to any school within a district that that gives plenty of choice.

The Congressman would like to see testing for principals as well as teachers and favors merit pay within the public school system. He believes a constant evaluation of the teaching staff would make it easier for parents to choose the best school for their particular children. Mr. Kemp is especially fond of the magnet-schools program. He told the audience he backed tax-credits for private education.

When asked by Judy Woodruff of Public Television whether he would back multi-million dollar federal commitment to education, Mr. Kemp flatly and unhesitatingly answered, "Yes." Mr. du Pont had asserted that money should come from the states, not the federal government, a stand which one would expect Mr. Kemp to take. Perhaps Mr. Rollins was misinformed when he asserted Congressman Kemp's desire to keep power local. Mr. Kemp went on to say:

> There has to be a federal commitment with federal resources . . . I think we can both balance our budget and bring this economy to full employment without inflation . . . and also provide for the education and defense of this country within the existing framework of the best free-enterprise system on the face of this earth.

No one ever said Jack Kemp was not an optimist!

Social Security

Jack Kemp is attempting to woo both senior citizens and those voters who have little knowledge of the problems the Social Security system will face in years to come with his adamant stand to keep the status-quo on Social Security—as if such a thing were possible. The status-quo will have to go, and wishing won't make it any different.

In his widely quoted disparagement of Pete du Pont, the only candidate with enough courage to wrestle with the very real problems that are built into the system, he showed his own ignorance. ("a politician who would tamper with the Social Security system 'is a candidate for a frontal lobotomy.'")[35] Further on in the *New York Times* article, Don Feder reports that Kemp said that "FDR's brainchild 'must remain the bedrock of retirement security.'" "Bedrock" my foot![36] Mr. Kemp has supposedly looked into the program and determined that the Social Security system is overfunded and that it may be time to lower the payroll tax. He conveniently ignores the liabilities the system will face beginning in 2012 as the baby boomers start retiring. He's correct in his contention that a lower payroll tax would lift an oppressive burden from employers and make them look more favorably upon hiring new workers and could well decrease the current unemployment rate and aid in reducing the deficit, but that's all he is correct about regarding Social Security. He points with pride to the fact that he withstood Senator Dole's attempt to get a handle on the deficit problem by, among other things, freezing COLAs of Social Security recipients.[37]

The Associated Press printed the following answer to the questions they put to Mr. Kemp (and all other candidates) regarding Social Security:

> I believe the Social Security system is the bedrock of retirement security and I will uphold its integrity and continue to oppose any effort to reduce benefits to older Americans . . . Social Security is an insurance program not a welfare program. Middle and upper-income people have made contributions to the Social Security system over the years, and they deserve the full benefits they have earned.[38]

Mr. Kemp has proposed removal of the Social Security Trust Fund from the budget to take it out of politics and preserve its integrity.

Agriculture

Mr. Kemp relates much of our agriculture mess to the fact that floating exchange rates are detrimental to exports.

He believes going to a gold standard will help alleviate much of the farm problem. He recognizes that the inflation of the 1970s followed by the deflation of the 1980s hurt the farmer more than most segments of society. He told an audience in Ames, Iowa, "With the right monetary reform, market prices could recover instead of support prices falling." He is not alone in his proposal that we lift agricultural subsidies only when other countries agree to do the same.

Mr. Rollin told the gathering at the SLC that Mr. Kemp does not want to let government walk away from the small family farms and simply let agri-business take over. Mr. Kemp, he maintained, recognizes the importance of exports and believes the way to increase our export market is to make the dollar strong. Great! After Secretary Baker spent all that time and effort at the Plaza Accords forging agreements with Japan and West Germany to weaken it. What is needed, according to Mr. Kemp, is a sound monetary policy (and we've heard that before). He feels the farmers will continue to need some subsidies and should be weaned gradually from their dependence via lower interest rates.

Housing

Congressman Kemp has gained support both in Congress and outside for his proposed solutions to the nation's housing problems. Urban Homesteading, whereby a public housing tenant is allowed to gain a stake in the community by purchasing his dwelling over time, has led Mr. Kemp into a unique relationship with Robert Woodson, the founder and head of the *National Center For Neighborhood Enterprise*, which completely backs the Congressman's idea.

The Role Of Government

Mr. Kemp attempts to draw inner-city minorities to his message, much in the manner of Jesse Jackson, and purposefully sets himself apart from the establishment image conveyed by George Bush and Robert Dole.

> Getting the government off the backs of the American people will be no one's slogan in 1988 ... Making government efficient and effective will be the thing this time. I've never understood why conserva-

tives positioned themselves against government.[39]

Perhaps the following quotations might help clarify the reasoning for Mr. Kemp:

> A government big enough to give you everything you want is big enough to take everything you have.
>
> *Gerald Ford and Barry Goldwater*

> Fear is the foundation of most government.
>
> *John Adams*

> Society is produced by our wants, and government by our wickedness.
>
> *Thomas Paine*

> Government's only business is the choice of evils. Every law is an evil, for every law is an infraction of liberty.
>
> *Jeremy Bentham*

> If men were angels no government would be necessary.
>
> *James Madison*

> Governments will alwys misuse the machinery of the law as far as the state of public opinion permits.
>
> *Emile Capouya*

Mr. Kemp appears to be a maverick, pleasing neither party. Whether pleasing an individual voter here and there—even an influential one like Mr. Woodson—will be enough to win him the presdential nomination, has yet to be seen.

Pat Robertson

Pat Robertson can trace his lineage to Benjamin Harrison, a signer of the Declaration of Independence, and on through two Presidents, William Henry Harrison and Benjamin Harrison, until he finally gets to his father, A. Willis Robertson. Like Senators Bush and Gore, Pat Robertson's father was a member of Congress, having served in both Houses for a total of thirty-four years.

Marion G. ("Pat") Robertson was born in Lexington, Virginia, on March 22, 1930. All through his teens Pat Robertson was involved in sports—football, boxing and wrestling. Even now he lifts weights, jogs and enjoys tennis and golf. In 1948, at the age of 18, he enlisted in the U.S. Marine Corps Reserve. He was commissioned as a 2nd Lieutenant upon graduation from college (B.A. in history, Washington and Lee University, 1951) and served in Korea in 1951.

It is interesting that questions have been raised about the veracity of both preachers in the 1988 race for the presidential nomination. Jesse Jackson has been accused by Barbara Reynolds in her book *Jesse Jackson: The Man, The Movement, The Myth* of falsifying facts, and Pat Robertson has filed suit against former Congressman Pete McCloskey of California and Congressman Andrew Jacobs of Illinois, who accused him of using the influence of his father, then a Senator, to avoid combat while in Korea. Apparently Pat Robertson has referred to himself as a "Marine combat officer" when speaking of the time he served in Korea.

At any rate he returned to the states in 1952 and was promoted to 1st Lieutenant and served as a legal officer in Quantico. In 1954 Pat Robertson married Adella Elmer of Columbus, Ohio, who was to become the mother of his two daughters and two sons. Mr. Robertson received his law degree from Yale in 1955 and went on to the New York Theological Seminary, where in 1959 he received a Master of Divinity degree. He was ordained a Southern Baptist minister in Norfolk, Virginia, in 1961.

Pat Robertson is the candidate with the most years of formal education and also holds the distinction of being, if not the most successful (how does one measure success?) in business, at least the candidate with the longest uninterrupted entrepreneurial experience. Pat Robertson started CBN (Christian Broadcasting Network) which is seen in all fifty states and sixty foreign countries, in 1959 with $70 initial capital and has expanded it over the last quarter of a century so that it now provides wholesome entertainment to millions of households. The Reverend Robertson also has a television station in the Middle East (ME-TV) and business endeavors in fifteen foreign countries.

> Operation Blessing is a major private sector relief agency which assisted nearly 9 million needy Americans nationwide in 1985. The 700 Club Crisis Counseling Center expects to receive approximately 5 million phone calls this year for distressed and destitute people. 115,000 adults and children in urban ghettos were taught to read through the "Sing, Spell, Read and Write" program.[40]

If that were not enough, the Reverend has founded and headed a construction company, a full-service advertising agency and a company to make motion pictures and television series. The *National Legal Foundation*, with three hundred lawyers dedicated to fighting to preserve religious freedoms, was also his brainchild.

Abortion

Abortion is the number one issue of many of Pat Robertson's supporters. In late September 1987, over 1,000 people gathered in Ames, Iowa, and chose Robertson over Kemp as their pro-life candidate. The Ames group was approximately three times the size of the Right To Life Group that you will remember preferred Congressman Kemp.

There is no doubt that Pat Robertson is determined to see that Roe v. Wade is overturned. He supports the Reagan administration's Pro-Life Bill (HR1729), which permanently prohibits federal funding of abortion, and opposes Grove City legislation (HR1214), which would require private, religious hospitals that accept Medicare-Medicaid patients to perform abortions. He is an advocate of the Tauke-Sensenbrenner amendment, which would protect hospitals from the preceding provision. The Reverend Robertson believes that life begins at conception and, therefore, abortion is murder and is always wrong, except in cases where the mother's life is at stake.

Qualifications

When C-SPAN asked Mr. Robertson's supporters in Ames why they thought Pat Robertson was qualified to be President of the United States, they received a variety of responses.

One lady thought he had a background in law—"as good a background as any other candidate," she said.

A gentleman thought Pat Robertson was qualified by reason of

> His integrity and competence and his legal background. His excellent understanding of constitutional law ... He's been stereotyped as a minister, but I believe he's a statesman ... He has a legal background, he has an economic background, he has a background in education and journalism, he's the head of a university. As a journalist he's traveled around the world and visited with heads of state. He's knowledgeable and aware of what's going on in the world and I could say more!

Another man answered that Pat Robertson was the "chosen man for the times." He told C-SPAN that the problem facing the nation which concerned him the most was education. "It makes me feel so bad that there's kids coming out of school that can't even read or write."

Another gentleman referred to Pat Robertson as:

> A man who's head and shoulders above all the other candidates, as a man who's being led by the spirit ... He's well informed in all kinds of areas. Business areas, economic areas, international—he's had international experience. He's got the criteria to be the best president we've ever had ... Morality is the most important thing. Morality in our government, morality in our country. A nation that believes in God will be lifted up. A nation that doesn't believe in God and practice God's commandments will go down. That's the sum and substance of the whole thing.

By September 17, 1987, Pat Robertson had gathered 3.3 million signatures from supporters and made it official that he would announce his candidacy for the Republican nomination for the presidency of the United States on October 1, 1987.

Education

Pat Robertson and Pete du Pont are the only two candidates for the '88 presidential nomination to support an educational voucher system—albeit one that would not "interfere" with private education. Vouchers would permit parents of educationally disadvantaged children—indeed parents of all children—to raise the quality of education for their children. As Pat Robertson wrote in the June 1987 issue of *Conservative Digest:*

> The present welfare system makes no provisions for education "vouchers." There is no method that allows parents and children to "choose" one type—or standard—of education over another ... how do you learn that one school may be better than another for someone who dreams bigger than the "system" allows? How can we convince the "system" that even if you are poor and black, a future scientist cannot afford to choose his training ground on the basis of a school-districting map.[41]

The Reverend Robertson spoke to the annual convention of the National Association of Evangelicals in March 1987 in Buffalo, New York:

It isn't whether children pray or not pray—the problem is, are they being inculcated in morality and religious values throughout all their education or are they being given a totally secular education based on atheism and humanism, at the taxpayer's expense? . . . If we . . . will work in the courts and work in the political arena and work in the public airwaves and work in the churches by way of education and by way of prayer and by wy of action, then I sense as part of the great religious revival that is coming to the United States of America, that, in the not-too-distant future, we can say to our children and our grandchildren, "We give you one nation under God."

This speech terrified humanists who believe neutrality should be the goal to which public education aspires. Of course neutrality necessarily means no *one* religious view espoused over another, and so by default the secular-atheist-agnostic-humanist point of view triumphs.

At Constitution Hall in Washington, D.C., on September 17, 1986, Pat Robertson made a speech titled, "A New Vision For America." In it he said:

Our schools, with what is called "progressive education," have become progressively worse. We have in our society 27 million functional illiterates. Each year we add 2.3 million to their number. Instead of being the most literate nation on earth, we rank number 14 among the developed nations in literacy and we are falling fast . . .[42] The "progressive education" advocated by John Dewey and his followers is a colossal failure and must be abandoned.

For our children's and our grandchildren's sake we must insure that control of education is returned to their parents and caring teachers in local communities, and taken away from a powerful union with leftist tendencies.

There can be no education without morality, and there can be no lasting morality without religion. For the sake of our children, we must bring God back to the classrooms of America!

Welfare

In his article for *Conservative Digest*, he quoted Claude Brown, author of *Manchild In The Promised Land:*

It used to be that young black men and women viewed the low-income community as a way station to a better place. You were taught that each generation had a responsibility to do better than the one that went before. You were told that if you worked hard enough, there was a hope of going on. Today, these neighborhoods are no longer way stations ... they are *warehouses for the poor.* And there is no hope of going on ... Somehow, we have failed to teach the latest generation the lessons they need to go on.

The Reverend Robertson doesn't see that being black and being poor is the real problem. We all can point to any number of "poor blacks" who have "made it." He agrees with many sociologists, black and white, that:

For too long the wealth of black families has been drained by a welfare system ... that forgot the critical importance of the values embodied in strong families—discipline, hard work, ambition and self-sacrifice, patience and love.[43]

He justly criticizes the current welfare system for giving assistance directly to young mothers, bypassing the fathers and consequently relieving them of any responsibility they may otherwise have felt for providing for their families. AFDC (Aid to Families with Dependent Children—the welfare system) mothers are constantly forced to choose between the fathers of their children and a welfare check.

And what happens to "welfare children"?

They grow up in an environment that is more often a haven to drug traffickers than a home to them ... anti-family, anti-human, anti-life. It is in this environment that the children of welfare are dying—killing themselves and killing one another ... the leading cause of death for young black men in this country is murder ... black men account for only 6 percent of our population but they represent over 50 percent of our prison population.[44]

Drugs

The Reverend Robertson takes a hard stand against drugs, including alcohol, in our schools. He claims the marketing of drugs to high school students is a $120 *billion* annual business in this country. He wants to see mandatory sentencing without possibility of parole for dealers who sell drugs to children under age eighteen. Of course there isn't a candidate running for the presidential nomination that does not agree that the nation needs to come up with a better system to eliminate the importation of drugs, its distribution within the country and its abuse. Drugs all too often lead to crime and, according to Pat Robertson,

> It is crime, not poverty, that keeps working people in their homes at night—away from part-time jobs ... It is violence that keeps people who want to move up, and move on, away from night-school classes.[45]

Employment

The Reverend Robertson supports a minimum wage for younger workers, arguing, along with the Reagan administration, that such a program would give thousands of presently unemployed teenagers a chance to acquire skills, work habits, self-esteem and a work record which will ultimately lead to a better job.

He sounds a lot like Pete du Pont who likes to talk about "empowering people" when he says,

> Our goal is to empower these people, to raise them up to self-reliance where possible and to encourage independence, not to generate dependency.[46]

He ridicules the EJA (Emergency Job Act of 1983), claiming it cost approximately $325,000 "per unemployed person actually aided by this program ... between March 1983 and June 1984, the economy created 6,390,000 civilian jobs, while the EJA created 35,000. So, the private sector generated about 99.5 percent of all the new jobs.[47]

In order to create more jobs in the private sector Mr. Robertson would repeal the Davis-Bacon Act of 1931, which requires federal contractors to pay prevailing wages (otherwise known as union wages), which now adds 10 to 15 percent to all federal projects. The Chamber of Commerce estimates that repeal of Davis-Bacon would save the federal government over $2 billion with the added benefit of creating more than 100,000 new jobs.

Like most of the other candidates, Mr. Robertson would like to see more partnerships between government and the private business sector. An original idea is his "Individual Business Accounts" concept, which would provide tax incentives for those who invest in stock issued by new small businesses. This would of course stimulate new business activity. He would also like to encourage capital ownership, as exemplified by the ESOP (Employee Stock Ownershp Plans). He shares Louis Kelso's[48] views that the expansion of capital ownership would benefit the country and broaden the access to the American Dream, which can seldom be attained today by wages alone. "Expansion of incentives for the ESOP approach for small business would enhance productivity, promote community strength and motivate workers."[49]

Trade

Pat Robertson, being a businessman who has had to watch the bottom line, is more agitated than most other candidates by our trade deficit. He agrees with many popular economists who fault the American practice of concentrating on quarterly returns rather than focusing on long-range business patterns. Of course, this is dictated by the pension fund managers who, to a large extent, control business policy in this country.

Like any good Republican, Mr. Robertson abhors tariffs or any other protectionist measures and would seek to expand free but *fair* trade by keeping our markets open to all, but at the same time gaining equal access. He doesn't mince words but says what we all want to hear: "Either (addressing other nations) give us free and fair access to your markets—or we will shut down America's markets to you."

Agriculture

As for agriculture, Pat Robertson supports mediation and loan restructuring as opposed to farm foreclosure. (So what else is new?) He also supports phasing out farm subsidies over a reasonable period of time. Whether he considers Pete du Pont's five-year plan "reasonable" or not is not clear. Since Pat Robertson is one of the last to declare his candidacy for the presidential nomination (October 1, 1987) he has not gone into as many specifics with regard to his farm program as have his Democratic opponents, many of whom have been stomping Iowa for over a year. He would like to extend opportunities for farm exports, and who wouldn't, but how? He wants to stop sending taxpayer dollars to foreign farm businesses that throw American farmers out of work. How they are getting our tax dollars and what to do about it will be revealed as the Reverend Robertson starts "catching up" in Iowa and his campaign heats up.

Social Security

Pat Robertson sides with Pete du Pont in the controversy over Social Security without agreeing on specifics. He agrees that benefits must be guaranteed for current recipients but that a gradual shift to private IRA-type pensions for younger workers will be the only salvation for the program. When asked the by-now-familiar questions put by the Associated Press to all the candidates: ("Will you keep Social Security benefits and the annual cost-of-living increases exempt from budget cuts?" and "Do you favor any means test for Social Security benefits?"), he answered:

> By the year 2015, the Social Security system as we know it will be bankrupt . . . I have been advocating a gradual movement toward a compulsory private system of Social Security which would free future retirees from the vagaries of the electoral process . . . We should absolutely guarantee the integrity of current retirement benefits to the elderly and the retiring now. But we need to begin to phase in a compulsory private program for younger workers.[50]

Deficits

Pat Robertson believes that deficits are fiscally and morally wrong. Such an attitude, if adopted by every Congress person, would guarantee a speedy end to all our deficits. Government excesses drain the economy, take resources from the private sector and allow government bureaucrats to use, waste or redistribute the nation's wealth.

Mr. Robertson would like to see the Grace Commission's recommendations acted upon and would support a move toward more privatization in order to take advantage of the profit motive and other incentives for efficiency which are notoriously absent in bureaucracies in this or any other country. He is a staunch backer of the Gramm-Rudman legislation and any other program which would discipline our legislators and ensure that reductions in the deficit are made consistently and according to a prearranged schedule.

Taxes

Right in line with his thinking that workers should be allowed to keep more of their earnings is his attitude toward taxes. The Reverend Robertson faults the 1986 tax reform which did away with accelerated depreciation. He argues that in order for people to put their money into speculative enterprises, there must be incentives. Whether the government should provide those incentives is really a moot point, since it assuredly does—incentives and penalties whether we like it or not are provided via the tax code. He told Mr. Schneider:

> I think we need to recognize that whenever you have an organ that is spending a trillion dollars a year, that has 2.6 or 2.7 million employees, that is giving checks to over 50 percent of the American people, that organ is enormously powerful and it is obviously being used right now to bring about certain types of behavior.[51]

No Redneck Preacher

William Schneider gave the following account of his interview with Pat Robertson in preparation for his article which appeared in the July 1987 issue of *The Atlantic Monthly:*

> Robertson was equally businesslike on the subject of the federal budget. He favored cutting $100 billion out of it immediately. "I don't think we can wait on it," he said. "I think it can be done, and it can be done by prudent management." ... Robertson felt that some agencies should be dismantled ... "not just improved business management but whole departments." Among them were the Legal Services Corporation, Amtrack, Conrail, and the Departments of Education and Energy.[52]

William Schneider has declared that "Robertson is no redneck preacher" who sees religion as the answer to all the country's ills. However, no one would deny that Pat Robertson's greatest support comes from the born-again Christians, the group that comprised approximately 15 percent of all voters in the 1984 presidential election. Joe McQuaid, editor of the New Hampshire *Union Leader*, told C-SPAN that Christians are well organized in New Hampshire and all over the country and he expects to see Pat Robertson get a lot of votes just by espousing old traditional values and without any startling new ideas.[53]

Pat Robertson himself claims that 94 percent of Americans believe in God. In this context he has said that it is stupid for 94 percent to give the 6 percent minority control over virtually every aspect of public life. (Referring no doubt, to the absence of creches in city squares, Christmas Pageants and Christmas Carols in schools and, of course, the prohibition on prayer in the public schools.) He argues, along with many others, that separation of Church and State means only that no particular religion should be sanctioned or preferred by the State above any other, but not that the State should ignore all religions. He and his followers believe that the State, mostly through its courts, has infringed in recent years on the private morality and personal liberty of its citizens. Liberal court rulings have imposed the values of a vocal and active minority on everybody. Most of Mr. Robertson's supporters are opposed to feminist causes, busing, quotas, affirmative action, gay rights, sex and AIDS education in the schools, the banning of prayer and legalized abortion. What liberals see as an enhancement and expansion of individual rights, the far-right views as an encroachment on individual rights and an expansion of government.

In late April 1987 Pat Robertson addressed the Jefferson Society Forum at the University of Virginia at Charlottesville. He asked his audience:

> What makes America so good? Why do people want to be here? Why do more immigrants want to get in than we can allow? We need no wall to keep people in . . . The Founding Fathers recognized that freedom is something that cannot be taken away from us. It is a gift of God. (It is) taken away only by risk of incurring God's wrath.

He went on to explain that the concept of self-restraint is at the heart of freedom and that freedom itself depends on morality. Public morality, he said, depends on religious principles.

Fear Of The Unknown

Before the nation got to know Ronald Reagan they were afraid of him. They had heard that he was an extremist—a war monger—a kook, dangerous and to be feared. The man himself dispelled the myth.

I think Pat Robertson will initially encounter the same hostility. Rumor has it that if elected he would *force* his personal values and religion on all citizens. Remember, New Hampshire gets first crack at the candidates, and as Joe McQuaid told C-SPAN, ‘‘*Forcing* is against New Hampshire’s independent streak!’’

Section Four

The Watergate Legacy

The Watergate Legacy

Evolution Of The Nominating Process

Presidential campaigns and our party system have evolved over the years. James Madison was picked by Thomas Jefferson as his successor, Martin Van Buren was Andrew Jackson's choice and William Howard Taft was backed by Theodore Roosevelt. James Monroe was unopposed in 1821. William Henry Harrison who had lost his bid for the presidency in 1836 was the subject of the nation's first uproarious campaign in 1840, based on no particular platform but on pure war hero ballyhoo. (Harrison, who had defeated Indians at Tippecanoe Creek in November 1811, thus his nickname 'Ol Tippecanoe, was a hero of the 1812 War.) Perhaps the long drawn out campaigns, such as we are experiencing in the 1980s, would have exposed his lack of judgment and prevented the country from enduring the inauguration and death of a president in a single month. The inaugural day, March 4, 1841, was miserably cold and rainy. Nevertheless, in an attempt to live up to his campaign image as tough and masterful, President Harrison appeared bare headed and unprotected on a strapping white horse. He died of pneumonia thirty days later on April 4, 1841.

The eleventh president of the United States, James Knox Polk, was the country's first "dark horse" winner, nominated by his party as a compromise candidate on the ninth ballot. James Polk may also be the only president to take his campaign promises seriously. It is said that he used his wife as his secretary and the two of them worked day and night for four years to reduce tariffs, restore an independent federal treasury and to add the California and Oregon territories to the nation. At the end of four years, having made good on his promises, he packed up and went home.

In 1848 the Whigs again rallied a boisterous winning campaign around a war hero with no thought of issues, and again their war hero died in office. This time it was said that exposure to the hot sun while attending ceremonies for laying the cornerstone of the Washington Monument was responsible for Zachary Taylor's term of only sixteen months. (The weather was blamed for a lot of deaths 150 years ago.)

The Democratic Convention was deadlocked in 1852 and Franklin Pierce's name, which had only been submitted on the thirty-fifth ballot, was accepted on the forty-ninth. In 1880 James Garfield was nominated on the thirty-sixth ballot. Grover Cleveland, who in his bid for a second term in 1888 was defeated by Benjamin Harrison, was the only president in history to win a second term (1892) after being out of office for a span of years. Warren Harding was nominated on the tenth ballot in 1920 after being picked by the "Boys" in the smoke-filled-room.

1960 was a transition year in the nominating process. In that year there was a merger of backroom and grassroots politics. Nominations were still controlled by the parties but the grassroots efforts of the candidate and his family between 1956-1960 ensured John Fitzgerld Kennedy the Democratic nomination on the first ballot. The violent 1968 Democratic Convention completed the transition. After 1968 there was a shift in control of the nominating process from party leaders to the grassroots. Primaries, which lessen the influence of party leaders and congressional colleagues, have more than doubled in the last two decades. There were seventeen primaries in 1968 and thirty-five scheduled for 1988. Neither George McGovern (1971-72) nor Jimmy Carter (1975-76) were the choice of party leaders, but they both exemplified grassroots power; power that has meant ever since that every candidate has to be taken seriously.

Alan Eherenhalt, political writer for the *Congressional Quarterly*, found that if it were up to Congresssional Democrats they would choose Thomas S. Foley, House Majority Leader, as the 1988 party nominee for president. But instead of allowing party bosses, the traditional king-makers, to at least start the ball rolling, more and more we see candidates choosing themselves, engaged in sometimes heroic efforts of self-nomination. Bruce Babbitt's 397 bike ride across Iowa and $300,000 of television advertising purchased in the spring of 1987 is an example of the new process.

Many people think a convention, similar to the system already in use in Massachusetts and Colorado, to nominate talent chosen by those "who know" (colleagues and various political leaders) and then a primary to narrow the professionally-picked list, would be a compromise in the right direction. This would bring forth the more quiet competent men and women, not only those who are adept at tooting their own horns and are ambitious enough to do so. According to proponents of this idea, the party members who received a specific set percentage of votes, 15 percent or 20 percent for example, would go on to a national primary. It may give too large a role to professional politicians for some people's taste, but it reserves for the voters the ultimate decision as to the nominee.

Debates have replaced straw polls as political feedback and most people agree the change is for the better. The earliest 1988 Democrat v. Republican debate occurred in Des Moines, Iowa, in May 1987 between Bruce Babbitt and Pete du Pont, the darkest of the dark horses. Another early Iowa debate featured Jack Kemp and Richard Gephardt just prior to the debate in which all seven (at that time) Democratic hopefuls participated. Of course the feedback from debates is no more accurate than it was from straw polls. Now on a scale of one to seven, with four being neutral, viewers voice immediate impressions and computers crunch out numbers. Among the seven in Dubuque in August 1987, Msrs. Gephardt, Dukakis and Simon were all declared winners.

As for Iowa and New Hampshire, the opinion of their usefulness as a barometer for the nation varies even among political experts. Many like to point out that since the New Hampshire preferential primaries began in 1952, no candidate has won the presidency without first winning that state. Jude Wanniski, in an article for the *National Review*, August 1987, claimed

> In a sense, the national electorate saves time and effort by trusting in the voters of New Hampshire to do the first serious sorting out of the candidates.

In the Iowa caucus participants will gather in 2,495 caucuses in ninety-nine counties. Mr. Wanniski believes the Iowa caucuses are less representative of grassroots support than are the New Hampshire primaries, while Don McLeod in an article for *Insight* claims the Iowa caucuses "may be the last real grassroots politics in America."[1] Ron Brown, a political professional formerly associated with Kennedy campaigns, claims that money and the calendar has distorted the election process. He believes that neither Iowa nor New Hampshire are representative of the American electorate and that it is absurd to have their citizens play the same role over and over every four years. Raymond Strather declared that the process demeans the presidency. Leslie Stahl of NBC says the elections have become an industry in Iowa and New Hampshire. Robert Beckel, the gentleman who handled Walter Mondale's campaign, agrees that the election process has gotten out of hand. He says the process is so long and so demeaning that it shapes, not enhances, the candidates.[2]

The strain placed on candidates and funds by having thirty-five primaries stretching from February 20th to June 5th has stimulated a series of reform proposals. One proposal set forth by the Hunt Commission (North Carolina Governor James Hunt headed the study) would set twelve weeks aside in which all delegates must be chosen. Others say the long campaign period will show who has the physical stamina, the mental toughness, the political instincts, the quality staff and organization that will ensure a winner—provided, of course, the skeleton closet remains empty.

Disgusted with having the citizens of Iowa and New Hampshire whittle the potential candidates down for the rest of the nation, Democratic leaders in the South decided Super Tuesday would be their chance to put two cents into the nominating process early on. In 1988 the first twenty-state southern primary was scheduled for March 8th. (Not all participating states are in the South.) But with so many delegates committed early, if trouble comes up later a party could easily find itself in a poor situation without the flexibility it needs.

Despite all faults the 1980s have come close to fulfilling the American ideal of mass participation in the political process. Few would disagree that current election procedures are an improvement over the old secret deals and smoke-filled rooms—and the parties have survived.

The Role Of TV

In her 1971 book, *The Case Against Direct Election of the President*, Judith Best is persuasive when she states that:

> The prospects are that the direct-election plan would increase the incidence of party splits, encourage the development of minor parties, undermine party control over the crucial task of nomination, postpone compromise, simplify and dramatize issues, increase the importance of homogeneous regions and one-party states, disturb the geographic party leaders and encourage the formation of doctrinaire and single-issue parties.[3]

Television and mobility have all but ended one-party areas[4] where, in the past, because of the winner-take-all feature of our current election process, even a second party has considered effort spent campaigning there useless. With proper TV coverage no effort is useless; all comers are possible viable candidates. In a state as large and populated as California, television is the most efficient way to reach the greatest number of people, although "reaching" does not guarantee acceptance. It is doubtful that one can exaggerate the importance of television coverage anywhere in the nation. Many jokes have been made about the plastic or blow-dried politician trained for the media, but television coverage is no joke. Joe Biden used TV to his advantage during the Bork hearings when he kept witnesses favoring Robert Bork's nomination waiting over six hours while he stretched out the testimonies of such anti-Bork illuminaries as William Coleman, Barbara Jordan and Andrew Young for the benefit of the evening news shows.

Paul Starobin of *Congressional Quarterly* reported that Senator John Danforth of Missouri admitted that

> The electronic media formed an "exceptionally important part of our national life—especially for officials ... We will drop anything ... for a morning talk show so we can speak for five minutes or less.[5]

The 38-year-old legislation known as the Fairness Doctrine requires broadcasters to cover matters of public importance and to provide opposing viewpoints. The print media is not so regulated but the discrimination was said to be justified because of the scarcity of broadcast frequencies. The same scarcity does not exist today when the nation has 10,128 radio stations, 1,611 TV stations and only 1,657 daily newspapers. Early in 1987 Congress passed a measure intended to make the Fairness Doctrine not merely a regulation but the law of the land, but the measure was vetoed by President Reagan in June.

The Meredith Corporation, a broadcast group in Des Moines, was cited by the Federal Communications Commission (FCC) for airing advertisements promoting the construction of a nuclear power plant. The corporation sued and a federal appeals court remanded the case to the FCC with instructions to consider the constitutional arguments set forth by Meredith. The FCC found that the Fairness Doctrine had a chilling effect on the coverage of important issues, was unnecessary as it would be in the broadcasters' best interest to broadcast such activities as good business practice (rival stations would do so) and it violated first amendment rights. Besides, with or without the Fairness Doctrine, the equal-time rule, which requires broadcasters to allow equal time to candidates competing for public office, is still in effect and airing opposing views of non-candidates continues to be the policy choice of most large stations.

On August 4, 1987, the FCC voted 4 to 0 to abolish the Fairness Doctrine, but Congress would not let it go at that. The ink was barely dry on the FCC's decision than so-called public interest groups were claiming minority viewpoints would no longer get a fair hearing. Ralph Nader called the decision "FCC's darkest hour" and Senator Ernest Hollings, chairman of the Senate Commerce, Science & Transportation Committee, declared the FCC's determination was "wrong-headed, misguided and illogical" and set about to undo it with some conniving that deserves to be spotlighted.

It was reported that in October 1987 a vote was taken in the Senate Commerce Committee without first notifying opponents that the Fairness Doctrine was even to be considered. To add to the feeling of subterfuge, the committee changed rooms several times before voting. The outcome was a decision to make the Fairness Doctrine law and to assess what is estimated to amount to $340 million in annual taxes on sales of broadcast stations and other users of radio frequencies.[6]

But there is more fancy footwork. The Senate is debating campaign-finance reform that would restrict negative broadcast advertising. Incumbents are vulnerable to the use of their voting records by challengers and there is little doubt they are hurt most by negative advertising. If a challenger can't make an effective attack, incumbents will always win. It would be unconstitutional to ban negative advertising outright, so S2, the Senate's main election reform package in 1987, would require that to qualify for public financing (voluntary, of course), a candidate must stay on the air during at least 50 percent of any TV commercial and personally deliver any attack made on an opponent. It is likely such an attack would boomerang. But then negative advertising is likely to boomerang anyway even without such fine tuned regulation.

Senator Evans has a proposal to force candidates to appear throughout TV or radio ads. Of course, a candidate is only *forced* (Remember the Constitution?) if he wants to qualify for the special low political ad rates that broadcasters are *already forced* (What Constitution?) to offer candidates. Other proposals go even further by requiring candidates to notify opponents of an attack or to *make broadcasters give* (Private property, Comrade?) candidates free TV or radio time to respond. Even defining an "attack" is a problem. S2 authorizes federal payments to candidates "attacked" by independent campaign committees so the candidates can buy time to respond. Congressman David Obey would provide free television time (apparently he hasn't yet learned that *nothing* is *free*) for a candidate to respond to the "attacks" of independent groups. Ostensibly, if forcing broadcasters to cough up the needed television time free of charge is unacceptable to the non-socialist majority in the country, then they'll just have to pay for their ideals and, like it or not, fund the television response time with tax dollars. (Calling tax dollars public financing doesn't change the facts.) The public would foot the bill for any amount over $5,000 needed to fend off an independent "attack," says generous Mr. Obey.

Those in favor of providing candidates with *free* air time use the same old tired argument, "Other countries do it." Of course, many of those countries are socialist and also do not have a first amendment guarantee of free speech to worry about. In a *Wall Street Journal* article on November 18, 1986, Arthur Schlesinger, Jr., pointed to recent elections in Brazil as an example for America to emulate. For two months before the election ". . . every Brazilian television network gave the parties free time every night from 8:30 to 9:30."

On pages 149-151 of her 1983 book *Politics and Money*, Elizabeth Drew advocates so-called *free* air time for politicians. She says:

> The broadcasters would oppose it, for obvious reasons; but the ownership of broadcasting stations is among the most lucrative businesses in America . . . stations in the large media markets are among the most profitable . . . (candidates) could be given air time without great financial risk to the stations.

As if the fact that stations are profitable has absolutely anything whatsoever to do with the principle involved here, unless of course, Ms. Drew is willing to concede that the principle is *deep pockets*.

I have my doubts about requiring a business to provide services without compensation. I don't wholeheartedly subscribe to the old saw that "the air waves belong to the people." Someone's energy and capital makes it possible to harness those airwaves. My other dilemma concerns the manner in which that time should be acquired. When one is in a position of power, as our elected officials are, it is easy to forget that this is first and foremost a free country. (*Free* as in liberty.) It is inconceivable that every station would *willingly* provide, even for a fee, prime time for political debates, especially when citizen apathy is high, as evidenced by the already-mentioned fact that almost two-thirds of those eligible to vote chose to ignore the 1986 elections entirely. Just consider the ratings a maverick station could pile up by showing *anything* else if all other channels were covering the candidates between 8:30-9:30 every night for two months.

In a collective economy public needs enjoy the same sort of built-in priority that private consumption enjoys in a capitalist economy. In the former all resources are available to the public sector and private consumption is restricted; in the latter public services are restricted to claims against the private sector—or should be. Unfortunately, as we are only too aware, the annual deficit in this country is a direct result of our elected officials trying to have it both ways and ending up spending more than they are willing to tax.

The Cost Of Campaigns

Recent reform proposals have centered around the cost of elections, congressional as well as presidential. In 1974 it was estimated that the cost per vote was 67 cents; ten years later, in 1984, the estimate had risen to $7.74 per vote.

According to campaign expert Professor Herbert Alexander of the University of Southern California, it will cost approximately $400 million to elect the President in 1988, up from $325 million in 1984. The 1968 presidential campaign cost $91 million, the 1972 presidential campaign cost $137.8 million, the 1976 presidential campaign cost $159.7 million and the 1980 presidential campaign cost $275 million, including primaries, conventions and general election expenses. Over one billion dollars was spent in electing people to all offices during the 1980 campaign. That makes Elizabeth Drew's contention that congressional campaigns can be financed by raising the check-off on tax returns to $2 ("Another dollar a year seems a small price to pay") hilarious. One would have to ignore the foregoing facts as reported by the League of Women Voters and believe an anonymous estimate relayed to us by Ms. Drew:

> One estimate, based on recent campaign costs, is that the system would cost about eighty million dollars per two-year election cycle.[7]

Although it is true that the exact sum spent by either party is unknown, nevertheless "self-financed" gobbledygook is only for those who believe in Tooth Fairies, Santa Claus and that Social Security benefits are self-financed. Keep the "eighty million dollars per two-year election cycles" figure in mind as you hear the tallies from dollars spent on the 1988 election. When they try and convince you "it won't cost *that* much, you *know* the estimates are low.

Public financing was intended to lessen the impact of private funds and to put candidates on an equal financial footing. The changes were meant to give state and local parties a say commensurate with the input of special national interests. Congress felt an obligation to help the parties encourage grassroots participation.

According to Elizabeth Drew, "Even by a conservative count Reagan's advantage over Carter in funds was greater than Nixon's over Humphrey in 1968, and almost as great as Nixon's over McGovern in 1972." Bad laws don't help. People will do what they want to do and finding a way around such laws only breeds contempt for law. Detailed laws are bad laws, for all contingencies can never be covered and splitting hairs becomes an obsession on both sides. For instance, according to Richard Stout, former press secretary to John Anderson, no report has to be made to the Federal Election Commission (FEC) when forming a foundation to study issues, but a report must be filed when forming an exploratory committee. There is a subtle distinction between a fund-raiser appeal and a solicitation for a contribution on behalf of a candidate.

The election law is detailed, allowing two cents per voter per state to be spent by the national parties in a presidential campaign (amounting to $4.6 million in 1980 per party). Actually, the Republicans spent $64.6 million and the Democrats $13.9 million by knowing their way around the current election laws and labeling expenditures accordingly. Ms. Drew's concern that "the real point is that a path around the intent of the law has been found"[8] is understandable, but it is the law, not the men clever enough to get around the law, that is at fault. Our officials are elected to make it possible for the people to do what they want to do without undue interference. Ridiculous government road blocks are easily and disdainfully circumvented.

A candidate used to raise about a third of his campaign funds before the election and could wait until the year of the election to raise the other two-thirds. The many early primaries and caucuses has reversed the ratio in 1988. It may be that our campaign laws will ensure that no one is ever elected to federal office who cares two hoots about deficit spending.

Those who recognize the dangers inherent in deficits are prevented from running. Donald Rumsfeld said in the summer of 1987:

> As a matter of principle, I will not run a deficit. The personal regret I feel in not making the race is dwarfed by my distaste for the idea of not being able to meet the financial obligations of a long, intense and expensive campaign.

No front-runner in history had ever been in as tough financial shape as Gary Hart was even ante-Donna Rice.[9] Mr. Hart led the Democratic polls but lagged in fund raising. He began the '88 race owing $1.3 million to his 1984 Campaign Committee. However Federal Election Committee files show "nineteen former presidential candidates, including John Connally and Jimmy Carter, still owe about $9 million."[10] And don't forget Senator John Glenn's mammoth debt still on the books from his 1984 run. Candidates and their families, as was stated earlier, are only allowed to contribute a maximum of $50,000 to their own campaigns, post-election as well as pre-election, which makes it that much harder to get out of debt. S2, the 1987 reform measure before the Senate, wants to make it even harder by lowering contributions from a candidate or his family from $50,000 to $20,000.

On September 22, 1987, the FEC announced that the Biden Campaign had qualified for matching funds from the U.S. Treasury and reaffirmed that Gary Hart's campaign did not. The Biden Campaign submitted documents covering $146,083 in contributions from 790 people in twenty-two states. The election regulations state that a candidate must raise at least $5,000 in at least twenty states in contributions of $250 or less from individuals in order to qualify for federal funds. The matching money applies to those individual contributions of $250 or less.

Gary Hart's Campaign failed to file the necessary documents to qualify before he dropped out of the race on May 8, 1987. Possibly his staff had other things on their mind at that time. If a candidate goes into debt, as Mr. Hart did, because he was courageous, idealistic or merely ambitious enough to make a try for what he believed in, should he be penalized to the extent mandated by our Rube Goldberg financing regulations? Current law prevents deficits from being paid off by large donors or a political party. This discourages fiscally conservative, but otherwise qualified, candidates.

Luckily Joe Biden learned from Gary Hart's mistake and quit the race for the Democratic presidential nomination only after the FEC ruled that he had qualified for federal money. The Biden Campaign had raised just under $4 million by mid-September 1987. Many contributors would like to know what happens to that money and why the federal government should add to it when there is no longer a campaign in existence.

Common Cause has referred to the old practice of taking the war chest into retirement as spoils, as kind of a "political IRA." According to federal election campaign laws, if they were in office prior to 1980, members of Congress may, upon retirement, spend any remaining campaign funds for "any lawful purpose." (How vague can you get?) However, PL96-187, passed in 1979, prohibits incumbents sworn into office after January 7, 1980, to convert campaign funds to personal use when they retire. This encourages an incumbent to spend his campaign chest rather than hoard it.

Former House Speaker Thomas P. O'Neill Jr., who retired at the end of the 99th Congress, spent, according to FEC records, $98,634 in an attempt to empty his campaign chest during his last year or so in office. A good deal of the money went for sporting events and other entertainment, including thousands of dollars to restaurants for himself and guests. He also contributed heavily to the campaigns of fellow democrats, charities and his church. Too bad he didn't offer some of it to the U.S. Treasury to reduce the public debt. Thousands of people do every year, you know, and according to the Bureau of Public Debt, gifts for FY1987 totaled $1,052,022.19 through June 1987.[11]

Unfortunately when Gary Hart retired he had fewer funds left over because, boy oh boy, did he have a place to put the money. Most of the $12,407 reported as leftover funds upon his retirement from the Senate went to retire the debt of his 1984 Presidential Campaign Committee.

The Dukakis campaign's involvement with the elimination of Joe Biden from the list of 1988 presidential contenders in October 1987 does not seem to have affected the governor's ability to raise money. At the time of Senator Biden's decision to withdraw from the race, Governor Dukakis had already accumulated more dollars than any other Democratic hopeful. His chief fund-raiser, Robert Farmer, set records in 1983 and that history allows the governor to take a principled stand when it comes to money.

> Mr. Dukakis insists he won't accept money from political-action committees, Massachusetts lobbyists or children under eighteen (who are commonly used by others as conduits for wealthy parents who want to give more than the $1,000 allowed by federal law). He won't take more than $100 from a Massachusetts state employee.[12]

Wealthy Greek Americans and others associated with big business were reportedly rallying to the governor's aid, but ironically small business groups withheld their support because of legislation requiring Massachusetts businesses over a certain size to offer health insurance to employees. The irony is that the governor identifies with the small businessman in many of his campaign appearances.

According to *Fortune*, the Democrats may need to raise $5 million each early on and the Republicans $10 million each.[13] It seems that meeting those goals will be no trick at all for either Michael Dukakis or Pat Robertson. More than three months before declaring his candidacy, Pat Robertson had amassed a campaign chest of $7 million, which in June 1987 was almost double the contributions that had been made to the Bush campaign.

Jesse Jackson is not looking for money to win the nomination for him in 1988 (he only hopes to raise a modest $3 million) but is counting on grassroots support. But although that strategy might work for the Reverend Jackson, no other candidate is willing to try it. It is safe to say that campaign managers are more likely to turn to bizarre methods of raising funds than to accept limitations. During the 1980 race Richard Gephardt's current finance chairman, Terence McAuliffe, wrestled a live alligator to raise $10,000 for Jimmy Carter. It is still unclear if he intends to do the same for the Congressman.[14]

The Democrats, who have generally proved less adept than Republicans at attracting small contributions through the mail, have come to rely on the generosity of Wall Street liberals. Walter Burnham of MIT refers to "Limousine liberalism" as a coalition between the "guilt-ridden rich and the dependent poor."[15] Despite Republican reverence for the entrepreneur, many self-made men are Democrats largely because they remember their modest beginnings and sincerely desire to help others up the ladder. Many who have inherited wealth let their guilt feelings drive them to liberal causes and share a benign view of government's role in furthering equality and economic justice (however "equality and economic justice" is defined).

Although Democrats are still a minority on Wall Street (75 percent voted for Reagan against Carter)[16] New York City itself has been the Democrats' territory for decades. Although wealthy, the Wall Streeters are not oppressed by regulation and have found it makes little difference to their business whether a Democrat or Republican holds the White House. A fee on securities transactions helps pay the costs of the Security and Exchange Commission (SEC), so although PAC money may have caught the interest of those in Congress who blocked a Reagan administration proposal for a similar fee to defray the costs of the federal Commodity Futures Trading Commission, contributions came mostly from the Commodity Exchanges themselves in New York and Chicago.

The Need For Reform

Elizabeth Drew claims that 1988 presidential hopeful Representative Richard Gephardt told her several years ago that:

> If you have the need to raise three or four hundred thousand dollars, you're taking an enormous amount of the members' time just to raise the money. And, whether it's conclusive or not, it has to have an increasing impact on the legislative outcome. Part of it's psychological. A kind of fever takes over. Members hear that someone else is raising five hundred thousand dollars, and they think they have to raise five hundred thousand dollars, and soon everyone thinks he has to raise five hundred thousand dollars, and it's disruptive to the public process.[17]

She also quotes Congressman James Shannon as saying:

> We on the Democratic side came out of the 1980 election and saw we got clobbered, in large part because of money. So the whole subject has come out of the closet. There has been all too much discussion

> around here about how what we do in the House and on our committees is going to affect our ability to raise money.[18]

Ms. Drew is looking for an electoral process that would give us the best kind of representation, and who isn't?

> My view is that if the money represents an unfair advantage it ought to be eliminated. Where is the ethics or morality in saying the system ought to be maintained because it benefits you, if the advantage is inherently unfair?[19]

One might counter by asking where the ethics or morality lies in claiming a system ought to be junked because it hurts you? Nothing is "inherently unfair." Fairness is a judgment call and always relative.

On page eighty-nine of *Politics and Money*, Elizabeth Drew quotes a lobbyist:

> When issues are not issues of conscience . . . and their (Congress person's) district or state doesn't have a clear interest, if you (lobbyist) raise enough money you can keep them from doing anything.

Why not? Under the conditions described, a party or parties interested enough "to raise enough money" should prevail, though one wonders why reason and intellectual persuasion shouldn't work just as well. Power frequently leads to blackmail in one form or another. Ms. Drew says the "grass roots" aspects of lobbyists are nonsense[20] and wants readers to believe the struggle in Washington, D.C., is between those with money, whom she indiscriminately refers to as lobbyists, and constituents. She is unlikely to concede that those with money are sometimes constituents—it is not always an either/or scenario.

Richard Gephardt told Elizabeth Drew back in 1982 that

> It shouldn't be possible for labor or management or environmentalists or anyone else to have this importance in the electoral process. That's not the way it should work.[21]

Yet one wonders how the system *should* work if groups of citizens with interests are not to be allowed input. Labor, management, environmentalists, even government, are all made up of individual citizens and in their desire to make their point zealots hope we will forget this fact. Exaggerated or otherwise, distorted information often leads to major and unnecessary remedies being applied to minor ailments that, if left alone, would often cure themselves. Ms. Drew says:

> A candidate entering politics now must systematically make the rounds of the interest groups and win their approval, and their money, by declaring . . . in favor of the legislative goals they seek. He is imprisoned before he ever reaches Congress. Once there, he must worry about maintaining the groups' support or about finding other groups to support him or about casting some vote that might cause monetary retaliation. He must measure every action in terms of what the financial consequences to himself might be. The difference between that and corruption is unclear.[22]

Governor Dukakis and others who refuse PAC money are proof that Ms. Drew's assertion is not necessarily true. How can Ms. Drew call being responsive to the people's interests (What else are "interest groups"?) a form of corruption? Not being responsive is more likely to add up to corruption in my book. So what to do?

Richard Nixon raised approximately $17 million from 124 contributors who gave a minimum of $50,000 each for the 1972 race. Over $1.7 million was raised from people who later received ambassadorships. Cause and effect? I admit it looked suspicious and who would not agree that the merest appearance of impropriety in our elected officials should be avoided? The Code of Professional Responsibility adopted by the American Bar Association in 1969 states that lawyers "should avoid even the appearance of impropriety"[23] because the appearance can be just as damaging as actual impropriety to public confidence in and respect for the law. It would seem that congressmen, many of whom are attorneys, should adhere to at least as strict an ethical code in carrying out their public functions.

Ms. Drew reports that Tom Downey, congressman from New York, claims used car dealers "bought their way to happiness" by spending $675,000 in the 1980 campaign to influence congressional votes to overturn the requirements of the Federal Trade Commission (FTC) that used car dealers list the known major defects of an automobile.[24] On the face of it, who would be against such a requirement? But there were concrete reasons to be against that piece of legislation and people other than car dealers thought it was a poor law. It is therefore unfair to claim that the votes were influenced by money when there was more to it than that. It is like saying if you are against Jesse Jackson's platform you are against blacks; a simplistic knee-jerk reaction made without sufficient inquiry. What Ms. Drew has left unsaid is just as misleading as what is inferred. She made a great deal out of the fact that the attempt by Congress to overturn the used-car regulations was overruled by an appeals court in October 1982, as if controversy between the legislative and judicial branches of government was a novelty. Elliott Levitas of Georgia has sponsored legislation permitting Congress to overturn agency regulation—so far without success. But to claim "moves to overturn agency regulations certainly do attract a lot of money" in an off-hand manner as Ms. Drew does, is to throw fuel on the fire. It is neither new or radical to question the legitimacy of regulatory agencies. Are they to be treated as a fourth branch of government? Are the agency heads and other bureaucrats to be given the same credibility as our elected representatives? To whom are they accountable?

Syndicated columnist George Will told David Brinkley's television audience on April 6, 1986:

> Lobbying is petitioning for redress of grievances ... There is no substitute in government, in the end, for trusting the integrity of your office-holders. Let them be trusted to listen to people and make the best case, and if they can't do that change the office-holders.

The only remedy consistent with our form of government is to have the citizenry act as watch dog. Minute regulation is not the answer. If an official votes in a manner inconsistent with his observed philosophy he should be called into account. If he is unable to explain his conversion to the point of view for which he voted to the satisfaction of the questioner, then, and only then, should the lure of money be suspected and he should be voted out of office pronto. However, to ascribe money as the motivation for all political acts and therefore to indiscriminately bind politicians hand and foot with detailed rules and regulations is to act irresponsibly. Even worse, it is to deprive the citizenry of this nation of the role the Founders intended.

Author John Updike told *Time* magazine (1987 Constitutional issue):

> The Constitution, as I understand it, trusts me with my own life within a set of laws and checks and balances that relieves us all from the need for great men and asks only, for our government, decent men.

Let's hope Mr. Updike is right, for it looks like even decent men are getting harder to find; most of them want no part of the onerous campaigns.

Attempts At Reform

In 1907 Theodore Roosevelt proposed public financing of campaigns, and this suggestion was responsible for the 1907 Tillman Act, which prohibited banks and corporations from contributing to federal campaigns. Although in 1909 William Howard Taft sponsored a bill requiring that political campaign expenses be made public, it took the Teapot Dome Scandal of 1921 to get something done. It led to the Federal Corruption Practices Act of 1925 requiring reporting of campaign receipts and expenditures. Unfortunately it was easy to circumvent and was rarely enforced.

The 1971 Federal Election Campaign Act (FECA) was the first election reform in forty-seven years. It established a Federal Elections Commission (FEC) to enforce the law, consisting of three Democrats, three Republicans and two non-affiliated members. The Act took effect on April 7, 1971, so you can imaging the scramble for funds that took place before that date. In order to qualify for federal matching fund, candidates were required to set up committees in at least twenty states and raise a threshold amount to show they were not merely frivolous candidates: $250,000 for the Presidency, $125,000 for the Senate and $10,000 for the House. The contributions were to be in increments of $100 or less ($250 for presidential campaigns) and loans and services would not count.

FECA limited a candidate's (and his family's) contributions to his own campaign to $50,000 and put spending limits on media advertising. This later restriction was repealed in 1974. FECA mandated that campaigns spending over $1,000 had to establish a political committee with disclosure of contributions and expenditures. Enforcement, according to the Act, was to be by the Clerk of the House and Secretary of the Senate for congressional candidates and by the Comptroller General for presidential candidates.

By the terms of the 1971 Act, radio and television broadcasters were required to charge political candidates the lowest commercial advertising rates. In the 1980s the mandate applied only to pre-election periods. FECA said labor unions and corporations couldn't contribute directly to any campaign but they could solicit, establish and administer "segregated funds" (PACs). The reform also provided for $1 check-off on tax refunds for taxpayers to fund presidential campaigns in the general election. According to the League of Women Voters:

> Approximately 25 to 30 percent of taxpayers avail themselves of this opportunity ... The 1971 Act forbade major party candidates who chose public financing from accepting private contributions.[25]

If all taxpayers used the check-off, based on 1971 figures, $74 million would be raised. In 1973 a committee estimated the cost of public financing for presidential elections to be $89 million, far more than Ms. Drew told us about in her 1983 book. Perhaps best of all, FECA forced congressional committees not involving national security to be held in the open. However Ms. Drew says this

> has strengthened the lobbyists' hand and reduced the legislators' ability to legislate ... Now the lobbyists sit right in the committee room keeping score. Sometimes they even signal to a member how to vote on a certain amendment.[26]

I find it hard to believe a member could keep his seat if the press reported the acts Ms. Drew feels certain occur. In November 1973 the Senate passed a bill which would have provided public money in congressional elections and presidential primaries, as well as requiring that only federal funds be used in presidential general elections. The intent was to reduce the influence of wealthy individuals in the election process; however, the House rejected the bill.

Many reforms were instituted in the 1974 amendments to FECA (PL93-443) which were signed into law on October

15, 1974 by President Gerald Ford. Spending limits had been set up by the 1925 Federal Corrupt Practices Act but, as was said, they were never enforced and were repealed in the FECA of 1971, making October 15, 1974, the date of the first *real* spending limits in this country. Unfortunately a restriction on spending prevents challengers from achieving the name recognition and platform for their ideas that is already possessed by incumbents.

The 1974 amendments established a six member bipartisan Federal Election Commission (FEC) but this time two commissioners were to be appointed by the President, two by the Speaker and two by the President Pro Tempore of the Senate. Individual contributions were limited to $1,000 per candidate for each primary and each general or run-off election, with a total contribution allowed of no more than $25,000 to *all* candidates. The reform limited contributions from political committees and national or state party committees to $5,000 per candidate for each election and set a limit of $1,000 for expenditures on behalf of a candidate as long as made *independently* of the candidate. A $10 million total spending limit was set for each qualified major party candidate in a presidential primary race with a $20 million each limit set for total spending by the nominees in the general election, to be pegged to the CPI. The 1974 amendment further provided that federal funds of $2 million, adjusted to CPI, be given to each major political party in order to cover the cost of the national nominating conventions. It was the intent of the 1974 amendments to strengthen the major parties and prevent a proliferation of splinter parties. The amendment also changed slightly the system of matching funds for presidential candidates in primary elections. Funds would be allowed only after a candidate raised $100,000 himself, in amounts of at least $5,000 per state, in twenty or more states consisting of individual contributions of $250 or less. The law required candidates to establish a principal committee through which all contributions and expenditures would be funneled and reported. It also required detailed reports be filed with the FEC. As in 1971 (FECA), labor unions, government contractors and corporations were allowed to establish segregated funds for political purposes only (PACs).

James Buckley, Eugene McCarthy, the New York American Civil Liberties Union, Stewart Mott and *Human Events* all brought suit, contending restrictions on spending in the 1974 election law were unconstitutional. David Keene, a Libertarian lawyer, handled the case.[27] The Supreme Court said the 1974 election reform violated the first amendment rights of citizens by restricting their spending to $1,000 for any election. The Court equated freedom of speech with contributions of money and found that limits on campaign spending are valid only if voluntary. If a candidate decided to forego public financing and its controls, fine, only his opponent would get *double* the public financing amounts normally alloted and have all limits lifted as well. ("Do as I say, OR ELSE—and some call it *choice*!) The Court ruled also that independent expenditures were to be unlimited (there hadn't been any to speak of prior to 1974) and upheld contribution limits on individuals and PACs, the provision for public financing as well as the rules requiring disclosure of contributions and expenditures. It ruled the Commission had to be appointed *solely* by the President with advice and consent of the Senate.

Again in 1976 President Ford signed amendments which changed the 1974 law by:

1) setting a limit of $5,000 per year for individual contributions to PACs and $20,000 per year to the national committee of a political party;

2) restricting multi-candidate committees to donations of no more than $15,000/year to a national committee of a political party;

3) allowing no more than $50,000 to be spent by a candidate or family on his campaign if the candidate intended to receive public funds;

4) mandating the establishment of an independent Federal Election Commission (FEC).

But our legislators keep amending amendments. The 1979 reform, among other things:

1) said local party organizations didn't have to report activity costing $5,000 or less;

2) declared services up to $1,000 worth don't count as contributions to the candidate;

3) stipulated that a candidate's name appear in all campaign committee titles;

4) required frequent reports of donors and amounts of any contributions exceeding $200;

5) required reporting of independent expenditures of $250 or more;

6) allowed the national parties to spend unlimited amounts to get-out-the-vote, including bumper stickers, brochures and such expenses;

7) upped federal contributions to the major parties from $2 million to $3 million each in order to cover the cost of the National Nominating Convention.

But even after all the reforms it is possible for a single individual to donate up to $50,000 to influence an election. What about the overall limits of $25,000 to all federal candidates during an election cycle? That can be circumvented by considering the election cycle as two years. The first year a person could give $25,000 to candidates and the second year give $20,000 to a party and $5,000 to PACs. So the limits on contributions are much higher than it would appear at first glance.

If the whole truth be told, the Democrats thought the 1979 change would give them an advantage. They reasoned that since union dues and other soft money could be funneled into getting out the vote, they would more readily rival the Republicans in ability to spend. However, they forgot the Republicans weren't going to sit still while the Democrats played catch-up with soft money. The Republicans soon began raising soft money on a grand scale befitting their skill in this area. Soft money is primarily used to free hard money and is most often used to raise funds by the Democrats and to get around limits by Republicans. It can be used diversely: for volunteer expenses, up to $30 per day per volunteer, or to build a four-story building. In 1980 $2.2 million was spent by the Republicans on the Eisenhower Center in Washington, D.C., to house the National Republican Congressional Committee.

Instead of individuals contributing directly to candidates, one more step was added; individuals contributed to their parties and the parties directed the money to states where it would do the most good. In 1980 Democrats contributed $590,000 to their Senate candidates and Republicans contributed $5 million to theirs. In 1982 the Democrats contributed $2.3 million to their Senate candidates but by 1982 the Republicans had raised their contributions to $9.2 million.

Questions have arisen as to whether money to be spent on the state level can be raised in nationwide solicitations and also whether ads to support a party in one state that are clearly and knowingly broadcast in another, are legal? For example, Illinois money has been responsible for broadcasts which reach into and influence Indiana voters. Unlimited funds can now be given by individuals and corporations, ostensibly to a state, but in practice to help any specified candidate. Money raised under this guise is not a contribution and is not reported, at least at the federal level, however state requirments vary. So the 1974 reform, which aimed at wiping out large individual and corporate contributions, was in effect nullified by the 1979 fix.

After Buckley v. Valeo (1976) the flow of money wasn't stopped, only rechanneled; more proof that people will do what they want to do and if frustrated will find a way around any obstacle. Independent committees became a new route for soft money, as the law allows unlimited independent expenditures by PACs and individuals to support or oppose as long as there is no direct connection with a candidate's campaign. The law stipulates that independent organizations should not consult with a candidate. It's an absurd regulation. A friend of a friend could, and often does, "consult." Sometimes the candidate and the independent committee use the same consultants. There is no such thing as truly independent spending. The press relays all the information needed to coordinate efforts on a candidate's behalf, albeit unwittingly. If a national party intentionally gives a candidate the results of a poll that could prove useful, it is considered a contribution but on the other hand nothing prevents them from giving a reporter the same information.

One independent committee, the Congressional Club of Jesse Helms, Senator from North Carolina, said in its brochures: "As an independent campaign, Americans for Reagan can spend an unlimited amount of money on behalf of Ronald Reagan." It was distinguishing itself from PACs and their limitations. Independent committees run ads ostensibly to help the local party but which in fact may help the national effort. They pay for state and local candidates with corporate contributions, and if federal campaigns are helped thereby, well . . .

During the 1980 primary and general elections independent expenditures for Carter amounted to $46,000; for Reagan, $246,000. All in all Ronald Reagan attracted $12.2 million. $1.7 million was spent by the Naitonal Conservative PAC (NCPAC), whereas the Congressional Club spent $4.1 million on Reagan's behalf. That was the year (1980) that *Common Cause* sued four independent committees working on Ronald Reagan's behalf. The case reached the Supreme Court which in January 1982 split 4 to 4 over the question of constitutionality.[28]

Elizabeth Drew talks about breaking the spirit of the law while attempting to hold to the letter and seems to suggest more letters (detailed stricter regulations) will take care of the spirit. Another suggestion of hers is to have any candidate who benefits from the actions of an independent committee assume responsibility for the committee's actions.

But independent committees are not the prime target of campaign reformers who prefer to center their main assault on PACs.

PACs

In the forties Labor established Political Action Committees (PACs) in order to offset contributions by wealthy individuals. The American Medical Association and other professional and business groups soon followed suit. For instance the Association of Manufacturers established BIPAC (Business Industry Political Action Committee). The AFL-CIO began COPE (Committee On Political Education) which contributed $900,000 to the 1982 race, while other PACs controlled by the AFL-CIO unions contributed $1 million.

Eighty percent of all PACs don't solicit the general public and are referred to as "connected PACs." They are organized by and affiliated with corporations and unions which must keep PAC money in "separated segregated funds." The more regulated an industry is the more likely it is to have a PAC. Non-connected PACs raise money from the public.

Now days campaigns have PAC directors who coordinate solicitations from PACs and offer what they refer to as PAC-Kits which explain the views of a specific PAC.

At the end of 1974 there were approximately 600 PACs, 89 of them corporate. Eight years later there were 3,400 PACs, 1,497 corporate and 350 controlled by labor. The PACs spent $23 million in 1976 and $80 million in 1982. The 1982 average winner of a House seat received one-third of his campaign funds from PACs.

If PACs can qualify as multi-candidate committees, they are allowed to increase their contribution limits to $5,000 per federal candidate per election, otherwise the $1,000 limit applies. To qualify they must prove they have been in existence at least six months, have received contributions from at least fifty persons and contributed to a minimum of five federal candidates. PAC limits are for each primary, run-off and general election, plus PACs can give up to $5,000 to an unlimited number of other PACs. The possibilities are limitless. It is good strategy to run a primary debt, since a person who wants to give in a general election can give twice as much if the primary campaign still needs contributions. *Common Cause* would like to see the contributions by PACs cut in half by changing the law to allow multi-candidate PACs only $5,000 per election cycle instead of the current maximum of $15,000 each when primary, run-off and general elections are all taken into account.

Alaska's senior senator, Ted Stevens, has an amendment which would cut the current $5,000 PAC (per election) contribution limit to $3,000 (per election) and raise limits on individuals from $1,000 to $1,500 (per election). Remember what per election signifies. Currently individuals can really contribute $3,000 not $1,000 to a candidate—*$1,000 in the primary, $1,000 in any run off and $1,000 in the general election*. Merely getting on the ballot for a general election counts as a primary, thereby ensuring at least a $2,000 contribution limit.

David Boren of Oklahoma was a sponsor of S655, which was adopted by a Senate vote of 69 to 30 on August 12, 1986, but failed to make it through the House. It would have, among other things, lowered PAC contributions from $5,000 to $3,000 per candidate per election and provided for up to 80 percent public financing for Senate campaigns. According to S655, Senate candidates could qualify for federal funds by raising the lower of $250,000 or 20 percent of their states' limit in small contributions. Eighty percent of the funds raised must come from in-state. Once qualified a candidate would be awarded his state's limit minus what he had already raised. Such a plan would have cut down on the time and effort now required to raise campaign funds. Opponents cited the regulations as one more set of loopholes to master and pointed out that, besides, the plan would unfairly favor incumbents.

Money to gain a nomination is largely raised from individuals rather than PACs, but in 1980 the presidential candidates received $1.56 million (pre-convention) in direct PAC contributions which didn't qualify for federal matching funds. The 1980 general election was funded with public money, $29.4 million each distributed to Jimmy Carter and Ronald Reagan.

PACs used to give to entrenched incumbents, which meant no one could ever afford to challenge. In 1980 that changed and PACs helped defeat many incumbents; in fact business PACs directed approximately one-third of their contributions to challengers that year. In a continuing effort to nullify the incumbency barrier, a 63,000 member organization (AMPAC) contributed over $4 million to various challengers during the 1986 campaign, but many other PACs did not and in 1986 PACs ended up favoring House incumbents over challengers six to one.

Mike Synar of Oklahoma, Don Glickman of Kansas and Jim Leach of Iowa co-sponsored a bill in 1982 which would have allowed House candidates to accept a limit of $75 thousand from all PACs and Senate candidates anywhere from $75 thousand to $500 thousand according to the size of their state. Congressman Leach fears a dominance by big business and labor with local constituents having less and less to say about how our policy is formed. For that reason he is a strong supporter of public financing of congressional as well as presidential campaigns.

As of June 30, 1987, ten House members reported having received more than half a million dollars each and eleven Senators reported receipt of a million dollars or more, all for their 1988 reelection campaigns. According to FEC reports, for the first half of 1987 Democratic House and Senate members had raised almost double their Republican counterparts—$12.6 million to $6.4 million and had stockpiled a grand total of $94 million.

Four Democrats were among the top five recipients of PAC money in both the House and the Senate. The Senate leaders in order were Lloyd Bentsen of Texas, James Sasser of Tennessee, Robert Byrd of West Virginia and Donald Riegle of Michigan; the lone Republican who occupied the number three spot was Orrin Hatch of Utah. Over 70 percent of Senate Majority Leader Byrd's total receipts came from PACs, whereas top hoarder Lloyd Bentsen claimed that his $1,128,769 from PACs was less than 30 percent of his total receipts. Dan Rostenkowski of Illinois led the House in PAC receipts followed by Robert Matsui of California, William Gray of Pennsylvania and Byron Dorgan of North Dakota for the Democrats. A Republican, Minority Leader Bob Michel, took the number three spot on the House side and although $149,800 looks like peanuts compared to contributions to the Senators, it accounted for slightly more than 83 percent of Mr. Michel's total receipts.

It seems a lot of Senator Bentsen's money came from the same donors who had their funds returned after the fuss made over the $10,000 bacon and eggs Breakfast Club the Senator ran early in 1987. Why is Senator Bentsen so popular? You don't suppose it has anything to do with his chairmanship of the powerful Finance Committee where both tax and trade legislation is written? As for the others, aside from Senate Majority Leader Byrd and House Minority Leader Michel, we find that in the 100th Congress Senator Sasser serves on the Budget Committee, the Banking, Housing & Urban Affairs Committee and the Appropriations Committee where he chairs the Military Construction Subcommittee. Senator Riegle serves on the Budget Committee and chairs the Securities Subcommittee under the Banking Committee. Senator Hatch serves on Judiciary and Labor and Human Resources. Representatives Dorgan and Matsui serve on the powerful Ways & Means Committee which Mr. Rostenkowski chairs. Mr. Gray is chairman of the Budget Committee. Any questions?

Incumbents of both parties tend to raise money long before they need it, their sole reason being to frighten any would-be challengers.

The *Conservative Digest* estimates that the typical Senate freshman will be committed to raise $125,000 every month for the next six years to keep up with campaign costs and prepare for a challenge.

Congressman Dan Rostenkowski hasn't had a real challenge since his first run in 1958. No worries about retaining his seat but still he received $495,000 in 1982 and won with 84 percent of the vote. PACs see him as a sure thing. He once told Elizabeth Drew,

> Anyone who thinks of running against me knows two things: one, I get back to my district; two, I've got a fund. And if I had to raise a lot more, I could.[29]

No wonder Mr. Rostenkowski opposes public financing of campaigns—he doesn't need it.

Representative James Quillen of Tennessee, another safe incumbent, used half of his campaign funds ($250,000) toward the endowment of a chair that bears his name at Quillen-Dishner College of Medicine at East Tennessee University. How's that for gaining name recognition on a daily basis? Yes, the contribution met the test of benefiting the 1986 campaign. George Bush showed up and the picture of the two politicians together appeared all over Mr. Quillen's district as front page news.[30]

Expenditures under House rules are broad.[31] Any use of campaign funds that personally benefit the member rather than the campaign is not permitted. In practice anything can be found to benefit the campaign—especially the candidate's comfort and good spirits while on the campaign trail. Obviously, many of the contributions sought and received are needed far less by the candidate than by the, many times, sacrificing contributor. (Reminiscent, perhaps, of the PTL and Tammy and Jim Bakker.) Campaign chests have been used for travel clubs, wedding and other gifts to constituents, ball games, formal attire, party expenses, legal fees, to brighten offices, for meals, trips and projects that may take some imagination to recognize as "reelection activities." Population changes are another reason many incumbents are forced to spend heavily on campaigns; to new residents even an incumbent is an unknown.

Some incumbents hoard contributions and sometimes

accumulate enough to run for the Senate. John Duncan of Tennessee spends $50,000 annually to feed his constituents at a down-home barbecue. About as near to "unchallenged" as a politician can get, he nevertheless spent over $300,000 in his 1986 campaign. Sam Gibbons ran for Florida's 7th District in 1986 spending over $550,000, which had the desired effect of discouraging any potential challenger.[32] Over half a million dollars spent by a twelve-term incumbent who ran unopposed! Is this a sane system or what?

Fred Wertheimer, president of *Common Cause*, a Washington, D.C., based lobbying group, has referred to the fact that presidents Ford and Carter, both incumbent presidents, lost their bids for reelection under the reforms instituted in 1974-76. This only proves that incumbency works *against* a person when he makes mistakes from a highly visible platform. The burden is on the incumbent to shoot himself in the foot, and if he does, and only if he does, will voters turn from the pedestal to see what the less visible challengers have to say. An incumbent has it all locked up under our present system. He doesn't have to win, he's already won, he only has to lose by saying or doing something to turn the people away from him.

Some content incumbents use excess funds to help colleagues, hoping that there will be a return favor, perhaps on a vote here and there in the future. Although this does not buy absolute loyalty, no one can put a price on the good will that is undoubtedly purchased by such a practice. For example, Henry Waxman, a California congressman, gave $40,000 to eight colleagues who served on the Commerce Committee. Coincidentally, Mr. Waxman was trying to win the chairmanship of the Health and the Environment Subcommittee and coincidentally seven of the eight voted for Mr. Waxman. Yet, as with the used car dealers and Nixon's ambassadorships, who can say for sure if cause and effect are at work here? Would the votes not have been cast *but for* Mr. Waxman's contributions? Ms. Drew cites this incident as an example of circumventing the rules.

With their own PACs, these "wealthy" politicians can help an individual or group that desires to aid a specific candidate and has maxed-out (already contributed the amounts allowable under the law). These are the types of activities that unintentionally give the appearance that power is being purchased. There is no good reason for an incumbent to have his own PAC and this practice should be discontinued.

The National Association for Association PACs (NAFA-PAC) was founded in 1980 to share information, as was the National Association of Business PACs (NABPAC) which advises its members and has as its slogan DEMOCRACY IS NOT A SPECTATOR SPORT. Ken Cole is the president of NABPAC, which represents 2,000 trade associations and corporate PACs. Mr. Cole has proposed doing away with PACs headed by members of Congress by restricting contributions to the two-year election cycle and not permitting funds to be carried over from one cycle to another. AMPAC agrees that incumbents shouldn't head their own PACs, shouldn't be allowed to raise funds more than two years before a reelection bid and suggests they specify the office being sought in their solicitations.

Public Financing Of Campaigns

Senator William Roth of Delaware has referred to public financing as "food stamps for Senators." There is no limit to how much money a candidate can spend to get elected *unless* he intends to use public funds. To qualify for public money a candidate must adhere to campaign spending rules which allow a maximum of $10 million plus inflation based on 1974 dollars plus 20 percent of the total which works out to a 1988 spending ceiling of almost $27 million dollars to gain the presidential nomination.[33] Party nominees, according to 1987 FEC calculations, can spend $44,460,000 in the general 1988 election.

Under the provisions of S2, the Senate's latest campaign reform proposal, candidates for the United States Senate would be asked to agree to voluntary spending limits based on the population of their states. S2 would authorize grants of public funds to general election candidates willing to abide by primary and general election spending limits. The proposal for 1988 is $950,000 in states with low populations, up to $5.5 million in California. Funds would come from an expanded version of the income tax check-off. The general election limit would be $400,000 plus a sum calculated by multiplying 30 cents by the number of eligible voters up to four million—only 25 cents after four million with a top for California of the $5.5 million, as already mentioned. But the reality is both contenders for California's Senate seat spent double that amount in 1986. Senator Alan Cranston barely managed to retain his seat after an expenditure of $11 million, and his unsuccessful challenger, Ed Zschau, tried even harder and spent $11.8 million.

S2 would also limit PAC contributions. Senators would be allowed a maximum of $190,950 in low population states up to $825,000 in California. PAC limits to candidates for the House would be set anywhere from $100,000 to $150,000. During the 1986 race congressional candidates spent $450 million, up 20 percent from the previous election, with $132 million of those funds provided by PACs.

AMPAC and BUILD PAC normally give $15,000 a year (maximum allowed by law) to the Democratic Senatorial Campaign Committee, but both by-passed the annual fund-raising dinner held in April 1987 to show their displeasure with the Senate's latest campaign reform bill, S2, which, if passed, would severely restrict PACs.

On Sunday, September 20, 1987, on its "Road To The White House" series, C-SPAN (Cable Satellite Public Affairs Network) provided the FEC campaign spending limits estimated in dollars before the passage of S2. Estimates for eighteen states were flashed on the screen. (*Congressional Quarterly* has the information for all the states if a reader is interested.)[34]

Iowa	745,149
New Hampshire	444,600
Minnesota	1,093,616
South Dakota	444,600
South Carolina	874,972
North Carolina	1,685,923
Alabama	1,004,987
Florida	3,226,373
Gaorgia	1,572,816
Kentucky	965,971
Louisiana	1,120,392
Maryland	1,194,729
Mississippi	655,162
Missouri	1,327,753
Oklahoma	846,162
Tennessee	1,270,488

Texas	4,194,178
California	7,095,460

On June 16, 1987, Senator Robert Byrd remarked

> So I hope that we will not be persuaded too much by those who protest loudly about public financing, about what all this is going to cost the taxpayers when, in fact, the taxpayers already do this voluntarily, in the case of presidential elections.[35]

Voluntarily is the key. Public financing of congressional campaigns, say opponents, would cost $100 million just for starters. (There you go laughing again!) Waving public funds in front of a candidate makes the whole scheme about as voluntary as paying taxes.

The House has its own set of campaign reform bills before the 100th Congress. HR2462, sponsored by Congressman Al Swift of Washington, instead of offering public funds outright for voluntarily accepting limits, substitutes discounted advertising, broadcasting and mailing rates. Ingenuity is never more valuable than when used to skirt a law! On July 1, 1987, the Senate Democrats tried Al Swift's compromise. They suggested that if a candidate is found exceeding the spending limits, his opponent would be given funds from the U.S. Treasury to make up the difference. (What deficit?) The Republicans still wouldn't buy S2. In June, Senator Byrd had been ready to give in on public financing but would not budge on spending limits. As Majority Leader, the Senator from West Virginia tried time and again to interrupt the Senate filibuster staged against S2 by the Republicans. S2 is considered to be partisan legislation with only three Democrats voting with all but two Republicans. After the seventh try for cloture, Senator Byrd on September 15th shelved the bill, at least for the duration of 1987.

Still another suggestion for campaign reform is to set up a national payroll withholding system for voluntary contributions. Employees would sign a card authorizing $1 a week of their pay (quite a jump from the modest $1 a year contribution on the tax return) to be directed to the party they choose. Employers could send the money to the IRS along with the periodic income tax and Social Security withholding, to be forwarded to the specified parties.

On May 6, 1987, an amendment to S2 proposed by Senator Frank Murkowski of Alaska was rejected 50 to 48. The Senator wanted to eliminate $100 million alloted in FY1988 to public financing of congressional campaigns and assign the money to veterans programs instead.

But money has never been the whole ball game. John Connally spent $12.6 million, a phenomenal sum in 1980, and it bought him only a single delegate to the Republican convention. The National Association of Realtors spent $496,000 to run its own campaign, including radio and TV ads (in order to get around contribution limits), in an unsuccessful attempt to help former Senator James Jones of Oklahoma. The American Medical Association had a similar experience in its effort to defeat Andrew Jacobs in Indiana, who was against higher Medicaid fees for doctors. They spent $315,000 without success, whereas Jacobs spent only $8,000 and won. Republicans spent $50 million in the last weeks of the 1982 campaigns, making the grant total: Democrats–$27.5 million; Republicans–$186.5 million. However, the role money played in that election is pure speculation. Although winners outspent losers in twenty-seven out of thirty-three Senate races, Republicans lost twenty-six House seats in 1982.

It is a fact of life that in a race between a known and an unknown the known is almost sure to win. Spending limits only make it harder for challengers to overcome the advantages incumbency provides. Incumbents are already known due to media coverage in the previous election and during their term. Franking privileges during their tenure means that unless challengers are free to solicit substantially larger contributions they will not be able to compensate for these benefits. It is hypocritical and condescending to act as though incumbents and challengers were starting out on the same foot.

Right after the Second World War congressmen had an average of three personal staff members; in the 1980s the average was up to seventeen, meaning some had a lot more than seventeen. A political scientist at the University of Maryland, Michael Malbin, found that when allowance was made for staff, office expenses, phone, travel, computers, mailings and so forth, an incumbent came out an estimated one million fifty thousand dollars ahead of any challenger. Not surprising then that between 95-98 percent of all incumbents win reelection.

A talk showhost on a popular San Francisco radio station a few years ago ran a half-hearted campaign to unseat all incumbents. A bit mindless and undiscriminating perhaps, but when it comes down to it, even those who are trying to do what is right (in each voter's subjective opinion) may deserve to be ousted for lack of competence in convincing their colleagues. A fresh batch of Congress persons may be just the tonic the nation needs.

Common Cause is indignant about the honoraria paid to House and Senate members who often appear before lobbying groups, generally at breakfasts, talk about issues that are affecting the group, answer questions, listen to comments and pick up a check for one or two thousand dollars. Both House and Senate rules prohibit members from accepting any gift valued at $100 or more from lobby groups but fees for speaking are legal. The amount of honoraria paid by all groups topped $7 million in 1985, up from $5.4 million in 1984. When Vice President George Bush speaks he generally receives between $35,000 and $100,000 in contributions. Senators are allowed to keep honoraria totaling 40 percent of their salary, which has, as we all know, been increased. In 1985 they were permitted to keep only 30 percent of a lesser salary so these guys know how to look after themselves. House members are still allowed to keep only 30 percent of their salaries but few ever reach that limit as they are normally given far less than their colleagues in the Senate. Most honoraria comes from local community organizations, educational institutions and public-policy groups whose main interest is in obtaining information, not attempting to influence.

Why the fact that business and lobbying organizations are getting into the act should cause *Common Cause* such concern is unclear to me. Does *Common Cause* really think this is buying votes? Then the answer is for the electorate to make certain they elect men and women of integrity. Some politicians turn down the fees and some turn them over to charity but do not decline the invitation to exchange ideas with the groups who invite them to speak. Why should these so-called lobbyists pass up a chance to influence legislators who have already too much control over their lives? Does Mr.

Wertheimer[36] think the groups would not want to exchange thought with legislators if money were not involved and that public officials would not accept invitations *but for* the dollars involved? Mr. Wertheimer knows this is nonsense. Articulate researched persuasion is the key to changing a legislator's mind and not dollars. And, as I said before, if this isn't the case then it's time to replace our legislators, not deny interests (''special'' interests is redundant) their chance to influence their future. The fact that ''lobbyists'' and ''special interests'' are almost considered dirty words can be traced to the snow-job by the press over the years. A representative government is based on the efforts of lobbyists and special interests. The alternative is to elect philosopher kings and leave them to their ivory towers (now the realm, thank goodness, of not so influential academicians) to decide issues that will affect our lives.

As a June 19, 1987, editorial in the *Wall Street Journal* put it:

> Common Cause and other sincere supporters of campaign-finance reform fail to see that the excessive influence of money on politics is merely a symptom of the underlying problem: the government's growing power to determine economic outcomes—subsidies, loans, protection against competition, entitlements, the defense pork barrel. Washington decides who benefits. Nobel laureate F.A. Hayek explained the process more than forty years ago: ''As the coercive power of the state will alone decide who is to have what, the only power worth having will be a share in the exercise of this directing power.''

Suggested Reforms

It may be a myth that an elected official must curry favor with the folks back home in order to remain in office. The Center for Naval Analysis, a Washington, D.C. research firm, found pork-barrel spending and guarding against district cut-backs was not helpful in getting incumbents reelected. Professors Robert Bernstein and James Payne of Texas A&M drew the same conclusion from their separate studies. They found that once elected and in office, representatives are able to do as they please without checking with their constituents. Even those who voted against spending back home were not punished, as is generally believed. The ''why not?'' is revealing and uncomfortably damaging to my plea to permit citizens to act as responsible guardians. It was found that most constituents could not even recall their representative's name, let alone his or her voting record. The excuse that politicians must spend and spend to please their constituents or risk being replaced is, according to the professors, nothing more than a myth—but one that the majority of politicians have helped perpetuate.

Some citizens believe for what our government officials do they get very little compensation. On the other hand how many people would take over their positions free of charge? Right now, remember, it costs over $3 million and years of pleading to attain a seat in the Senate (over $11 million in California). The opportunity to do something worthwhile and with a lot of ego gratifying glory is compensation enough for ninety-nine out of one hundred persons. Have you ever heard of a shortage of candidates, and if so would the reason really be too little compensation? I doubt it. But, in addition, there are side benefits. Just as students, authors and artists are famous for living on peanut butter and tuna in attics or basement rooms, sacrificing for the future "pay off," so politicians emerge from their years of service with "pay offs." What law firm wouldn't snap up a retiring Senator, just to put his name on their letterhead? And that's for starters!

After thirty-four years in Congress, Tip O'Neil, former Speaker of the House, during the first half of 1987 appeared in ads for American Express, Lite Beer and Hush Puppies. In his first six months of retirement he delivered approximately fifty speeches at $20,000 each. He was reportedly offered $20,000 just for standing in front of the warship *U.S.S. Constitution* and saying a few words. He received a $1 million advance on his book, *A Man Of The House* and that's on top of his $80,000 a year federal pension.[37]

The "pay off," although it may not be as large as Mr. O'Neil's, comes from serving in almost any branch of government—even when not elected. James Kilpatrick speaks of the economic and moral considerations that must be understood in determining the pay for public officials. He says,

> It is impossible to say what salaries are necessary to prompt talented men and women to run for Congress, to seek places on the federal bench or to accept top positions in executive agencies.

But then he goes on to admit

> Able men and women always will aspire to the prestige of the federal bench. A vacancy has only to develop before a dozen candidates make their ambitions known.[38]

It is possible to attract good people to positions of power without offering compensation but by appealing to their altriusm and patriotism and, yes, their egos. And, no, I'm not talking about a nation ruled by the rich, although *rich* is nothing shameful but something to which most of us aspire. To attain wealth one has had to do many things well. Experience with success is not to be shunned, although America has a love affair with the underdog and a distrust of the successful. And those who did not prove themselves by earning the leisure and financial security necessary to accept an honorary position, but rather inherited wealth, should be commended for their attraction to public service rather than scorned. But just as it is not necessary to be wealthy to serve in the peace corps, one need not be wealthy to hold public office, only qualified to contribute (at least qualified enough to convince voters) and in a position to make personal sacrifices if need be. Many companies even now support special employees in intern-type programs in Washington, D.C., as a service, a civic duty if you will, to the nation, and also perhaps for the prestige that reflects on the company.

Upon his retirement in 1986, Senator Barry Goldwater of Arizona gave an interview to Haynes Johnson of the *Washington Post* in which he provided his own set of facts to back up my contention that many Congressmen work less than they used to and not as hard as a lot of their constituents. He mentioned three-day weeks—late to meetings—staffs that have grown from approximately 2,000 over twenty-five years ago to more than 30,000 today.

Some officials suppose they were elected to write more regulations in the form of bills and amendments, much the way a doctor feels compelled to write a prescription to give a patient his money's worth. Senator Goldwater recalled that in 1952 the Congress voted on fewer than two hundred bills, whereas Congress in the 1980s has consistently voted on closer to 800 or 900 bills each session. But the Senator, as you-know-who says, hadn't seen anything yet. According to one of James Kilpatrick's columns, by the end of its first day the 100th Congress (and with Senator Goldwater no longer there to stem the tide) saw the introduction of 500 bills in the House and 283 in the Senate.

In September 1987, when announcing his intention to retire from the Senate after more than thirty years, Senator William Proxmire of Wisconsin told his colleagues:

> The people of this country think the Congress is the pits because we in the Congress tell them we are the pits. I have listened to many members of this body who have made a career out of attacking the Congress.

My first impression of the Senator's charge is that he underestimates the intelligence of the people—again. Surely people don't believe something because Congressmen tell them it is so. Perhaps Senator Proxmire forgot the old adage about actions speaking louder than words. For example, during his first nine years in Congress, Leon Panetta returned to the Treasury a total of $511,151 in office and payroll savings and the return from many of those years of his own pay increases. The savings came from such economies as limiting districtwide mailings, using reduced-fare flights, low-cost rentals of office space and equipment and careful management by his Washington and district field offices—and from having a supportive and sharp wife. (A bit reminiscent of President and Mrs. Polk.) All that and he was present for 96.2 percent of all House votes during 1985.

At the *Center for Excellence in Government* in January 1987, Harry Hughes, ex-governor of Maryland, advised that no one who has ever run against government and bureaucracy has accomplished anything. You can't break the system you have to use to get things done. Perhaps that is the message Senator Proxmire wanted to leave with his Senate colleagues. No matter how you look at the words, they are a far cry from the opinions of now retired Senator Barry Goldwater of Arizona.

Senator Goldwater seemed to think people's low perception of Congress, and politicians in general, was deserved. This may shock many citizens who criticize merely as sport. Fault finding ties with baseball as the great American pastime. Most of us are too far away to know if criticism is deserved and so send barbs "just in case." That's why when Senator Goldwater volunteered, "I don't think I've served in many good congresses," it was truly sobering. The senator advised a change in election practices which were excluding good people from running for office by requiring them to raise an inordinate amount of money.

Although I have been critical of Elizabeth Drew's assumptions that money *caused* specific votes, on page 95 of *Politics and Money* she convinced me of the need for reform. Ms. Drew describes an appearance by retiring Congresswoman Millicent Fenwick of New Jersey on "Meet The Press" at the end of 1982:

> Representative Millicent Fenwick, Republican of New Jersey, spoke of "the danger of perceived or actual corruption," which was, she said, "far more serious, I think, than the public is aware." She added, "When a complete stranger or almost complete stranger will tell you quite frankly, 'yes, I'm going to vote that way, because I took fifty-eight thousand from such-and-such group and they want it,' I call that corruption."

I must admit the unwillingness, or perhaps inability, to name names bothers me in the above reported conversation. If there are ne'er-do-wells such as the described "stranger" then I would think it would be any citizen's civic duty to discredit them, and especially the duty of a Congresswoman. But discrediting is not enough unless *the people* act on the information. If the ordinary citizen doesn't care, then we get what we deserve.[39]

The *Congressional Quarterly* reported in its June 20, 1987 weekly report that four congress persons were found in violation of House rules and were not disciplined. (The rest of us commoners should be so lucky and so should George Hansen have been when he earlier appeared before this same committee.)

Charlie Rose of North Carolina, a senior member of the House Administration Subcommittee on Elections, "borrowed," interest-free, $63,995 from his campaign funds and may have used the proceeds for personal expenses (a violation) judging by the coincidental purchase of a Jeep and beach house at the time of the "loans." Mr. Rose on September 16, 1987, tried to dismiss the seriousness of his actions by asserting borrowing from campaign chests is "common practice among members of the House."

> The panel (House Ethics Committee) found that Oakar (Mary Rose Oakar of Ohio) broke House rules and federal law, when she paid a former staff member more than $45,000 in salary for nearly two years after the aide had moved to New York City.

Ms. Oakar bought a town house in 1986 with another aide whose salary she raised by $10,000 one day after the purchase and by an additional $3,600 a month later. Somehow the Committee reportedly found no impropriety here because two other employees received raises also. Unbelievably the Congresswoman had the gall to say, "I hope people will respect my sense of integrity." (And two plus two equals five!)

Professor Ogden O. Allsbrook, Jr., of the University of Georgia has recommended a Constitutional Amendment to limit all elected representatives to one term in order to foster a genuine concern for the health of the nation and to remove the distraction of future elections. He points out that so far incumbent politicians have found deficits a more palatable alternative than defeat at the polls—again perpetuating the myth that constituents know what their representatives are up to.

Three 3-year terms for Representatives and three 6-year terms for Senators with a limit of 18 years of service is an alternate suggestion which has been making the rounds on Capitol Hill, although not enthusiastically.

It is well to remember that Congress persons, Senators and the President are all elected in various manners and for different terms precisely in order to prevent temporary majorities from controlling the entire government. Rather than a single term most people would prefer a limit of two, three or even four terms in order to encourage expertise and continuity. There are others that believe the framers of the Constitution, by prescribing a two-year term for Representatives, intended to make certain there was a constant supply of fresh faces in Congress. Certainly they never intended influence to be wielded for twenty or thirty years in the capitol by a single individual, far less a family. Article I Section 4:2 of the Constitution states that Congress shall assemble at least once in every year. There seemed no need to limit terms of office.

Ruling in a country founded on the premise that "the best government is the least government" was never meant to be a career. Yet there have been several "dynasties" over the years on Capitol Hill extending between generations. Take former Senator Albert Gore, Sr., whose political career in Washington spanned thirty-two years (1930-71) and whose son, at the beginning of his career today, has already added another ten.

Members of Congress, although unwittingly, are themselves the most persuasive advocates for one term and many spoke to Elizabeth Drew in the fall of 1982.

> Most of us are physically and intellectually exhausted from doing the work here and running home most weekends to campaign, so you have a tired Congress that can't concentrate.
>
> *Mike Synar of Oklahoma*[40]

> If members know that can happen to them (refers to ability of challengers to raise a great deal of last minute money), it means they will be looking over their shoulder every damn vote.
>
> *David Obey of Wisconsin*[41]

> There has been all too much discussion around here about how what we do in the House and on our Committees is going to affect our ability to raise money.
>
> *James Shannon of Massachusetts*[42]

On C-SPAN in April 1986, Henson Moore, then a candidate for Senator from Louisiana, told his interviewer that he favored limiting the terms of Congressmen. According to Mr. Moore, who was at that time a member of the House of Representatives, Congress does almost nothing during January and most Mondays and Fridays as it is. He said he would like to see political office treated as a *part-time position*—five or six months and then back home to live under the laws they have legislated and to make their living as artists, doctors, insurance salesmen or what have you. He went on to comment on the amount of time he was required to campaign on top of being away from his home state while Congress was in session. He wondered for all of us just what kind of men and women our current campaign practices are attracting. Certainly, he surmised, no kind, caring considerate family men and women—that sort of person is out of the race from the beginning under our system. Pat Schroeder found this out, to her distress.

Of course most members of Congress don't take kindly to the thought of a single term any more than they do to the suggestion that their pay be lowered and that they legislate less and spend more time being productive members of society. I'm not supposing such reforms will ever get through Congress, and that's why I'm issuing a grass roots call for reform—reform which must come from the people's demand for a Constitutional Amendment.

Fat chance, you say, and you may be right. Although more than ten thousand Constitutional amendments have been proposed in Congress since 1789, only thirty-three have won the necessary approval of two-thirds of both Houses and a mere twenty-six have passed the final hurdle of adoption by legislatures in three-quarters of the states. So who said it was going to be easy?

In the *Ohio State Law Journal*, Spring 1987, Professor Philip Oliver of the University of Arkansas suggested limiting the term of Supreme Court justices to eighteen years. Since there are nine justices, one seat would become vacant every two years on a staggered basis. This, Professor Oliver argues, would give every president the opportunity to appoint, with consent of the Senate, two members to the Court, or four members if the president had the confidence of the people and was reelected. Reappointment to the Court would not be allowed.

Under Professor Oliver's proposal there would be little advantage in a justice timing his retirement to coincide with the term of a president who shares his views. The most blatant examples, according to the professor, of justices clinging to their appointments well beyond the dictates of their years, are Chief Justice William Howard Taft and Justice William O. Douglas, although it is likely that 79-year-old Justice Thurgood Marshall and 81-year-old Justice William Brennan are doing the same thing today.

When voters select a president, they do so knowing the president may be called upon to fill vacancies on the Supreme Court, but it is not a sure thing. Why leave an important political act like naming a justice to the Supreme Court to chance, asks Professor Oliver, when a Constitutional Amendment can bring a desirable balance to the process? Professor Oliver points out that President Taft made six appointments in a single term, President Nixon made four in five and a half years and President Carter was not able to name a single justice to the Court. If each president automatically had the power to name two full-term justices, each presidential election would share nearly equal importance in shaping the Court.

Opponents will surely plead the sanctity of the Constitution, but Professor Oliver is prepared for them. He claims that since its inception, America has been experiencing an evolution in democracy. In the beginning neither presidents nor senators were elected by the people and only very few people had the right to vote. Although the president is still chosen by the electoral college, the 17th Amendment in 1913 put an end to the old practice of having state legislatures appoint Senators. Thomas Jefferson, according to the professor, was from the beginning opposed to life tenure for federal judges. The original thirteen colonies and most states admitted prior to 1830 provided life tenure for their judges but were not above correcting the error later on. Today, again according to Professor Oliver, every state but Rhode Island limits judicial terms.

Those who seek a more efficient government may be courting disaster. Who wants to see a thousand bills introduced into Congress in one day? The 783 record previously mentioned is already too much. If anything we need to slow our representatives down. But the *Committee On The Constitutional System*, headed by Senator Nancy Kassebaum of Kansas, former Secretary of Treasury Douglas Dillon and Washington, D.C., attorney Lloyd Cutler, believes that efficiency means better government. They have considered reform to forbid ticket splitting in order to ensure a president a legislative majority, reform to permit members of Congress to serve in the President's Cabinet in order to give Congress a stake in White House policies, reform to increase the terms of Representatives to four years and Senators to eight with elections to coincide with presidential elections[43] and reform to increase the term of the president to six years. They have even considered reform to make the American government more parliamentary, more like England's government, although according to *Time* magazine[44] Senator Kassenbaum backed away from such an idea.

An idea to model our government on Switzerland's (which was first modeled on ours) crops up now and again. The Swiss have a Federal Assembly (our Congress) consisting of a National Council (our House of Representatives) and a Council of States (our Senate) whose members are popularly elected. The National Council has two hundred members (one deputy per 22,000 people) who serve four-year terms. The Council of States consists of forty-six officials, two chosen from each canton and one from each half canton (like our states). Every four years the Federal Assembly elects the Federal Council of seven men who hold the nation's highest executive authority (instead of our one president). Members of the Federal Council are elected for four-year terms but are almost always reelected. The seven ministers, as they are sometimes called, each preside over a division of government: (1) exterior; (2) justice; (3) finance; (4) economy; (5) military; (6) foreign affairs; and (7) transport, communication and energy. The ministers are chosen to create a balance between the various cantons and the different political parties. Each of the seven members of the Federal Council rotate each year in the office of President of the Council and of the Confederation. The facultative referendum makes it possible for the people to demand a direct popular vote on any existing or proposed law and to initiate a vote on almost any issue. Even constitutional amendments can be initiated. Voting days are set for weekends to ensure the maximum number of voters, who must be at least twenty years old. In 1971 Swiss women were given the federal vote and representation in the National and State Councils, Canton Parliaments and Courts. In 1984 a woman was elected to the Federal Council for the first time, meaning Switzerland will have a female president before the United States.

I have digressed into Swiss government because some people have suggested the Swiss referendum and seven executives be attempted in this country. My own fascination with predictions by famous men of the past[45] has made me seriously consider the possibility of having a more diverse executive branch.

> The executive power in our government is not the only, perhaps not even the principal, object of my solicitude. The tyranny of the legislature is really the danger most to be feared, and will continue to be

so for many years to come. The tyranny of the executive power will come in its turn, but at a more distant period.

Thomas Jefferson

We need to look at America's philosophical evolution over the past two hundred years not to try and bring back the past—we're a different nation with different needs than we had two hundred years ago—but so we don't repeat our mistakes. But we must also examine our past so we don't lose what it is that was responsible for our greatness.

Congressman Al Swift of the state of Washington chaired hearings on "Campaign Finance Reform" which were aired on C-SPAN in July 1987. Fred Wertheimer of *Common Cause* presented his views before the House Administration Subcommittee. Mr. Wertheimer was asked by Representative William Thomas of California to state the problem with our current election process "succinctly." Mr. Wertheimer answered:

> Too much money is being spent in campaigns, too much time is being spent raising it, too much PAC money is influencing the electoral process and the Congressional process and challengers are getting far too few dollars to be able to compete whether they're Republicans or Democrats ... you create a system where money given by interest groups influences decisions and I think that system becomes a corrupt system.

He told the Committee that *Common Cause* supports HR 2717 because it is legislation which, in Mr. Werthcimer's view, provides maximum flexibility. He told the committee he would like to see matching funds replace PAC money in all federal elections. He went on to warn, however, that "we've seen the creativity that accompanies any campaign laws."

The next witness was Scott Thomas, chairman of the Federal Election Commission (FEC), who said the FEC had submitted twenty-four legislative recommendations to Congress in March 1987 but that he intended to focus on three main recommendations before Mr. Swift's Committee.

First Mr. Thomas stated the FEC would like to see the elimination of state expenditure limits on presidential candidates, as they are arbitrary and easily circumvented and therefore difficult for the FEC to enforce. Next, the FEC suggested Congress prohibit fraudulent solicitation of funds (would seem unnecessary as *fraud* is always prohibited), and third that the FEC be notified when a PAC qualifies as a multi-candidate political action committee.

I mention Mr. Thomas' testimony because after the many reform proposals we have discussed and the twenty-four recommendations sent to Congress by the FEC, these three seemed mediocre. But then the recommendations are not political but only to make the FEC function more efficiently, I would suppose. A revealing look, I thought, at the FEC.

Because the next witness seemed especially representative of the "common man," I am presenting most of his testimony here and almost word for word. Mr. C.V. Le Force of Concord, California, chairman of the Realtors' PAC (NAR) testified:

> Campaign reform is based on two questionable allegations: (a) that PACs are playing too large a role in funding campaigns; and (b) that campaigns are too expensive . . . PACs are legitimate and desirable, they get people active and voting. NAR has a high turnout of voters. PACs broaden the political base of giving and provide a vehicle for participation to many citizens that did not exist before. PACs are a collective effort. They allow like-minded individuals to pool their resources, to contribute to more campaigns than an individual could. PACs are pluralistic . . . they compete with other PACs to make their voices heard. All PACs do not give to the same candidate. PACs can oppose each other's goals and we believe this makes for good debate and enhances our Democratic process.
>
> In politics, competing claims are being negotiated. More PACs give each PAC less influence—the more the better—it dilutes influence and expands participation. Legislation should broaden participation in the election process . . . We don't believe that Congress is for sale . . . The criticism that PACs are attempting to buy legislation with contributions rather than supporting principles is a very, very harsh indictment of the integrity of the members of Congress as well as the individual NAR PAC contributors. The most effective curb against influence-peddling in a democracy is free and open debate, strong political competition and an assurance of a level playing field in any campaign.

Mr. Le Force then suggested some fundamental questions regarding proposed election reform:

> Do the suggested changes make the election process more or less fair?
> Do they curtail participation by the public?
> Do they inform the public?

Mr. Le Force's group thinks not.

> Taxpayer financing of campaigns is wrong, it won't work, it isn't affordable, it creates a monster and the general public doesn't want it.

When asked by Mr. Swift for a summation, Mr. Le Force said:

> NAR believes we should increase the limits of individual contributions, that we should curtail the length of campaign fund raising, we should ban leadership PACs, we should curtail franking privileges, we should limit post-election contributions by PACs and we should eliminate and zero out any campaign war chests.

I would recommend Mr. Le Force's testimony to all elected officials as proof that the "common man" is far wiser than is generally recognized.

The Outcome in '88

I don't know who will be the 41st President of the United States, but as I write the gentleman who said the following stands a pretty good chance and I like what he has to say:

> The wonderful, but awesome thing about America is that it all depends on us, on "We the people." On the decisions we make, the examples we set, and the practical, far-reaching leadership we provide in the years ahead. That means electing men and women like those brilliantly practical bands of patriots that met in Philadelphia two centuries ago. Between them, they wrote an inspiring first chapter in the story of America. But the beauty and the challenge of the American story is that it's a never-ending one. Its greatest passages may be written in the century ahead . . . It's up to us to write them.
>
> *Robert Dole, 1987*[46]

Notes

Section One

1. 89th Congress–Second Session, and 90th Congress–First Session, 1968, P. 21.
2. 1876 Samuel Tilden (D)–50.9 percent of popular vote; Rutherford Hayes (R)–47.9 percent of popular vote. Votes were contested in the South and some hanky panky went on to give Hayes all of Oregon's votes. The Electoral College showed Tilden–84, Hayes–185. A Commission was appointed to look into the matter because the House was controlled by Democrats. The election of 1876 was definitely under a "cloud of fraud."
3. 91st Congress–First Session, 1969, p. 520.
4. *Voting For President*, by Wallace Sayre and Judith Parrish, p. 54. The authors favor the winner-take-all system because it works. The popular vote by states has not deprived the popular vote winner of the presidency since 1888.
5. Ibid, 117.
6. Ibid, p. 133.
7. *The Case Against Direct Election of the President*, by Judith Best, p. 217.
8. Ibid, p. 162.
9. Sayre and Parrish, p. 111.
10. Carl Rowen's column, September 3, 1987.
11. *Who Votes* (1980), by Raymond Wolfinger and Steven Rosenstone, p. 105.

12. Ibid, pp. 109, 111.
13. *Wall Street Journal*, April 15, 1987, article by David Shribman.
14. *Atlantic Monthly*, January 1987, "The New Shape of American Politics" by William Schneider, p. 41.
15. *The American Deficit: Fulfillment Of A Prophecy?* by Helen P. Rogers.
16. *Atlantic Monthly*, January 1987, p. 43.
17. *Atlantic Monthly*, January 1987, p. 53.
18. *Democracy in America*, by Alexis de Tocqueville, Chapter entitled "Effects of the Tyranny of the Majority Upon the National Character of the Americans"
19. *The Commonwealth*, September 14, 1987, p. 403.
20. *Wall Street Journal*, October 1, 1987.
21. Ellen Goodman's, column October 6, 1987.
22. *Atlantic Monthly*, April 1987, "The Democrats in '88" by William Schneider, p. 57.
23. *Atlantic Monthly*, July 1987, "The Republicans in '88" by William Schneider, p. 82.
24. *Congressional Quarterly*, June 27, 1987, "Congress & the Country" by Alan Ehrenhalt, p. 1415.
25. *Time*, Sept. 7, 1987, "The Year of the Refusniks" by Laurence Barrett.
26. Ibid.
27. *Atlantic Monthly*, April 1987, p. 46.
28. *Atlantic Monthly*, January 1987, p. 47
29. Ibid.
30. *Atlantic Monthly*, April 1987, p. 38.
31. C-SPAN, Sept. 7, 1987, featured a panel of political pollsters.
32. *Congressional Quarterly*, June 27, 1987, "Congress & the Country" by Alan Ehrenhalt, p. 1415.

Section Two

1. Figures through the courtesy of the American Productivity Center, Houston, Texas.
2. *The Coming of the New Deal*, by Arthur Schlessinger, Jr.
3. *San Francisco Examiner*, December 31, 1986.
4. *Los Angeles Times*, January 19, 1987.
5. The story of Jesse Jackson's stuttering as a child I heard directly from his lips when he spoke at the International Platform Association in Washington, D.C., immediately following the Democratic National Convention which was held in San Francisco in 1984. I have not come across any mention of his stuttering in the biographies I have read and wonder why not.
6. *Current Biography*, January 1987.
7. *Time*, June 22, 1987, p. 29.
8. *New Republic*, June 1, 1987, "Ronald Biden" by Fred Barnes, p. 18.
9. *Time*, July 27, 1987. "The Duke of Economic Uplift" by Walter Shapiro, p. 23.

10. *Atlantic Monthly*, April 1987. "The Democrats In '88" by William Schneider, p. 49.
11. For a fascinating expose of OBEs (off-budget enterprises) see *Underground Government: The Off-Budget Public Sector*, by economists James T. Bennett and Thomas J. DiLorenzo. Because OBEs are permitted to issue tax-exempt bonds, they borrow at favorable rates, which crowd private borrowers out of the capital markets. Off-budget spending has increased by more than 30,000 percent in less than a decade.
12. *Wall Street Journal*, July 15, 1986. "Proposition 2½ Is MA' Dirty Little Secret" by Warren Brookes.
13. During the candidates' debate on August 22, 1987, in Dubuque, Iowa, Mr. Dukakis said, "only five percent of new jobs are defense related in Massachusetts."
14. *Time*, July 27, 1987, p. 22.
15. *Insight*, July 27, 1987, "Strong Hand at State's Helm" by Don McLeod, p. 15.
16. Letter to the Editor of the *Wall Street Journal* February 5, 1987, by Governor Michael Dukakis of Massachusetts.
17. *Wall Street Journal*, January 19, 1987.
18. *Wall Street Journal*, February 5, 1987, the Dukakis letter.
19. S1265, introduced May 21, 1987, requires employers to offer coverage to employees who work at least 17.5 hours per week (dependents covered too). Employers would be made to pay at least 80 percent of the premium (close to $1,000 a year per employee). Employers would be forced to pay 100 percent of the premium for employees who earn less than 125 percent of the federal poverty line. Estimated (always low) cost equals $25 billion per year.
20. *Atlantic Monthly*, July 1987, p. 82.
21. *Atlantic Monthly*, April 1987, p. 51.
22. Ibid, p. 50.
23. Ibid, p. 50.
24. See *Social Security: An Idea Whose Time Has Passed*, pp. 17-20.
25. *New Republic*, June 1, 1987. "Gephardt's Inside Moves" by Morton Kondracke, p. 22.
26. *Wall Street Journal*, April 30, 1987, p. 58.
27. *Atlantic Monthly*, April 1987, p. 51.
28. *Insight*, July 27, 1987. "Restoring Future's Old Shine" by Don McLeod, p. 16.
29. See discussion on pp. 54-56.
30. Address to Southern Legislative Conference, August 1987, Little Rock, Arkansas.
31. *Congressional Quarterly* (Weekly), April 4, 1987, p. 602.
32. President Garfield was shot on July 2, 1881, by a "Stalwart Republican" who had been denied an appointment as Consul to Paris and died September 19, 1881—becoming the fourth president to die in office.
33. *New Republic*, June 1, 1987, p. 4
34. *Wall Street Journal*, June 29, 1987, p. 18.
35. *Insight*, July 27, 1987, p. 17.

36. *Jesse Jackson: The Man, The Movement, The Myth* (1975) by Barbara A. Reynolds, Nelson-Hall, Chicago.
37. *Jesse Jackson and the Politics of Race* (1985) by Thomas H. Landess and Richard M. Quinn, Jameson Books, Ottawa, Illinois, p. 242.
38. *Jesse Jackson: The Man, The Movement, The Myth*, p. 30.
39. Ibid, p. 31.
40. *Up From The Ghetto* (New York: Cowles, 1970) by Phillip T. Drotning and Wesley South.
41. David Broder's column, September 27, 1987.
42. *Jesse Jackson and the Politics of Race*, from Foreword by Reverend Ralph Abernathy.
43. Ibid, pp. 102-103.
44. *Atlantic Monthly*, April 1987, p. 58.
45. *Time*, August 17, 1987. "Respect & Respectabiity" by Robert Ajemian, p. 17.
46. *Jesse Jackson and the Politics of Race*, p. 244.
47. *Jesse Jackson: The Man, The Movement, The Myth*, p. 29.
48. *Fortune*, May 11, 1987, p. 133.
49. *Jesse Jackson: The Man, The Movement, The Myth*, p. 32.
50. Ibid, p. 33
51. The question occurred before the Southern Legislative Conference in Little Rock, Arkansas, in August 1987.
52. For an expansion of this idea see *The American Deficit: Fulfillment of a Prophecy?* by Helen P. Rogers.
53. *Insight*, July 14, 1986, article by Warren Brookes.
54. *The American Deficit: Fulfillment of a Prophecy?* by Helen P. Rogers.
55. *Atlantic Monthly*, April 1987, p. 57.
56. William Schneider attributed this last line to *Time* magazine.
57. Debate held among seven Democratic candidates for the presidential nomination which took place August 22, 1987, in Dubuque, Iowa.
58. Before the Texas Legislature, April 24, 1987.
59. *Newsweek*, May 11, 1987, p. 88
60. *The American Political System* by Peter Woll and Robert Binstock, p. 372.
61. *Wall Street Journal*, March 28, 1984.
62. For further discussion see *Social Security: An Idea Whose Time Has Passed* by Helen P. Rogers.
63. See discussion on pp. 42-45.
64. Senator Paul Simon speaking in Iowa, Summer 1987.
65. Secretary of Education William Bennett before the Senate Labor & Human Resources Committee, January 14, 1987.
66. Senator Paul Simon speaking in Iowa, Summer 1987.
67. *Scientific American*, May 1987, "A Surge in Inequality" by Lester Thurow.
68. See *Social Security: An Idea Whose Time Has Passed* by Helen P. Rogers for a discussion of why retirement savings opportunities need to be expanded, not contracted.

Section Three

1. Prescott Sheldon Bush was Senator from Connecticut 1952-1963.
2. Quote attributed to Leo Nadeau, George Bush's gunner during World War II, and found in an article on Bush written by Gerald Seib which appeared in the September 14, 1987, edition of the *Wall Street Journal.*
3. *Wall Street Journal*, August 26, 1987, "Nearly All Aboard the Grainy Train" by James Bovard.
4. Ibid.
5. See *Social Security: An Idea Whose Time Has Passed* by Helen P. Rogers.
6. Ronald Reagan and George Bush both received University degrees in economics.
7. *Washington Post*, June 13, 1987.
8. Ibid.
9. Ibid.
10. *Congressional Quarterly*, January 31, 1987, p. 207.
11. Ibid.
12. *Associated Press*, June 14, 1987.
13. *Atlantic Monthly*, April 1987, p. 70.
14. Bob Dole to *Washington Post* June 6, 1987.
15. *Atlantic Monthly*, July 1987, p. 70.
16. Ibid, p. 69.
17. Archer-Daniels-Midland Co. is the largest recipient of government ethanol subsidies.
18. *War On Waste Digest*, July 1986, "A Honey Bunch of Subsidies" by J. Peter Grace, p. 3.
19. Ibid.
20. Ibid. (According to Mr. Grace, 119 million pounds of honey was stored by the government in 1984!)
21. *Wall Street Journal*, August 26, 1987, "Nearly All Aboard the Grainy Train" by James Bovard.
22. Elizabeth Dole, who resigned in September to help her husband's campaign, was at one time the only woman in President Reagan's cabinet. She served as Secretary of Transportation.
23. *Conservative Digest*, April 1987, "The DuPont Farm Opportunity Plan," pp. 16, 18.
24. Ibid, p. 19.
25. *New York Times*, June 2, 1987, from article by E.J. Dionne, Jr.
26. *C-SPAN Update*, April 20, 1987.
27. *Insight*, May 18, 1987, "Riding Ideas on the Campaign Trail" by Ralph Hallow, p. 54.
28. *Atlantic Monthly*, July 1987, p. 76.
29. Alexander Haig's father died at an early age and he was raised entirely by his mother. He was her only son.
30. Alexander Haig saw combat in Korea and Vietnam. Exposure to war is supposed to make one a man of peace and General Haig asserts that claim.
31. *Atlantic Monthly*, July 1987, p. 71.
32. Ibid, p. 74.

33. Ibid, p. 77.
34. *Policy Review*, Spring 1986.
35. *New York Times*, June 2, 1987, article by Don Feder.
36. Consult *Social Security: An Idea Whose Time Has Passed* by Helen P. Rogers.
37. See page 152.
38. *Associated Press*, June 14, 1987.
39. *Wall Street Journal*, April 29, 1987, "Divided Right" by David Shribman.
40. Campaign literature provided by the Robertson Headquarters.
41. *Conservative Digest*, June 1987, "The Wealth of Black Families" by Pat Robertson, pp. 35-36.
42. Other studies have placed America in 49th place.
43. *Conservative Digest*, June 1987, p. 39.
44. Ibid, p.36.
45. Ibid, p. 37.
46. Ibid, p. 39.
47. Material provided by the Robertson Campaign Headquarters.
48. Louis Kelso is a San Francisco-based attorney who first developed the ESOP concept.
49. Robertson campaign literature.
50. *Associated Press*, June 14, 1987.
51. *Atlantic Monthly*, July 1987, p. 80.
52. Ibid, p. 78.
53. Interview with C-SPAN, August 21, 1987, in "Road to the White House" series.

Section Four

1. *Insight*, July 27, 1987, "The Land of Corn and Candidates" by Don McLeod, p. 10.
2. These comments took place on September 3, 1987, at *Harpers* New School for Social Research. Richard Stout appeared via C-SPAN at the American Film Institute Forum on September 7, 1987.
3. *The Case Against Direct Election of the President* by Judith Best, p. 213.
4. A one-party area is where a single party has won 55 percent or more of the popular vote.
5. *Congressional Quarterly*, April 25, 1987, p. 785.
6. *Wall Street Journal*, October 22, 1987, report by Bob Davis.
7. *Poltics & Money* (1983) by Elizabeth Drew, p. 156.
8. Ibid, p. 109.
9. Donna Rice was the model linked by the press to Gary Hart, an incident which ostensibly led to Mr. Hart's withdrawal from the 1988 presidential race.
10. *Fortune*, June 8, 1987, "Who's Ahead In the Money Race" by Ann R. Dowd, p. 59.
11. Make donations to reduce the debt to Bureau of Public Debt, Dept. G, Washington, DC 20239-0601. See invitation from "Citizens For A Debt-Free America" printed in the Appendix.

12. *Wall Street Journal*, September 21, 1987, article by Brooks Jackson.
13. *Fortune*, June 8, 1987, p. 59.
14. Ibid, p. 68.
15. *Politics and Money*, p. 51
16. According to a 1982 American Stock Exchange poll.
17. *Politics and Money*, p. 51
18. Ibid, p. 51.
19. Ibid, p. 156.
20. On p. 97 of *Politics and Money*, Elizabeth Drew says, "Some of the interest groups talk about how their political decisions are made at the 'grassroots,' but of course that, for the most part, is nonsense." How can she be so certain?
21. *Politics and Money*, p. 51.
22. Ibid, p. 95.
23. ABA Code, Canon 9.
24. *Politics and Money*, p. 79.
25. *Choosing The President 1984: A Complete Guide to Understanding the Presidential Election Process* by The League of Women Voters Education Fund, p. 38.
26. *Politics and Money*, p. 83.
27. Buckley v. Valeo (Supreme Court, January 1976).
28. Justice O'Connor was excused because of a possible conflict of interest. Her husband had served on the Finance Committee of an Independent Fund Raising Committee. As of Spring 1983, *Common Cause* was still appealing the issue before the Federal Election Commission.
29. *Politics and Money*, p. 69.
30. As I write George Bush showed up at the hospital bed of Jessica McClure, the baby that was rescued from a well in Midland, Texas, and had the world watching her recovery with love and anticipation.
31. See *Congressional Quarterly Almanac 1986*, p. 46.
32. *Congressional Quarterly*, September 12, 1987, p. 2185.
33. *Fortune*, June 8, 1987, p. 59.
34. *Congressional Quarterly*, August 29, 1987, special report "The Nominating Process," p. 1991.
35. *Congressional Quarterly*, June 27, 1987, p. 1391.
36. Fred Wertheimer is the founder and president of *Common Cause*.
37. *Wall Street Journal*, June 29, 1987, article by Gilbert Fuchsberg.
38. James Kilpatrick's column.
39. See Sam Ervin and Plato on this subject.
40. *Politics and Money*, p. 89.
41. Ibid, p. 21.
42. Ibid, p. 51. Representative Shannon lost his bid for the Senate to John Kerry in 1984 and is now Attorney General in Massachusetts.
43. See page 242.
44. *Time*, Constitutional Issue 1987.
45. See *The Amerian Deficit: Fulfillment Of A Prophecy?*by Helen P. Rogers, where the quote from Lenin ("America will spend herself out of existence") is examined.
46. *Washington Post*, June 13, 1987.

Bibliography

Books

Choosing the President 1984: A Complete Guide to Understanding the Presidential Election Process by The League of Women Voters Education Fund

Who Votes? by Raymond Wolfinger & Steven Rosenstone

Campaign Journal: The Political Events of 1983-1984 by Elizabeth Drew

Voting for President: The Electoral College and the American Political System by Wallace Sayre & Judith Parris

The Case Against Direct Election of the President: A Defense of the Electoral College by Judith Best

Politics and Money: The New Road to Corruption by Elizabeth Drew

The American Voter by Campbell, Converse, Miller & Stokes

The Changing American Voter by Norman Nie, Sidney Verba & John Petrocik

The United States by Hofstadter, Miller, Aaron, Jordan & Litwack

The American Political System by Peter Woll & Robert Binstock

Government by the People by Burns, Peltason & Cronin

The Emerging Republican Majority by Kevin Phillips

The Electoral College: A Note on American Political Mythology by John Roche

The Federalist edited by Jacob Cooke

The New Age of Political Reform by Alexander Bickel

The American Electoral College by Roger MacBride

Presidential Elections by Nelson Polsby & AaronWildavsky

The Electoral College by Lucious Wilmerding
The American Voter by Agnus Campbell et al
Teledemocracy: Can Technology Protect Democracy? by Christopher Atherton
Perspectives on the Reagan Years by Hugh Heclo
*Race for the Presidency: Winning the 1988 Nomination*by Rhodes Cook (Congressional Quarterly)
Guide to U.S. Elections (Congressional Quarterly)
Underground Government: The Off-Budget Public Sector by James T. Bennett and Thomas J. DiLorenzo
Social Security: An Idea Whose Time Has Passed by Helen P. Rogers
Jesse Jackson: The Man, The Movement, The Myth byBarbara A. Reynolds
Jesse Jackson and the Politics of Race by Thomas H. Landess and Richard M. Quinn
Up From The Ghetto by Phillip T. Drotning and Wesley South
The American Deficit: Fulfillment of a Prophecy? by Helen P. Rogers
The Coming of the New Deal by Arthur Schlessinger, Jr.

Periodicals and Newspapers

Atlantic Monthly
Business Week
The Commonwealth
Congressional Quarterly
Forbes
Fortune
Insight
New Republic
Newsweek
Policy Review
Scientific American
Time
Los Angeles Times
New York *Times*
San Francisco *Examiner*
Wall Street Journal

Appendix

You are invited to participate in a historic endeavor.

To honor our predecessors, to ensure hope and opportunity for ourselves and our children, to restore a legacy of liberty and initiative for future generations, citizens of the United States of America have begun to voluntarily retire the public debt of the federal government.

In proportion to the success you have achieved by the exercise of your talent, energy and freedom as a citizen of this nation, make your tax deductible gifts payable to the U. S. Treasury, Public Debt Reduction Fund.

Furthermore, it is anticipated that our leadership and purpose will inspire our public servants to meet the challenge of the future with competence, efficiency, and thrift.

Contributions may be sent to:

Bureau of Public Debt
Department G
Washington, D.C. 20239-0601

Citizens For A Debt-Free America
2550 S. Sunnyslope Road
New Berlin, Wisconsin 53151
(414) 782-1305

CHART A

	BABBITT	DUKAKIS	GEPHARDT	GORE	JACKSON	SIMON
BORN	Los Angeles, CA June 27, 1938	Brookline, MA November 3, 1933	St. Louis, MO January 31, 1941	Washington, D.C. March 31, 1948	Greenville, NC October 8, 1941	Eugene, OR November 29, 1928
MARRIED	Harriet Coons 1969	Katherine Dickson 1963	Jane Byrnes 1965	Mary Elizabeth (Tipper) Aitcheson	Jacqueline Lavinia Davis, 1962	Jeanne Hurley 1960
CHILDREN	2 sons	1 son, 2 daughters	1 son, 2 daughters	1 son, 3 daughters	5 children	1 son, 1 daughter
LAWYER?	Yes	Yes	Yes	No, but studied law 2 years	No	No
EDUCATION	Notre Dame BS 1960 Harvard Law JD 1965	Swarthmore BA 1955 Harvard Law JD 1960	Northwestern BS 1962 Univ. of Michigan JD 1965	Harvard BA 1969 Vanderbilt School of Religion 1972 Vanderbilt Law School 1974-76	A&T Greensboro, NC BA 1963 Chicago Theological Seminary	University of Oregon Dana College, Nebraska
OCCUPATION SINCE AGE 21 WHEN NOT IN POLITICAL OFFICE	Special Asst. to Dir. of VISTA, 1965-67 Atty. with U.S. Office of Economic Oppor-tunity, 1965-67 Private Law Practice in Phoenix 1967-75	Lawyer, 1960-62 TV Moderator, 1970-74 Lecturer at Kennedy School of Government 1979-82	Lawyer, 1965-71	Journalist Homebuilding Business	Preacher & Social Activist Exec. Dir. "Operation Breadbasket" 1966-71 President "PUSH" 1971-83	Journalist Teacher
POLITICAL OFFICE	Atty. General, AZ, 1975-78 Governor of AZ, 1978-86	State Legislature, 1962-70 Governor of MA, 1975-79, 1983-	St. Louis Alderman, 1971-76 U.S. Representative, 1977-	U.S. Representative, 1977-85 U.S. Senate, 1986-	None	IL State Representative, 1954-62 IL State Senate, 1962-69 Lt. Governor of IL, 1969-73 U.S. Representative, 1975-85 U.S. Senate, 1986-

CHART B

	BABBITT	DUKAKIS	GEPHARDT	GORE	JACKSON	SIMON
ECONOMY	Advocates Workplace democracy, employee ownership and profit-sharing.	Favors subsidies and partnerships between government and private sector.	Would institute a national energy policy and increase minimum wage.	Advocates a national energy policy and would revitalize Small Business Admin.	Would use union pension funds for public works to increase employment.	Proposes WPA-type jobs program, anti-trust enforcement and UDAGs.
EDUCATION	Prefers grants to loans, more federal funds, job training and own Medicaid proposal.	Prefers grants to loans and more federal funds.	Favors more federal funds, grants over loans and higher but not merit pay for teachers.	Prefers grants to loans and more federal funds.	Would stress early years, favors more federal funds and prefers grants to loans.	Would stress early years, favors more federal funds and prefers grants to loans.
DEFICIT & TAXES	Would target programs, raise income taxes and restrict home mortgage deductions. Opposes oil import fees and excise taxes.	Would reduce deficit by stepping up collection of delinquent taxes and by stimulating economic growth.	Supports a fee on oil imports, higher minimum tax for individuals and higher tax on corporations.	Would cut defense expenditures and raise taxes.	Would raise taxes on business and the wealthy, collect delinquent taxes and emphasize job opportunities to gain more revenue.	Has own version of balanced budget amendment. Favors excise taxes and oil import fees. Opposes raising personal income tax rates.
AGRICULTURE	Would concentrate subsidies on small farmer only.	Believes leadership is the answer to the farm problem.	Harkin-Gephardt farm bill reschedules debt and uses mandatory quotas for production.	Advocates better farm credit policies and would put a "floor under the farmer."	Favors world cooperation, would return land to bankrupt farmers and provide more funds.	Favors more small farm subsidies and more uses of ethanol.
SOCIAL SECURITY	Advocates means testing and taxing high income beneficiaries.	Supports status quo and is against means testing.	Opposes means testing, would move trust fund, merge Medicaid & Medicare and provide long-term care.	Supports status quo and is opposed to means testing.	?	Opposes means testing and would remove trust fund from budget.
TRADE	Rejects Gephardt amendment but has his own elaborate plan for trade.	Approves parts of Gephardt amendment but has his own plan.	Author of Gephardt amendment to HR3.	Rejects Gephardt amendment. Would negotiate international exporter agreements.	Supports Gephardt amendment. Emphasis on int'l authority and commitment to economic justice.	Supports Gephardt amendment and would stop the export of American jobs.

CHART C

	BUSH	DOLE	DuPONT	HAIG	KEMP	ROBERTSON
BORN	Milton, MA June 12, 1924	Russell, KS July 22, 1923	Wilmington, DE January 22, 1935	Philadelphia, PA December 2, 1924	Los Angeles, CA July 13, 1935	Lexington, VA March 22, 1930
MARRIED	Barbara Pierce 1945	Elizabeth Hanford second marriage	Elise Wood 1957	Patricia Fox 1947	Joanne Main 1957	Adelia Elmer 1954
CHILDREN	4 sons	1 daughter	3 sons, 1 daughter	2 sons, 1 daughter	2 sons, 2 daughters	2 sons, 2 daughters
LAWYER?	No	Yes	Yes	No	No	Yes
EDUCATION	Yale BA 1948	University of Arizona, Washburn JD 1952	Princeton BSE 1956 Harvard Law JD 1963	Notre Dame West Point BS 1947 Naval War College 1960 Army War College 1966	Occidental College BA 1957	Washington & Lee BA 1951 Yale Law JD 1955 New York Theological Seminary Masters of Divinity 1959
OCCUPATION SINCE AGE 21 WHEN NOT IN POLITICAL OFFICE	Businessman – oil wildcatter	Prosecuting attorney for Russell County, 1953-60	Family firm and law practice 1963-68	Army career President & CEO of United Technologies	Football career for 13 years	Preacher University President Television executive and personality.
POLITICAL OFFICE	U.S. Repr., 1966-70 Ambassador to U.N., 1971-73 Chief Liaison Officer, People's Rep. China, 1974-75 Dir. of CIA, 1976-77 V.P. of U.S., 1980-	KS State Repr., 1951-53 U.S. Repr., 1960-68 U.S. Senate, 1968-	DE General Assembly, 1968-70 U.S. Repr., 1971-76 Governor of DE, 1977-85	Cmdr. in Chief NATO 1974-78, Secty. of State, 1981-82	U.S. Repr., 1970-	None

CHART D

	BUSH	DOLE	DuPONT	HAIG	KEMP	ROBERTSON
ECONOMY	Sees deregulation and job training as high priorities.	Would encourage deregulation, relax anti-trust and limit product liability. Opposes UDAGs.	Has plans for a national training bank which will create new job opportunities and a skilled workforce.	Advocates changes in anti-trust law.	Would reinstitute gold standard and fixed exchange rate. Supports enterprise zones & reduced taxes.	Favors ESOPs, "individual business accounts" and youth minimum age. Would repeal Davis-Bacon Act.
EDUCATION	Sees education as our competitive edge for the future. Would promote higher standards and accountability.	Favors voluntary prayer, competition and improvement. Would target federal aid.	Supports vouchers, competition, merit pay, teacher evaluations and testing of students.	Favors tuition tax credits and supports higher standards and self-financing.	Opposes vouchers and favors tuition tax-credits, teacher testing and magnet school programs.	Supports vouchers and prayer in schools.
DEFICIT & TAXES	Would concentrate on further spending cuts but would not balance the budget via a tax increase.	Tried to freeze COLAs for all entitlements in 1985. Is *serious* about deficit reduction. Favors a line-item veto and oil import fee.	A supply-sider who believes the nation can grow out of its debt. Opposes tax increases.	Favors line-item veto, new budget process, investment credits and equal cuts in budget across the board.	Opposes Gramm-Rudman. Thinks we can grow our way out of debt. Would act on Grace Commission recommendations.	Supports privatization, Gramm-Rudman and would act on findings of Grace Commission. Believes there is no need to raise taxes.
AGRICULTURE	Would phase-out subsidies only if trading partners do the same. Favors subsidies for ethanol.	Chief architect of 1985 Farm Bill. Favors subsidies for ethanol but opposes limiting other farm subsidies.	His Farm Opportunity Plan would reduce *all* subsidies over a five-year period until there are none.	Believes free and fair trade will solve the farm problem.	Thinks stable exchange rates and gold-backed currency will help the farm problem.	Supports mediation and loan restructuring as well as phasing-out subsidies.
SOCIAL SECURITY	Supports status quo and opposes means testing.	Favors taxing some benefits but opposes cuts in Medicare & Medicaid.	Proposes IRA-type program to run parallel to Social Security. Would guarantee current benefits.	Will do everything necessary to sustain system as we know it.	Claims trust fund is overfunded and would remove it from budget. Would lower payroll taxes.	Wants to guarantee benefits to current beneficiaries but shift younger workers to IRA-type pensions.
TRADE	Opposes House Trade Bill (HR3) and Gephardt amendment.	Supports Bentsen-Danforth trade bill and opposes Gephardt amendment.	Free trader. Wouldn't sign GATT agreement unless it opened some new markets to U.S.	Believes deficit reduction will reduce interest rates and help trade. Opposes tariffs.	Sponsor of Kemp-Gramm bill. No tariffs and no protection, just reciprocal free markets.	Anti-tariffs but wants to expand *fair* trade and advocates a reciprocal "access or else" stance.

Index